# Mapping the Four Corners

THE AMERICAN EXPLORATION AND TRAVEL SERIES

# Mapping the

## NARRATING THE

Robert S. McPherson
Susan Rhoades Neel

University of Oklahoma Press ✸ Norman

# Four Corners

❊    ❊

## HAYDEN SURVEY OF 1875

*Publication of this book is made possible through the generosity of*
*Edith Kinney Gaylord.*

❉   ❉   ❉

*On page iii,* Chittenden and Holmes made extensive notes and sketches of the geology, topography, and archaeology they encountered in southwestern Colorado, southeastern Utah, northeastern Arizona, and northwestern New Mexico. With an eye for economic growth as well as mapping, their notes served as an accurate assessment for future development. *Courtesy U.S. Geological Survey, W. H. Jackson Photo 1112a.*

LIBRARY OF CONGRESS CATALOGING-IN-PUBLICATION DATA Names: McPherson, Robert S., 1947– | Neel, Susan Rhoades.
Title: Mapping the Four Corners : narrating the Hayden survey of 1875 / Robert S. McPherson, Susan Rhoades Neel.
Description: Norman : University of Oklahoma Press, 2016. | Includes bibliographical references and index.
Identifiers: LCCN 2015048907 | ISBN 978-0-8061-5385-8 (hardcover)
ISBN 978-0-8061-6921-7 (paper)  Subjects: LCSH: Four Corners Region—Description and travel. |
Hayden, F. V. (Ferdinand Vandeveer), 1829–1887—Travel—Four Corners Region.

Four Corners Region—Description and travel—Sources. | Surveyors—Four Corners Region— Biography. | Indians of North America—Four Corners Region—History —19th century. | Four Corners Region—Geography. | Four Corners Region— Surveys. | United States—Territorial expansion—History—19th century.

Classification: LCC F788.5 .M38 2016 | DDC 919.792/59—dc23
LC record available at http://lccn.loc.gov/2015048907

*Mapping the Four Corners: Narrating the Hayden Survey of 1875* is Volume 83 in The American Exploration and Travel Series.

The paper in this book meets the guidelines for permanence and durability of the Committee on Production Guidelines for Book Longevity of the Council on Library Resources, Inc. ∞

# Contents

# *Illustrations*

## Maps

# *Preface*

ON A CLEAR TUESDAY MORNING IN EARLY AUGUST OF 1875, William Henry Holmes, a topographer with the U.S. Geological and Geographic Survey of the Territories, looked out on a landscape characterized by the *New York Times* as "a sterile fastness."[1] He stood at the precise spot where the territories of Utah, Colorado, New Mexico, and Arizona met. From this vantage point, Holmes could see Shiprock nearly forty miles to the southeast and Ute Mountain nearly as far to the northeast, and even farther in the distance westward to Monument Valley and the Comb Ridge monocline. Few places in the continental United States were more remote at that time than the region Holmes looked over. He was there as part of a team of scientists, under the direction of Ferdinand V. Hayden, who worked for the federal government, surveying the vast reaches of the trans-Mississippi West. The press of the day often referred to Holmes and his Survey comrades as "explorers," but that was a misnomer. They were not there to discover but to map. The land that the Geographic Survey party traveled and recorded that year, though remote, was neither unknown nor uninhabited. Indeed, Holmes stood next to a cairn of rocks placed earlier in the year by another surveyor, signifying the boundary where the four territories met. For Holmes and his compatriots, the task was to translate the land of the Four Corners into a distinctly American visual language of utility.

As later years proved, he accomplished this task beyond his wildest dreams. Today, in the exact spot that he stood, there resides a $5 million visitors' center with fifty-six vendor booths, restrooms, and a wheelchair-accessible monument commemorating the spot where the four states now meet. All of this is built upon the mapping system

Holmes employed. Certainly, the three federal agencies (Bureau of Land Management, Forest Service, and Park Service), as well as the four states and the two Indian tribes (Utes and Navajos) on whose reservations the facility resides, are happy with this accomplishment, as were the 292,226 tourists who visited it in 2014.[2] But there is also some irony here, especially for the Utes. As joint partners with the Navajos in managing the monument, they are willing participants in encouraging tourism to attract primarily non–Native American visitors onto their land. In 1875, they did all they could to resist the mapping, which they understood as encouraging white encroachment on their ancestral lands. In those times, surveying and drawing lines on a map were the harbingers of land lost and cultural devastation to American Indians and their way of life. Ute history provides a classic example of just how devastating these harbingers were.

Who were these white men who ventured so far into the Four Corners homelands of the Utes and Navajos? To Marshall Sprague, prolific historian of Colorado's past, they were "Hayden's Rover Boys." He portrays them as young men "armored by their absorption in the marvels of science," who tried to "conceal their youthfulness by wearing ferocious beards"; they were "thoroughly educated at places like Harvard and the University of Pennsylvania," as they "plunged into the wilds without the slightest thought of danger," but were "neither too timid nor too reckless as they roamed the wilderness."[3] This is a fair assessment of many of the Survey's members. It certainly was true of Albert C. Peale, who sat in his tent for a number of rainy days devouring novels until the weather cleared so that he could ascend and descend in an afternoon a peak named after him—the second highest in Utah outside of the Uintah Mountain range. It was also true of William Henry Jackson, frontier photographer par excellence, as he trudged up and down canyons and mountainsides with his 20" by 24" camera and glass photographic plates. And it was true of Holmes himself, a skilled geologist, ethnographer, and artist. Each of these men brought a certain expertise that added significantly to the success of the venture.

This was also true of the "western men"—the packers, outfitters, and guides—who managed the everyday tasks of moving their surveyor compatriots through Indian country. Many of these employees had worked for the Hayden Survey in previous years and knew how to keep "Easterners" out of trouble. Take Shep Madera, one of the head packers, for instance, who could wrangle a mule, bake flaky biscuits, quote Shakespeare, and even stand on his head. When it came time for a brush with the Utes or chasing bears in the woods, his cool wisdom saved lives. Then there was Tom Cooper, another chief packer, who was so in tune with the movement of the horses and mules in the herd he was responsible for that he prevented their theft one night—a theft that would have otherwise left his party stranded a hundred miles from its resupply depot. Even "Judge" Porter, an African American cook, not only hustled fine grub, but shared some definite opinions that entertained men around the campfire.

Perhaps most important for those of us interested in the history of the Hayden Survey, many members of the 1875 field crew were prolific writers who recorded daily and weekly activities of the different elements of the Survey. One, Cuthbert Mills, was a professional journalist, invited by Hayden to tag along and post reports to the *New York Times*. But several of the regular employees of the Survey who had scientific or logistical duties also sent articles to eastern newspapers about their activities in the field. Indeed, this had been a customary practice of the Hayden Survey since it began work in 1871 in the Yellowstone area. Robert Adams, who had been with Hayden since the Yellowstone Survey, and Edwin A. Barber, who had been with the Survey since 1873, filed newspaper articles, as did A. C. Peale. Charles Aldrich, who oversaw the Hayden supply camp in 1875, sent long, descriptive articles to the *Chicago Daily Inter-Ocean*. In addition to these published reports, some members of the 1875 field teams kept diaries, including Peale and Jackson. Holmes wrote detailed field notes that included many personal observations of events, along with extensive scientific notes and drawings. All of these materials provide an incredibly rich record of the Survey's activities in the Four Corners region. The story of their work, sometimes mundane, occasionally dramatic, but always filled with curiosity and keen observation, covers their travels as they make their way from the Rocky Mountains into the canyon and plateau country of the Four Corners. With their observations of the lives of the Penitentes and Catholic padres in southwestern Colorado, of the Utes living in their beloved mountains, of the Hopi mesas and the Anasazi ruins—with an Indian fight thrown in for good measure—the "Hayden Boys" provide an interesting glimpse into the past.

In this book, we have assembled a selection of diary entries, field notes, correspondence, and newspaper articles written in 1875 by members of the Survey. Some documents have never been published before, while others are reprinted here for the first time in context. Rather than using these accounts in their entirety, we have chosen to arrange selected excerpts into a chronological narrative. For some of the more dramatic moments in the months-long expedition, we provide multiple passages about the same event. Otherwise, elements were selected because they move the reader through time and space as various groups of surveyors went about their activities; or because a particular selection provides compelling descriptive detail about the natural and human-made landscapes through which the Survey crews passed; or because they illustrate the working practices of nineteenth-century field scientists and the practical routines of travel and camp life.

Ultimately, this is their story, told in the words of the men who lived it. The reader not only has a first-hand account of what it was like to be among these surveyors as they traveled in the Four Corners area, but to hear it in the prose of that day, which comes in a variety of formats, ranging from brief diary entries and scientific field notes to lengthy newspaper articles.

The tone of these extracts varies, and we, as authors, have worked to retain the distinctive voices that provide depth and complexity to the story. We have also made some editorial interventions in order to make the text as integrated and comfortable to read as possible. Paragraph breaks have been added in places, especially to lengthy newspaper articles. Modern spellings for common words were adopted and references to personal names and place-names standardized. Colloquialisms and slang commonly used in the nineteenth century, however, have been retained. Terms like "squaw," "buck," and "savages" were used by Survey members, scientists as well as reporters, most often in casual reference but sometimes with deliberate pejorative intent. Although such language grates on modern ears, its historic usage provides valuable insight into the cultural assumptions underlying the activities of the Hayden Survey, which is one of the reasons we believe publishing these original sources is so important.

Our hope is that readers will find in these passages more than just an adventure story of some highly literate professionals placing lines on a map or another chapter from an already full book about American Indian opposition to the westward movement. The words of the Hayden "boys" make us witnesses to a remarkable place, astonishing in its complexity and beauty, and to a moment in time when ancient, traditional, and modernizing cultures collided. Here are some insiders' views of the settling of the West—views of men creating maps while experiencing a hearty adventure—at a time when much was new.

# Acknowledgments

L ET'S FACE IT. THE AUTHORS OF THIS BOOK ARE MOST indebted to the men of the Hayden Survey who wrote so well and kept meticulous notes. As historians working with materials created more than 140 years ago, we appreciate the care taken in field reports, diaries, journals, newspaper articles, and published government documents that provide a day-by-day accounting on both a formal and personal level. Anyone who has worked with official reports knows that often much gets screened out of the final product, especially some of the more interesting behind-the-scenes activities and discussions. Here we are privy to much of what transpired, for better or for worse, through the eyes of those who lived it. As one reader suggested, "I felt like I was privy to the email accounts of the Hayden Survey.org." We agree.

Add to this, William H. Jackson's contribution. How many frontier expeditions were fortunate enough to have a professional photographer of his caliber along to visually record, at that moment, what members of the expedition encountered? And when circumstances did not permit a photo—there were no cell-phone "selfies" with the Utes in pursuit—he later sketched or painted a picture to capture the moment. Jackson's fine-grain photos, however, were important not only as illustrations for that shutter snap in time; they continue to give additional information beyond the event. For instance, one day while one of us (McPherson) was working with an archaeologist friend intimately familiar with Montezuma Canyon in Utah, the fellow pointed out that in one of Jackson's photos of an Anasazi (Ancestral Puebloan) site could be seen part of a Ute cornfield. Few, if any, such pictures exist, and Jackson had made at least one archaeologist very happy to understand this part of Ute material culture well over a hundred years later. Other members of the Hayden Survey of 1875 made their own significant contributions in the fields of geology and cartography by naming places upon the land, identifying important locations (some of which became national monuments), and specifying useful natural resources—all while mapping the country.

Moving forward in time, we would like to express deep appreciation to a number of organizations and individuals. Foremost is the staff at the American Heritage Center, University of Wyoming, Laramie. They were extremely helpful in obtaining materials in the Jesse V. Howell Collection. Howell did the lion's share of gathering newspaper articles and correspondence of many of the Hayden Survey members. We acknowledge the work of P. K. Hurlbut, who had the energy to retrace the steps of the Gardner-Gannett party to locate the site where the men trashed their equipment and made their escape from the encircling Utes. His correspondence concerning this led us to some enjoyable days in the field, pinning down the specific location. Archaeologist Winston Hurst was of great assistance, not only in fieldwork aspects, but also in developing the maps used in this book.

The vast amount of material collected on the topic needed to be shaped. Thanks to the suggestions and encouragement of Chuck Rankin at the University of Oklahoma Press, we received clear guidance that moved us to a finished product that was manageable for both us and the Press. But no one deserves greater thanks than teacher and archivist Bob Blair, who made access to his entire collection of Jackson photos available to us as well as assisting us in procuring them from different repositories. Bob, who republished Jackson's *The Pioneer Photographer*, has also served as a Jackson photo archivist for the Scotts Bluff National Monument in Nebraska and is now a leading expert on this photographer's work. More importantly, as colleague and friend, he unselfishly shared his time and talent in getting just the right pictures. His efforts are greatly appreciated, as are those of Winston Hurst, who drew maps of routes taken by different elements of the 1875 survey. Thanks also go to the Scotts Bluff National Monument Library; the U.S. Geological Survey Library, Denver; the National

Anthropological Archives, Smithsonian Institution, Washington, D.C.; the American Heritage Center, University of Wyoming; the Palace of the Governors, Santa Fe; the History Colorado Center, Denver; the Denver Public Library; and Brigham Young University, Provo, Utah, for providing permission to use their photos.

# Mapping the Four Corners

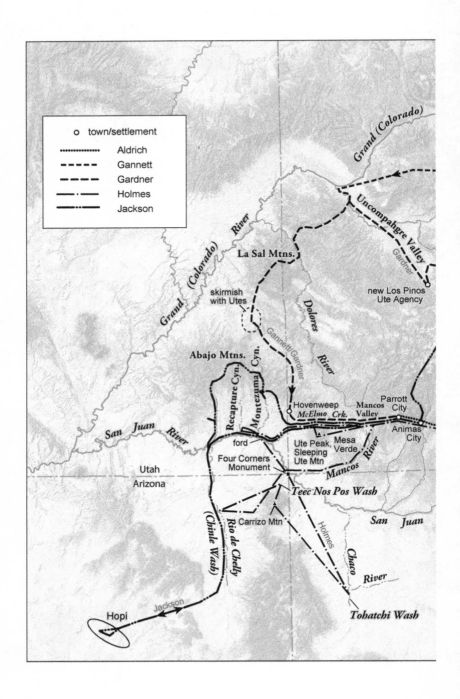

town/settlement

Aldrich

Gannett

Gardner

Holmes

Jackson

Grand (Colorado)

Uncompahgre Valley

Gardner

River

La Sal Mtns.

new Los Pinos
Ute Agency

Grand (Colorado)

skirmish
with Utes

Dolores

River

Abajo Mtns.

Gannett/Gardner

Recapture Cyn.

Montezuma Cyn.

Hovenweep

Mancos
Valley

Parrott
City

McElmo Crk.

San   Juan   River

Animas
City

ford

Ute Peak,
Sleeping
Ute Mtn

Mesa
Verde

Mancos    River

Four Corners
Monument

Utah
Arizona

Teec Nos Pos Wash

San   Juan

Carrizo Mtn

(Chinle Wash)

Rio de Chelly

Holmes

Chaco

River

Hopi

Jackson

Tohatchi Wash

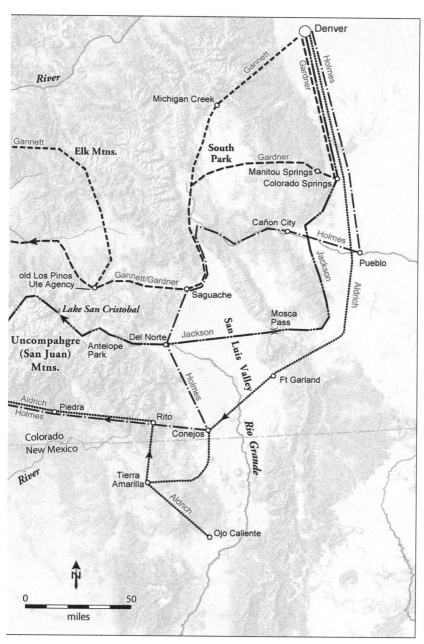

River

Gannett

Elk Mtns.

South
Park

Gannett

old Los Pinos
Ute Agency

*Lake San Cristobal*

Uncompahgre
(San Juan)
Mtns.

Antelope
Park

Gannett/Gardner

Saguache

Del Norte

Jackson

Michigan Creek

Gannett

Gardner

Denver

Holmes

Gardner

Manitou Springs
Colorado Springs

Cañon City

Holmes

Jackson

Aldrich

Pueblo

Mosca
Pass

San Luis Valley

Ft Garland

Holmes

Aldrich
Piedra
Holmes

Colorado
New Mexico

River

Rito

Conejos

Tierra
Amarilla

Rio Grande

Aldrich

Ojo Caliente

N

0                    50
miles

MAP I. Jackson's Map of Routes and Ruins. Map by Ben Pease, based on
a map by Winston Hurst. *Copyright © 2016, University of Oklahoma Press.*

3

# Introduction

IN THE SUMMER OF 1875, WELL AHEAD OF THE TIDE OF advancing settlement, a small team of government scientists set out to map the desert region lying along the borders of Colorado, Utah, Arizona, and New Mexico Territories. The team was working for the U.S. Geological and Geographic Survey (most often referred to as the Hayden Survey after its director, Ferdinand V. Hayden). Yet the activities of this expedition in these distant reaches of the West were very much part of a dynamic national culture searching for greater economic development and poised to embrace new scientific ideas and technologies. By 1875, Americans—Northerners and Southerners alike—were growing weary of the decade-long effort at post–Civil War Reconstruction. Turning from a troubled past to visions of a new industrial future, America entered an era of powerful corporations, technological innovation, and urban growth.

The nation's government was one of the strongest proponents of encouraging economic growth and assisting entrepreneurs to succeed. A good part of this success depended on available natural resources— knowing where they were, how they could be reached, and what it would take to turn them into products that fueled the growing economy. This was one reason that, directly after the Civil War, the trans-Mississippi West came under the close scrutiny of various surveying expeditions, such as the one to the Four Corners region, that not only mapped a heretofore unknown territory in preparation for sale, but also identified exactly what types of resources were present, how efficient transportation—railroads at this time—could be effectively introduced, and how best to wrest the land from American Indians living in the region.

The Hayden Survey's 1875 fieldwork in the Four Corners region was part of this decade-long effort by the federal government to understand the potential of the trans-Mississippi West. Leaving Denver in early June, the members of the Survey traveled by horse and mule across the Rockies and westward to the Colorado Plateau. There they divided into several working teams, each consisting of two or three scientists, wranglers, cooks, and, on one of the crews, a reporter from the *New York Times*. Working hundreds of miles from established settlements, these teams spent weeks in the hot, dry canyon and plateau country, making triangulations, puzzling out the region's complex geologic formations, and noting the presence (or absence) of resources that might be of value to economic development. Most of the territory that the scientists surveyed that summer was part of the traditional homeland of the Utes and Navajos. Encounters between the region's Native inhabitants and the Hayden scientists were mostly peaceful, characterized by curiosity and the mutual, if somewhat wary, interests of travelers in a harsh environment seeking fresh food and water.

Noted western photographer William Henry Jackson, in charge of the Photographic Division, departed from the other elements of the Survey on a special assignment that took him to the Hopi mesas in northeastern Arizona. There he briefly studied Hopi culture with the hope that ethnographic comparison might reveal how these nineteenth-century American Indians related to the remnants of ancestral Puebloan or Anasazi culture he had explored and photographed the previous year. During this field season, he continued to investigate the prehistoric ruins and material culture that had remained undisturbed for hundreds of years. While Jackson and other members of the Survey were not the first to marvel at what they found, they were the first to seriously study, scientifically record, and accurately illustrate elements of many of today's well-known ruins, such as Mesa Verde, Hovenweep, Poncho House, Casa del Eco, and other lesser-known sites.

In mid-August, after more than two months in the field, the survey-ing work came to an abrupt end as the scientists were forced by a party of Utes to abandon their equipment and flee to safety at the Survey's base camp in eastern Colorado. The specific provocations for the Ute attack on the Hayden Survey in August 1875 are unclear, but there is no doubt that the Indians well understood the broad implications of the scientists' work at a time when their traditional homelands were being restricted to a reservation whose boundaries shrank year after year. The Hayden Survey was not engaged in mapping boundaries for this reservation, but its overall goal, true of all the federal surveys in the West, was to integrate the region into the economic and cultural system of a rapidly expanding and industrializing nation. The process of "surveying" was more than merely measuring; it sought to define the land in terms of western concepts of nature and of capitalist concerns of value and usefulness. This meant rendering these concepts into tangible, usable, and communicable forms, such as maps, photographs, and published reports.

Preparation of these documents occupied the Hayden scientists when they returned from their summer fieldwork to the Survey's headquarters in Washington, D.C. This was their customary practice—a summer of fieldwork in the West followed by winter months in the East, processing data and disseminating information to the public, to fellow scientists, and to an influential coalition of politicians and business interests whose support made the Survey possible. Hayden's scientists did this work at a time when assumptions about nature, the meaning and conduct of science, the intersection of public and private enterprise, and the aesthetics of place were shifting within American culture. Hayden and his team helped create this changing world by contributing new approaches to the visual representation of scientific knowledge, the bond between publicly funded science and economic development, and the professionalization of disciplines ranging from anthropology to geology. The work of Hayden's men in the Four Corners during the summer of 1875 was typical of the Survey's activities throughout the 1870s. Reading the records left by these men makes us witnesses to the changing world in which they worked.

## F. V. Hayden and the Surveying of the West

The decade prior to the Civil War witnessed explorers venturing into parts of Utah and surrounding areas to make maps and gather information about the general lay of the land. Men like John W. Gunnison (1853), John C. Frémont (1853–54), John S. Newberry (1857–59), and John N. Macomb (1859) provided a glimpse into an area mostly unknown to white Americans. After the Civil War, with the nation poised for an era of geographical and economic expansion, the federal government undertook a major effort to survey the lands of the trans-Mississippi West. The Great Surveys, in both deliberate and unintentional ways, made white settlement and economic development of the remaining reaches of the continental United States possible. Two of these surveys, the U.S. Geographical Surveys West of the 100th meridian, headed by Capt. George Montague Wheeler, and the Geological Exploration of the 40th parallel, directed by Clarence King, operated under military auspices for the purpose of identifying sites for military installations in the West. John Wesley Powell's survey of the Green and Colorado River systems and F. V. Hayden's survey of Montana, Wyoming, and Colorado Territories were federally funded but operated under the direction of the Department of the Interior. Although these four surveys often competed with each other for funding and publicity, their work between 1867 and 1879 brought vast reaches of the far West to the attention of policy makers and ordinary citizens. Scholars continue to debate the relative merits of the four great western surveys, but most agree that the work of the Hayden Survey had lasting impact not only on the regions it investigated, but also on the conduct of civilian science within a democratic system.

Ferdinand Vandeveer Hayden, although trained as a physician, was more interested in geology than medicine as a young man. Fascinated by the natural world, Hayden was also attracted to the adventure of exploration. Soon after graduating from the Albany Medical College in 1853, he joined geologist Fielding Meek on an expedition to the Badlands of Nebraska Territory. With some funding from the Smithsonian Institution, Hayden spent the rest of the pre–Civil War decade studying the geology of the northern Missouri River and collecting fossil specimens. He participated in the expeditions of the area by U.S. Corps of Topographical Engineers lieutenant Gouveneur K. Warren and captain William F. Raynolds. On these governmental expeditions, Hayden served variously as geologist, topographer, collector, and surgeon. During the Civil War, Hayden performed duty as a Union Army surgeon and then as chief medical officer of the Army of the Shenandoah. At the conclusion of the war, he took a post as instructor of geology and mineralogy at the University of Pennsylvania, but he spent summers in the Dakota Badlands.

In 1867, Hayden received funding from the federal government to conduct a survey of the newly established state of Nebraska. The task was conducted under the auspices of the newly created federal agency known as the U.S. Geological and Geographical Survey of the Territories, with Hayden as its director. While in the field, he made the acquaintance of several engineers who were in the midst of planning extensions of the railroad system across the continent. With their encouragement, Hayden determined to expand the scope of the Geological and Geographical Survey farther west into Wyoming and Montana Territories. His ambitions for the Geological and Geographical Survey grew as his work encompassed more territory. During the Survey's first two years of operation, Congress appropriated a budget of $5,000 for the work. Thereafter, the annual budget increased to $75,000, although Hayden often supplemented this with special appropriations and private donations.[1] He remained head of the Geological and Geographical Survey, which came to be known simply as the Hayden Survey, until its disbanding in 1879 with the establishment of a single federal organization (the U.S. Geological Survey) to oversee any further western surveying.

Hayden sought to distinguish his organization as a civilian scientific enterprise, distinct from Wheeler and King's work for the U.S. Army, which Hayden characterized as being of limited utility. The army was not interested in science, he insisted, only in gathering enough geographic data to establish forts and maneuver troops. He wanted to do more than extend the traditional rectangular survey that had been used since the founding of the nation to plot land divisions. The old survey was good enough to establish boundaries between states and territories, but what was needed, in his view, was information about the land *within* those lines. Hayden's vision was of a science that served the larger purpose of economic development and settlement. His emphasis was on the value of science to enterprise, always pointing out to funders that his surveys identified mineral, timber, and agricultural resources. When Congress held hearings in 1874 on the conflict between the Wheeler and Hayden surveys in Colorado, Hayden pointed out that his work encompassed a broader range of utility.

Science and scenery were two items promoted by Hayden's surveys. Here, A. D. Wilson and Franklin Rhoda establish part of a map grid through triangulation on top of Sultan Mountain, Colorado, 1874. *Courtesy U.S. Geological Survey, W. H. Jackson Photo 01111.*

Over the course of more than a decade, Hayden strove to make his Survey a tool for orderly economic development in the West. In the process, he and the young scientists who worked for him transformed the nature of scientific investigation during a time when science was becoming professionalized and popularized. The era of the "gentleman" naturalist was giving way to trained men who made their living in specialized fields of inquiry. Hayden's Survey contributed to these changes by making science "visual" for the layperson, adopting new techniques of cartography, and defining science as a practical discipline—not just an avocation—while also promoting it as an adventure. His insistence on quick dissemination of the knowledge gained by his surveys through published reports, photography, and museum displays in a variety of forums—both popular and professional—stimulated scholarly debate as well as public interest in science. His insistence that civilian scientists best served the national interest helped establish the concept of federally funded scientific endeavor, while his skilled lobbying for appropriations set the model for a federal scientific bureaucracy.

Hayden gained his greatest public attention with the Survey's work in Yellowstone. Expeditions into the Yellowstone country in 1871 and 1872 took with them artists who provided stunning images of the landscape as well as scholars who saw that same landscape with a scientific eye. Pictures produced by Thomas Moran, the painter, and William Henry Jackson, the photographer, helped persuade Congress to set Yellowstone aside as America's first national park. Moran's and Jackson's work demonstrated to Hayden the political power of visual imagery, and he thereafter integrated artistic representation as a staple into each of his future surveys. This important connection of making science visually accessible to the public through the landscape provided the necessary tie to tax revenues for funding expeditions. Hayden's Yellowstone surveys also included a careful selection of guests, a practice that became one of the hallmarks of his work. These guests included reporters, who helped publicize the surveys, and private entrepreneurs or friends of politicians, who worked behind the scenes to lobby for funds to support Hayden's efforts. The 1875 expedition incorporated many of these elements that he had developed over the previous years.

Hayden's exploration of the Yellowstone country brought his Survey fame and increased political support. But the region was extremely isolated, making the logistics of fieldwork difficult and expensive, a situation not likely to change any time soon. The Northern Pacific Railroad's interest in the area was far from realized, and, as a consequence, economic consolidation and expansion of mining and agriculture seemed at that point distant. Hayden, committed to entrepreneurial science, wanted his work to be useful in economic development and, crucially, to be seen as useful by the politicians who held the Survey's purse strings. The logistical difficulties posed by the Yellowstone region's remoteness, in other words, were not the only impediment to Hayden's work. He wanted to survey territory where the processes of development were seen as more immediate. Thus, while there was much left to survey in Montana and Wyoming Territories, in 1873 Hayden turned his attention southward to Colorado Territory.

## The Hayden Survey in Colorado

Colorado struck Hayden as territory with greater, and certainly more imminent, economic potential. Work there would likely bring more public attention and political support for the Survey. It was not that Colorado was unknown territory where Hayden could make new discoveries. Indeed, quite the opposite was true. Colorado Territory had long been at the nexus where the northernmost reaches of the Spanish Empire met the westward-expanding Anglo-American nation and a diverse collection of indigenous cultures that were engaged in extensive networks of trade. Interactions among multicultural travelers and traders in the region continued throughout the nineteenth century, with little note of shifting political regimes. The region passed from the French to the Americans, then the Spanish, then the Mexicans, and finally back into American hands following the 1846–48 Mexican War.

Originally part of Kansas and Nebraska Territories, much of Colorado had briefly been claimed by the Mormons as part of their State of Deseret, but in 1850 the federal government established the region as part of the new territories of New Mexico and Utah. In 1858, the discovery of gold at Pike's Peak in the southern Rocky Mountains brought a rush of prospectors and entrepreneurs to the region. An effort by mining interests to create a new territory, which they wanted to call the Territory of Jefferson, failed, but when the festering national debate over slavery resulted in statehood for Kansas, western portions of that state were reorganized in 1861 as a new Territory of Colorado. It would take another fourteen years before it was successfully mapped.

Efforts during the Civil War by the Confederacy and the Union to assert control over the southwestern territories brought increased attention to Colorado, as did discovery of silver deposits in the Front Range of the southern Rocky Mountains. Soon after the war, interest in Colorado Territory grew as the railroad system extended westward. The Union Pacific Railroad reached Julesburg (in northeastern Colorado) in 1867, and connected with the Central Pacific two years later to form the first transcontinental railroad. In 1870, the Denver Pacific Railway completed a north-south link between the transcontinental line at Cheyenne, Wyoming, and the town of Denver in Colorado

Territory. A rapid transportation system like this accelerated economic development in the mining and livestock industries, which could now move their products to factory systems farther east.

Denver, one of several mining towns established during the Pike's Peak gold rush, had grown steadily over the 1860s, becoming the capital of Colorado Territory in 1867. Although Denver was still small, with a population of barely 5,000 in 1870, the arrival of the Denver Pacific and, a few months later, a connection to the Kansas Pacific line suggested that the city was poised to serve as a hub of development for the agricultural and mineral lands on the western slopes of the Rockies. Discovery of silver in the San Juan Mountains in 1872 only furthered the belief of entrepreneurs, politicians, and scientists like Hayden that Colorado was poised for a period of settlement and economic development. By 1873, statehood seemed likely, and Hayden believed that his survey could provide not only accurate maps, but also the kind of data about resources needed to guide political and economic decision-making.[2]

Hayden's view of Colorado Territory's economic potential was no doubt influenced by his association with backers of the Denver & Rio Grande Railroad. He had always believed that the interest of the railroads aligned with the goals of his scientific surveys. Both, he believed, sought an orderly and useful development of the West. He also understood that railroad corporations were the economic engines of the era and, therefore, that the leaders of those corporations wielded enormous political influence. Hayden solicited the support of these men, sometimes establishing personal friendships and, whenever possible, sharing maps and information that everyone understood as valuable for the construction of new rail lines, the development of natural and scenic resources (often on lands owned by the railroads), and the settlement of towns and farms whose goods would flow along the rails. "It is clear," writes James G. Cassidy in his biography of Hayden, "that when Hayden laid out his plans for the survey he often did so with reference to the activities of the railroads."[3]

One of Hayden's early railroad friends was William Henry Blackmore, an English financier with an interest in western development. During the Civil War, Blackmore had helped raise loans in Europe for the Union and had later marketed stocks overseas for the Union

Pacific Railroad. In the late 1860s, Blackmore acquired a portion of the Sangre de Cristo Land Grant with the idea of enticing English immigrants to the San Luis Valley as well as developing mineral resources in the San Juan Mountains. He first met Hayden in 1868, while both were in Laramie, Wyoming—Hayden as part of his survey of the transcontinental rail line and Blackmore to broker a possible merger between the Central Pacific and Union Pacific. Both men shared an enthusiasm for the West and also for photography. Blackmore hired Hayden to conduct a survey of his lands on the Sangre de Cristo grant. He took a keen interest in Hayden's work thereafter.

The Englishman helped finance Hayden's second trip to the Yellowstone country in 1872, also paying for William Henry Jackson's equipment and services. Hayden responded by inviting Blackmore, his wife, and nephew to join the Survey in Yellowstone. (Blackmore's wife died of pneumonia on the trip—becoming the only fatality in the history of the Hayden Surveys.) By 1873, Blackmore was one of the financial backers for William Jackson Palmer's proposed Denver & Rio Grande Railroad. Palmer had been the construction manager for the Kansas Pacific Railway, mapping the route for the rail line from Kansas City to Denver and overseeing the work to its completion in 1870. Once in Colorado, Palmer became convinced of the region's possibilities. Failing to persuade his bosses at the Kansas Pacific to build lines farther into the territory, he established his own railroad company. Palmer's vision for the Denver & Rio Grande was to establish a north-south line between Denver and El Paso. That idea soon gave way to the construction of narrow-gauge rail routes connecting the mining regions of Colorado and, later, providing a connection between Denver and Salt Lake City. Palmer believed that the railroad's success depended on having in-state smelting and processing plants for Colorado's (and eventually Utah's) precious metal, coal, and iron ore deposits. To develop these, Palmer formed the New York & San Juan Mining and Smelting Company, which invested in mineral-rich lands and the associated processing infrastructure.[4] This was important, as the tentacles of the railroad moved deeper and deeper into the interior of the territory, eventually leading to increased mining and the dispossession of the Utes from their ancestral homelands—an issue that hit the 1875 Hayden Survey squarely in the face.

Palmer's partner in the Denver & Rio Grande was William Abraham Bell, an English physician. Besides a shared interest in railroad investment, the two men had a passion for photography, especially of western landscapes. Together, they founded the town of Colorado Springs in 1870. Palmer built a twenty-two-room, Tudor-style estate called Glen Eyrie, where he hosted powerful politicians, businessmen, artists, and scientists, including Hayden. In 1873, Bell opened a grand hotel and spa at nearby Manitou Springs and later built his own English manor, Briarhurst. Palmer and Bell attracted many wealthy English investors to Colorado Springs, including William Blackmore's sister, Blanche, who built a stately home there. Hayden also owned land in Colorado Springs. These relationships with Colorado's railroad entrepreneurs clearly influenced Hayden's decision to move the Survey to the territory, although in his petition for funding to Congress in 1873, he stressed logistical rationales for this new direction. At the time, he estimated it would take five years to complete a survey of Colorado Territory.

In addition to the new geographical focus on Colorado, Hayden introduced changes in procedures and personnel to the Survey. His work in Montana and Wyoming had been criticized by some, including Hayden's rivals Clarence King and John Wesley Powell, for a lack of accurate and thorough cartography. The challenge of rendering a three-dimensional world in a two-dimensional format had confronted mapmakers for centuries. By the late nineteenth century, the goal of topographic surveying was to convey elevation along with horizontal distance and geologic structure. Hayden determined that the work in Colorado would focus on topographical surveying, combining the triangulation methods utilized by the British in India with identification of geological formations and location of mineral, timber, and agricultural resources. The ultimate goal of Hayden's work was to produce a series of thematic maps giving visual expression to the region's economic potential—geology, natural resources, topography—everything that settlers, miners, entrepreneurs, and policy makers would need for an orderly, efficient, and profitable development of the region. The project would combine topographical maps, showing geographic distance and elevation, with topographical sketches or sections illustrating stratigraphy across broad stretches of land.

To oversee the topographic work, Hayden engaged James Terry Gardner.[5] Although not formally trained as a topographer, Gardner had developed a reputation as a skilled practitioner while working with Clarence King, with whom he had been friends since childhood, on the survey of the Sierra Nevada. As King's 40th Parallel Survey concluded, Gardner considered an offer from Hayden to join his work in Colorado. King had never liked Hayden, so he urged his longtime friend to reject the offer, but Gardner admired Hayden's work and supported his commitment to applying modern techniques to the topographical survey of Colorado. Through his work with King, Gardner was well known within eastern scientific circles, and these contacts put him in touch with some of the brightest young students. He was therefore able to hire several young scientists whose work with the Hayden Survey became the beginning of their distinguished careers.

With Gardner's help, Hayden devised a system of fieldwork that proved to be remarkably efficient and highly productive. They divided the Survey into small field groups, each with a topographer and geologist working in tandem, supported by two or three packers and a cook. The support crews were essential to the success of the Survey. They needed to be skilled at managing stock; packing supplies and surveying equipment; traveling long, tedious miles in rugged country, and being companionable camp mates. Whenever possible, Hayden employed the same men each season, which developed a genuine camaraderie between the eastern scientists and the western working men. Their pay reflected the relative value of each group to the Survey: the scientists, who worked year-round for the Survey, received between $125 and $200; the packers and cooks, who worked only for the three-month field season, got between $60 and $70.[6]

The groups, or divisions as Hayden called them, worked independently of one another but with coordinated assignments for specific geographic areas. This organizational approach allowed Hayden to expand or collapse the Survey's work in response to congressional appropriations—the bigger the budget, the more divisions could be fielded. A division might include an additional scientist specializing in botany or paleontology, although geologists most often had the added task of collecting fossils and botanical specimens. None of the divisions included guides, scouts, or armed escorts, although on occasion a crew might temporarily take on an Anglo or Indian local to serve as interpreter and liaison. Hayden continued to invite reporters to accompany the Survey in the field, but after 1873 the number of patronage "guests" declined.[7]

In addition to the surveying divisions, Hayden created a separate group assigned to make photographic images. William Henry Jackson, who had worked with the Hayden Survey since 1870, headed the Photographic Division. Hayden was keenly aware that the publicity brought by Jackson's photographs benefited the Survey politically, but he also believed that his work was part of the scientific process of the Survey. He made that point in a report to Congress: "An unthinking public might imagine that the employment of photography in connection with the work of the Survey is more ornamental than useful, and that the sole business of the photographer is to secure in the field a number of pictures merely to please the eye, and not for practical and scientific use. . . . Besides the constant and important use made of these illustrations in the preparation of the geological and topographical reports, copies of them are now used by professors in all the principal colleges of the land to illustrate their geological teachings."[8]

As an indication of Hayden's appreciation for the scientific and political value of photography as well as his trust in Jackson's skill, diligence, and curiosity, the Photographic Division was free to roam wherever Jackson thought he could get great pictures. Like the other divisions, this one was small, usually Jackson and someone to serve as an assistant, plus two or three packers and a cook. Hayden's confidence in Jackson was amply rewarded during the years the Survey spent in Colorado. The photographer's 1873 picture of the Mount of the Holy Cross became one of his most famous images. Jackson was also a keen artist, and his sketches of geological formations, ancient ruins, pottery, other artifacts, and camp life form an important part of the Survey's rich historic record. He found cliff houses in the Mancos River Canyon in 1874, but did not enter far into the Mesa Verde area; it would be more than another decade before Richard Wetherill and Charlie Mason located Cliff Palace and the other sites for which this mecca of Anasazi ruins would become famous. What Jackson did find, however, was enough to capture Hayden's attention.

With the Survey's shift to Colorado, logistics for the fieldwork improved. As Hayden had anticipated, the railroad made it possible for Survey scientists to travel quickly from headquarters in Washington, D.C., or their homes back east to Denver. Often these men met during the train trip west, joining at stations along the new transcontinental lines. The Survey maintained an office in Denver during the field season, but scientists and support crews rendezvoused at a campsite on Clear Creek, about six miles outside the city. Here James Stevenson oversaw the outfitting of the field crews. Stevenson, a self-taught geologist, had known Hayden before the Civil War and had served as his general assistant since the creation of the Survey in 1868. By 1873, Stevenson was handling the logistics, being described variously as general manager or executive director.

During their earlier work, Hayden and Stevenson had come to appreciate the value of mules for packing equipment and supplies in mountainous terrain. Most of the land to be surveyed in Colorado was inaccessible by wagon, so everything the field crews needed, from food to photographic plates, was carried by the sure-footed animals. Most crew members rode mules rather than horses, although at least one horse, a "bell mare" to help guide the mule train and keep the animals settled, accompanied each division. The mules were crucial to the success of the fieldwork, especially in the more remote and rugged reaches of the Survey's territory. Any threat to the mules, by accident or neglect, was a serious concern. Each animal had a name, noted in the Survey account books; crew members rejoiced at being reunited with a particular mule season after season or grumbled at being assigned a new one. Comments about the health, dispositions, and daily antics of these beasts of burden were frequently included in diary entries, letters home, and newspaper articles.

Since the Survey would be working for several years in Colorado, Stevenson arranged for ranchers near Denver to store equipment and board the mules during winter months. Through these local contacts, Stevenson made arrangements for supplies to be ready at the outset of the field season, thus saving his own staff time in acquiring the necessities and the equally time-consuming task of selling off stock and equipment at the end of the season. When the Survey crews assembled in June, this advance planning meant that the men could

Jackson's artistic eye and Colorado's dramatic scenery became a winning combination for Hayden's purposes. Mountain streams, towering peaks, and forested slopes—as found here in Baker's Park with Sultan Mountain in the distance—spoke to both entrepreneur and adventurer. *Courtesy William H. Jackson Collection, Scan #20100752, History Colorado Center, Denver, Colorado.*

take to the field within a week or less of their arrival in Denver. Once on the trail, surveying and photographic equipment was always close at hand, packed and unpacked at each camp by the skilled muleteers. The pace of travel was modest but steady, about ten to fifteen miles per day, allowing the scientists time to ride out in advance of the train to take measurements or collect specimens and then rejoin their colleagues for the evening's camp. Since their surveying tasks took the divisions as much as four hundred miles from Denver, Stevenson set up a resupply depot each year in an area, often near a mining camp, centrally accessible to all the divisions in the field at the time. These supplies were brought in by wagon trains traveling along different routes from the surveying divisions. This efficient approach to logistics allowed the divisions to work for a month or more, utilizing the supplies they had carried with them by mule, while the heavier wagon trains slowly made their way to the chosen depot. As this entire system of operation had developed over the years, it was standard operating procedure by 1875.

The multiyear survey of Colorado actually began in 1873. The surveyors first established a baseline near Denver; it followed the Kansas Pacific Railroad tracks for about six miles. Two additional baselines became necessary in subsequent years for checks on accuracy as the surveyors moved farther west. The U.S. Coast Survey had previously established an astronomical station at Denver and another at Colorado Springs, so the Hayden topographers knew the precise lines of longitude and latitude. From this baseline, the survey extended a network of primary triangles and, within these, secondary triangles. Gardner, with the assistance of Holmes, calculated Denver's elevation. This formed the basis for the future work of determining contour lines at two-hundred-foot intervals across the territory. Hayden also created a master cross section of Colorado's rock formations, against which the geographers could determine the stratigraphy of a specific locale from their field observations. Being able to trace any given formation's presence across a wide expanse of folds and uplifts was critical to understanding the geologic forces that had shaped the territory's landscape.

## THE HAYDEN SURVEY AND THE
## INDIGENOUS PEOPLES OF THE FOUR CORNERS

Hayden saw the work of his Survey in Colorado as a scientific endeavor. Its focus on geology, geographic description, cartographic accuracy, and even ethnography distinguished the Survey, in his mind, from the traditional purposes of surveying—to facilitate private land claims, for example, or to provide for military defense. He believed that his Survey had a far grander and more valuable purpose: to stimulate and guide the rapid, efficient expansion of the American economic system into Colorado. The implication of this vision for the region's American Indians was obvious. What had for centuries been Native space was to be reconceptualized according to notions of Western science and reorganized according to Western economic and cultural practices. Hayden's crews, with their carefully packed theodolites, tripods, and cameras, marched into territory that belonged to the Utes, whether by aboriginal claim and occupancy or through constantly shifting recognition given by treaties. In doing so, the Hayden Survey accelerated the loss of Native lands and helped solidify within the popular American imagination the idea that indigenous culture was part of a past that was inevitably, and rightly in the minds of most whites, being erased by the "progress" of a modern society.

The Hayden scientists carried with them assumptions about Native peoples that were current in nineteenth-century America. For all their curiosity about the region's ancient ruins, the Hayden men knew or understood little about the actual inhabitants of the area they intended to survey. The Utes' nomadic lifestyle, which was based on hunting and gathering; their suspicious, even at times warlike, demeanor toward surveyors; and their cultural beliefs reaffirmed the contemporary, nascent anthropological theory of the day. Social Darwinism, as it defined cultural traits, was an ethnocentric, hierarchical classification. Humankind, it asserted, passed through three stages of development—savagery, barbarism, and eventually civilization, the highest achievement. This approach to understanding people as "progressing" along a linear scale, considered everything from house types and clothing to social customs and cranial capacity to determine how close each culture was to reaching the ultimate goal of becoming like "civilized" Christian Anglo-Americans and others of the Caucasian race. Written accounts by members of the 1875 Survey underscore that these beliefs were part of the active understanding of some of the crew members.

Today there is a far more sophisticated understanding of just who the Utes were and how they adapted to a difficult environment. Current research suggests Numic-speaking peoples entered the Four Corners area close to the time of its abandonment by the Ancestral Puebloans (Anasazi or *mokwič/muukwitsi*), roughly between 1200 and 1300 A.D. Exactly when and where these American Indians came from is still open to debate. Without going into a lengthy explanation, the languages of the Utes, Paiutes, and Hopis all belong to the same language family, the first two being mutually intelligible, while the Hopis share some commonality but are much further removed linguistically from the other two tribes.[9] Given this relationship, it is interesting to note how members of the Survey held the Hopis in high regard and assigned the Utes and Paiutes a much lesser stature. The Utes refer to themselves as Nuche and think of themselves as mountain people, while the Paiutes are Pa-Nuche or Water Utes, in each case denoting one of the group's main resources in different ecological niches.[10] Historically, the Utes themselves considered the Paiutes as poor country cousins of lesser status.

The Utes hunted and gathered over a large geographical area, roughly 225,000 square miles, encompassing approximately the western third of the state of Colorado, most of Utah, and the northern part of New Mexico.[11] Economic necessity and cultural adaptation encouraged dispersion rather than unity, although many of the groups shared friendly relations, intermarried, and assisted each other in war and peace. Each band occupied specific geographical areas, which they visited on a seasonal basis for food, clothing, and medicine as such supplies became available in the mountains, basins, plains, or along the rivers. Their adaptation to these different environments gave each group not only its distinctive diet and cyclical migration pattern, but also its name. Modern anthropological literature divides the eleven historical Ute bands into the Northern and Southern Utes, a designation that these people in the past would not have used.

Summarizing the history of the Utes up to 1870, one finds a group of people who were usually friendly to the Spanish, Mexicans, and Anglo-Americans. There were times, however, when alliances shifted and the Utes fought those opposing their interests. With the end of the Civil War and a renewed interest in opening the West, greater attention focused on Ute territory. Their agent, W. F. M. Arny, even encouraged the loss of Indian lands by stating in his annual report of 1867 that several thousand white families could homestead in the area north and east of the Animas River, Colorado. By establishing a reservation, the mining and agricultural resources of the region would be opened for development and could be "done at comparatively small expense, for it is cheaper to dispose of these Indians in this way than to fight and exterminate them."[12] By establishing a military post between the reservation and the settlements, the Utes could be controlled, the settlers protected, and resources developed.

On November 6, 1868, President Andrew Johnson signed a treaty that placed the Northern and Southern Utes on two reservations,

decreasing their combined territory by one-third.[13] Representatives
of every band signed the treaty.[14] The reservation headquarters for
the Northern Utes was located at White River, while the headquarters for the Southern Utes was at Los Pinos. It was not long before
the Utes would lose 4 million acres of Colorado land. The process
started slowly in 1871 and 1872, with trickles of miners coming to the
mountains in the summer and leaving in the fall. The Las Animas
Mining District around Silverton, for instance, had scores of claims
filed in 1871 on over two hundred silver lodes in just the one district.[15]
This was clearly in violation of the treaty of 1868. Agents notified the
commissioner of Indian Affairs. When the government directed the
miners to depart, the military remained ready to remove the miners.
But mining lobbyists went to work in Washington, and the troops
were never sent. The result: more miners, camps that grew in size and
sophistication, and angrier Utes.

The next year saw the same. The governor of Colorado, Edward M.
McCook, went on record as believing that the relatively small number
of Utes did not require as large a reservation as they had received by
treaty. Surely, some of that land could be relinquished for mining and
general economic development. There was, however, the problem of
the treaty, and so on April 23, 1872, Congress authorized the secretary
of the Interior to hold negotiations with the Utes to see if they were
interested in giving up the southern portion of their land where miners
were entrenched. On August 26, a five-day council commenced at the
Los Pinos Agency. Present were McCook; Felix R. Brunot, chairman
of the Board of Indian Commissioners; Colonel Price, commander of
the Eighth Cavalry stationed at Pagosa Springs; and an assortment
of Indian agents and other government officials. Ouray served as
spokesman for the Utes and their representatives from the Tabeguache, Muache, Capote, Uncompahgre, and the Jicarilla Apache bands.
Fifteen hundred Indians, in all, gathered for the occasion.

Following preliminaries, the council got down to business. Throughout the meeting, both sides maintained a "most kind and friendly feeling."[16] For five days the testimony did not change. The government's
position was simple: "There is no desire to force you to do that which
you may not wish to do. . . . This action on your part must be voluntary
and be concurred in by the chiefs and by the people of the nation.

. . . We want you to be happy and enjoy life as long as you live. . . . We have come here to talk with you and see if we can help you."[17] At the same time the commissioners knew that "The miners are already present in such numbers that their expulsion by legal measures would be almost impracticable." One need not wonder as to the extent of the duplicity. There was no mistaking the Ute position. Ouray was direct: "The Ute Nation does not wish to sell one span of its lands. We have all we want and the government is bound to protect us. . . . We are not satisfied with these trespassers. We do not wish to sell any of this land."[18] The Utes felt that their position was clearly understood and that both sides agreed that there would be no loss of land.

The evening before the commissioners departed, Ouray assured them that the miners and others did not have anything to fear. The Indians were "unanimously determined upon peace" and believed that the Great Father was ready to enforce the agreements made in the treaty of 1868. The commissioners understood this, later writing, "[W]e became satisfied that at least for the present it would be impossible to conclude any satisfactory negotiations with them."[19] Case closed, or so it seemed. In a year's time, almost to the day, Commissioner Brunot was back, this time singing a different tune. The hue and cry from the mining community and other interested parties had been heard, loud and clear. Now the commissioner was there to take land.

Supposedly, the Indians in the 1872 meeting had been prejudiced by "outside parties," but had now changed to a more "favorable disposition." The three reasons given for the negotiations had not changed: too much land, too few Indians, and the real reason—"The people of Colorado are anxious to have that portion of the reserve not needed for Indian purposes thrown open to entry and settlement . . . in order that the agricultural and mineral resources thereof may be more thoroughly and rapidly developed."[20] Brunot led the discussions, with talks starting on September 6, 1873. He concluded that there seemed "little to encourage us in hoping for a successful termination," refuting the premise that the Indians had changed their minds. Little wonder, when one considers that Ferdinand V. Hayden and a group of his men had been surveying the reservation, "which excited the suspicions of the Indians"; that "parties of miners had repeatedly endeavored to pass by the agency and enter the reservation at places where the

Indians were not willing they should go"; and that these miners had told the Indians that the government in the East could not protect them and that, "whether they sold the mines or not, they were going to stay."[21] The fact that the government had done nothing to remove the miners from reservation lands earlier certainly encouraged the white men and frustrated the Indians. Ironically, the commission felt that the only advantage it had in negotiating with the Utes was an "oft-tested friendship" and their earnest desire to keep the peace and build a positive relationship.

The first round of discussions began with the Utes realizing there had to be some give. They offered to sell only the tops of the mountains that now held mines, but none of the valleys.[22] As part of the deliberations, members of the commission and the Ute chiefs visited some of the six hundred lodes and three hundred miners actively working claims. They were impressed, but more importantly, they were reassured that the good agricultural land they desired had now been taken off the table. Those prime southern lands were to remain as part of the Southern Ute reservation. Four days of discussion resulted in the Utes signing over 4 million acres of land in what is now called the Brunot Agreement. They also scheduled a trip to Washington, D.C., for those leaders who desired to go. Ouray summarized his view of the government's process by saying, "All Utes understand the line [boundary lines on maps], and it is as we say. The lines in regard to the mines do not amount to anything; it is changing them all the time—taking a little now and a little again—that makes trouble. . . . The miners care very little about the government and do not obey the laws. . . . With you it is different; you talk in the name of the Great Spirit; we understand that, and think it right and ought to have great weight."[23] Over two hundred Indians signed the agreement, relinquishing territory they could never regain. Congress ratified the agreement on April 29, 1874.

Whether one uses such euphemisms as "manifest destiny" and "the settling of the West" or less euphonic words such as greed, lies, and broken agreements, the results were the same. Within a year's time—almost to the day of the ratified Brunot Agreement—some of Hayden's men were meeting in Washington to discuss their movement into Ute territory that summer. Much of this field season would be

Following the 1873 signing of the Brunot Agreement, which gave miners access
to the San Juan Mountains in Colorado, some of the negotiating participants
went to Washington, D.C., where this photo was taken. *Front row, left to
right*, Guero, Chipeta (Ouray's wife), Ouray, and Piah (Ouray's brother); *second
row*, Uriah M. Curtis, Maj. J. B. Thompson, Gen. Charles Adams, and Otto
Mears; *back row*, Washington, Susan (Ouray's sister), Johnson, Jack, and
John. *Courtesy Denver Public Library, Western History Collection, photographer
unknown, X-30679.*

spent traipsing over Ute lands already lost and despoiled by a van-
guard of miners and cattlemen. Members of the Survey team would
soon record the effects of these industries, while also encouraging the
settlement of new areas. As mapmakers, these harbingers of civilization provided the tools for orderly land sales—the township and range
grid system on a map. As Ouray pointed out, the Utes understood
clearly what the "lines" on a map meant. Two disastrous treaties had
already confirmed that.

Ouray had other problems. The Utes traditionally never embraced centralized leadership. There was no single spokesman until the government appointed one to serve as a figurehead for negotiating and treaty signing. Ouray became that man, and while he worked to represent his people's interest, there were many Utes who believed he was self-serving, power-hungry, concerned only about his own band, a traitor for agreeing to any land loss, and out of touch with the Utes' concerns. Yet whenever there was a conflict, the government turned to him and expected an answer, whether he had the power to effect a favorable outcome or not. So when the unpopular mapmakers arrived on his doorstep in 1875, ready for a season of fieldwork, Ouray was in a difficult position.

ORGANIZATION OF THE
HAYDEN SURVEY'S 1875 FIELD SEASON

When Hayden, Stevenson, and Gardner prepared for continuation of the Colorado work in 1875, personnel and procedures were well established. Planning for this field season began in the spring at the Survey offices in Washington, D.C., but the real work commenced in early June when the whole group—almost forty scientists, packers, cooks, and reporters—gathered at the Clear Creek camp on the outskirts of Denver. Hayden remained in Washington, planning to visit Denver later in the summer.[24] He had divided the Survey into seven groups, each with a specific task and area of responsibility. Experienced topographers, who had operational control while in the field, headed each one of the divisions. Hayden assigned two divisions to complete work previously begun in central Colorado along the Front Range. Gustavus R. Bechler and Allen David Wilson led these divisions, which were to work in the Middle and South Park areas, including the drainages of the upper Arkansas and North Platte Rivers.[25]

The bulk of the effort in 1875, however, was to be done in southwestern Colorado, extending west and east about thirty miles into New Mexico and Utah. The previous year, the Survey had reached the 108th meridian. The goal for this year was to move from that point west, sufficiently past the 109th meridian so that the Survey's primary triangulation could be linked to John Wesley Powell's survey of the Colorado River. Powell had performed this work under the auspices of the Smithsonian Institution, but in 1875 Congress transferred his survey to the Department of the Interior. Hayden, always a keen competitor, saw this change as an opportunity to expand his own brief to include the Colorado River basin. Thus, this year's work of the western crews would have particular political importance for Hayden.

James Gardner was to lead the Primary Triangulation Division in Hayden's absence from Colorado, while also serving as general director for all the field crews. He had the key task of extending the great triangles connecting the entire region upon which the more detailed topographic work depended. This division had the largest territory to cover. Gardner and his assistant, Frank Pearson, would assume the surveying tasks. Also along was Robert Adams, Jr., who served as a general assistant. He had been with the Survey since 1872.[26] In addition to his formal duties, Adams filed reports with the *Philadelphia Inquirer.* Two experienced packers, Shep Madera and Clarence Kelsey, oversaw the mules and camp equipment. Jacque Charpiot, who had been with the Survey in 1873, returned as cook. As an indication of the importance Hayden accorded the primary triangulation work, a reporter for the *New York Times*, Cuthbert Mills, accompanied Gardner's division.

The Primary Triangulation Division had no work to do until it reached the Los Pinos Indian Agency, nearly four hundred miles west of Denver. Rather than joining his crew on the long trek to the starting point, Gardner undertook a special project, surveying the Cucharas-Trinidad coalfields, a region of particular interest to Hayden's friends, William Palmer and William Blackmore. It is unclear if Hayden assigned this task to Gardner or if Gardner undertook it on his own initiative, since he knew Palmer and had stayed at the railroad baron's famed Glen Eyrie estate in Colorado Springs. Regardless of who initiated the coalfield study, Gardner, on the Hayden Survey payroll, spent several weeks engaged in a study that clearly benefited a private company, while the division he was to lead marched without him across Colorado to take up their official duties.

Two groups received the task of secondary triangulation: the Southwestern Division, which would survey the area from the Uncompahgre Valley to the lower Grand River, and the San Juan Division, moving south and west along that river. Hayden placed the Southwestern Division under the direction of geologist William Henry Holmes. Hayden and Holmes had known each other since the 1850s. As a young man, Holmes, a native of Ohio, had wanted to pursue a career in art, but study in Washington, D.C., led to work with some of the leading naturalists at the Smithsonian Institution. His illustrations of birds, nests, and eggs for the well-respected Smithsonian scientist Spencer Fullerton Baird and of invertebrate fauna for paleontologist Fielding Bradford Meek brought Holmes to Hayden's attention. Though never formally trained as a scientist, Holmes became a master geologist and cartographer through his work with Hayden. Holmes was part of the 1872 Yellowstone expedition and thereafter became one of Hayden's most valuable and productive workers. His ability to render geological formations and stratigraphy with accuracy and beauty was one of his lasting contributions. Along with William Henry Jackson, Holmes played an important role in establishing the modern culture of visual science.

For the 1875 field season, two topographers, George B. Chittenden and Townshend Stith Brandegee, assisted Holmes. Brandegee was new to the Hayden Survey. He had a degree in engineering from the Yale Sheffield Scientific School, but his passion was botany, which he had studied under Asa Gray at Yale. Brandegee was teaching school in Colorado in 1875 when Gray recommended him to Hayden. His engineering background, combined with advanced study in botany, made him just the kind of well-rounded field worker that Hayden and Gardner favored—competent at the practical task of surveying but a keen observer with a scientific mind. Brandegee spent only the 1875 field season with the Hayden Survey, then went on to a notable career in botany, settling in California and publishing on the plants of Mexico and the Baja California region. Chittenden also had studied engineering at Yale. After Gardner hired him for the Colorado field survey in 1872, Chittenden became one of the Survey's most valued topographers, a position he held until the Hayden Survey disbanded in 1879.

Hayden's plan for 1875 was for the Southwestern Division to travel west from Denver by horse and mule to a point at the 108th meridian, where the previous year's work had ended. Although Holmes and his crew established a number of triangulation stations east of that point on the outward journey, their main task was surveying a 6,500-square-mile region west to 109° 30' and between 36° 45' and 37° 30'. This area included portions of the San Juan, La Plata, Mancos, and Dolores Rivers as well as McElmo and Montezuma Creeks.

Holmes also had the assignment of further exploring the prehistoric ruins on the Mancos River that had been located the previous year. Two experienced packers, Tom Cooper and Jack Pierce, with John Raymond serving as cook, joined the scientists of the Southwestern Division. Cooper and Raymond had been with the Hayden Survey for several years. There were no reporters in this group.

The Western Division, headed by Henry Gannett, would also work from where the 1874 crews had left off at the 108th meridian and continue westward into Utah. Gannett's men, however, were to focus on the area north of Holmes's assignment in the drainages of the Dolores and Uncompahgre Rivers. Gannett was another of Hayden's seasoned field scientists. A graduate of Harvard, he held a degree in civil engineering. While there, Gannett worked at the university's astronomical observatory. Then, at age twenty-five, he joined Hayden's 1871 expedition to Yellowstone. His skill in making longitudinal observations attracted Hayden's interest, but over subsequent years, Gannett also developed into a valued topographer.[27] The total area to be surveyed by this group was about 6,000 square miles. The most western reach of their assignment was the La Sal Mountains, approximately thirty miles across the Colorado border into Utah. Establishing a triangulation point in the La Sals was the key to connecting Hayden's work to that of Powell on the Colorado River. The Western Division was to march from Denver to Los Pinos, the Southern Ute Reservation agency, and from that point begin surveying along a lengthy arc extending north, then west, turning south and returning east to a point in the La Plata Mountains. It was planned that all the divisions would gather at that point in mid-August.

Two assistants, W. R. Atkinson and Albert Charles Peale, joined Gannett. Atkinson had been a professor of mathematics at Hiram College in Ohio, but left the position because of ill health. He sought work through the Ohio Republican Party machine; it was Congressman James A. Garfield, long a supporter of Hayden, who asked that

the young mathematician be given work with the Survey. By 1875, Hayden was less interested in patronage appointments to the Survey than he had been in earlier years. He now favored men trained in fields needed to accomplish the topographic and geologic work. But Atkinson's mathematical background struck him as potentially useful for cartography. In subsequent reports about the work, there were vague references to one of Gannett's crew "breaking down"; this may well have been Atkinson, whose health wasn't ideal from the outset. Although Atkinson joined one of the field crews, he never worked for Hayden again and none of the Survey's published reports and bulletins are attributed to him.

Albert Charles Peale, by contrast, was one of Hayden's most trusted field men. They had been together on the first trip to Yellowstone in 1871 and during every field season since then. When Peale joined the Survey, he was fresh from medical school at the University of Pennsylvania, where he had first met Hayden, who was a professor of geology at the time. Mineralogy, not medicine, was Peale's passion, and although he was sometimes called upon to use his medical training while in the field, he never formally practiced medicine. (Peale was often referred to as "doctor" and published using the honorific, "Dr.") During the Yellowstone surveys he served as a mineralogist, but with the relocation of the Survey to Colorado, his role was as geologist on the two-man topographer-geologist teams that formed each division. He was twenty-six years old when he started on this fifth summer's work. The season proved to be an especially demanding one, but Peale worked efficiently and, by all indications, happily. At the end of the season he returned to Philadelphia to marry his fiancée, Emilie Wiswell, to whom he had written nearly every night while in the field.[28] After the Hayden Survey disbanded in 1879, Peale worked for the U.S. Geological Survey, producing landmark studies on mineral springs, including those in Yellowstone National Park. Ben Northington and Charles McCreary were the packers and "Judge" Porter the cook for this group. Porter, the only African American member of the field crew, had been with the Hayden Survey since 1873.

In addition to these surveying parties, William Henry Jackson's Photographic Division took to the field again with two assignments. The first was to take spectacular photographs of the central Colorado

Rockies. These had been visited in previous years, but Jackson had not procured what he and Hayden believed were photos as exciting as his famed "Mountain of the Holy Cross." As Jackson noted in his 1929 autobiography, he concluded that the 5" by 8" camera he had used previously was "wholly inadequate" to the "proper representation" of the Rockies.[29] In 1875 he decided to bring a large format (20" by 24") camera to get photos unlike anything done before in such remote locations. His second assignment was to follow up on his discovery the previous year of prehistoric ruins in southwestern Colorado. Although he took along his cameras and intended to take many photos, the object of this part of the work was to determine the geographic extent of the remnants of the as-yet-unnamed ancient civilization. The plan was to travel south and west of the Mancos River and then along the San Juan into Utah. From there, Jackson intended to travel farther south and west into Arizona to the Hopi mesas. For the first leg of his journey, two packers, a cook, and Edwin Atlee Barber accompanied him. Although listed on the Hayden roster as a botanist or naturalist, Barber was mostly interested in Native cultures. He went on to a distinguished career as a specialist in ceramics, particularly the ancient pottery of Mexico and the southwestern United States.[30] In addition to his official duties with the Survey, Barber also filed reports on Jackson's activities to the *New York Herald*. For the trip to the Hopi mesas, Harry Lee, a Colorado miner, who served as guide, interpreter, and liaison with the Indians, also accompanied the Photographic Division.

Crew members and reporters referred to the Survey divisions in various ways. The Western Division was sometimes called the Grand River Division, and the Southwestern Division the San Juan Division. Most often reports referred to them by the name of their designated leaders and their primary responsibilities, a format adopted here in this book:

Gardner Division—Primary Triangulation Division
Gannett Division—Western or Grand River Division
Holmes Division—Southwestern or San Juan River Division
Jackson Division—Photographic Division

The work assigned to these groups took them more than four hundred miles west of Denver, into a region inaccessible by rail or wagon road and with few established settlements. As Hayden noted in his final report, "The areas for exploration this present season were much

This lithograph made from a photo of the primary leadership of the 1874 Survey shows four of the major participants involved the next year. *From left to right*, William H. Holmes, George B. Chittenden, Ferdinand V. Hayden, Ernest Ingersoll, and William H. Jackson. *Courtesy Scotts Bluff National Monument*, SCBL 932.

farther from the base of supplies than heretofore, rendering the labor greater, and causing great loss of time in travelling to and from these bases."[31] To supply the divisions working in southwestern Colorado, he intended to establish a supply depot in the La Plata Mountains on the eastern perimeter of the intended survey area, a site of considerable mining interest since the early 1870s. One of the new camps, Parrott City, provided a good location for a central supply point. Hayden retained Charles Aldrich to oversee the Parrott City supply depot. Aldrich had no particular qualifications for the job. He had been a newspaper reporter and editor in his home state of New York and later in Iowa. He was also active in Republican Party politics, serving on a variety of state and federal commissions; from 1860 to 1870 he served as chief clerk of the Iowa House of Representatives. An amateur naturalist, especially interested in ornithology and the preservation of bird species, Aldrich was acquainted with the distinguished ornithologist Elliott Coues, who had worked with Hayden; it was this connection that probably brought Aldrich to Hayden's attention. After an eventful summer with the Hayden Survey, Aldrich returned to Iowa and in his later life served as a representative in the Iowa state legislature.

Now, in June 1875, he went by train from Denver to Pueblo, the last stop on the railroad. From there, he traveled southwest to Tierra Amarilla, New Mexico, where he was to rendezvous with a wagon train of supplies that Stevenson had arranged to be sent from Albuquerque. Aldrich took the supply train north to Parrott City, a journey that proved more difficult than anticipated. Once there, he had little to do but wait for the various divisions to stop in for resupply. He spent part of his time getting to know the miners of the region, fishing, and posting news reports to the *Chicago Daily Inter-Ocean*.

One of the advantages of locating the supply depot at Parrott City was the presence of John Moss, one of the principal developers in the La Plata mining region and a man well known to the Utes. Hayden understood that the southwestern Colorado surveying divisions were working in a region where Indian relations were tense. In 1874, the Hayden crew assigned to survey on the Southern Ute Reservation (as well as on lands lost under the Brunot Agreement) was turned away by the Indians. Both Gardner's Primary Triangulation Division and Gannett's Western Division were scheduled to return to the same area the next year. Apprehensive of a similarly hostile reception, Hayden secured the services of Moss, who contacted Ute leaders with assurances that the surveyors were in the region for a general scientific investigation and not to survey the controversial new reservation boundaries. Gardner also visited Chief Ouray at the Los Pinos Agency in late June, offering similar assurances and admonitions about good behavior. Nonetheless, the Utes were clearly agitated, and the Hayden crews approached their territory with trepidation.

If the region's Native inhabitants were likely to be a concern for the Hayden Survey, so too was the environment. The region into which the Hayden divisions headed was not unknown, yet it was an alien landscape to Anglo-American eyes. Early American visitors to Colorado Territory thrilled at the Rockies; their great escarpments and mountain valleys perfectly embodied nineteenth-century aesthetics of the picturesque and the sublime, especially in contrast to the endless, flat plains east of the Front Range. The landscape of the Front Range was, to Anglo eyes, comprehensible and useful, at least potentially so, in practical and aesthetic terms. But this was not true where the western slope of the Rockies give way to the Colorado basin in the western third of Colorado. Here the land was profoundly different. Instead of the mountain peaks, forested slopes, and watered river valleys familiar to most Americans through artistic representation, if not actual experience, there lay a desert labyrinth of buttes and canyons arrayed in an intricate and potentially deadly series of mazes.

The Four Corners region affords breathtaking yet unsettling vistas that provoke an unnerving sense of being lost—trapped even—in a nonsensical topography in which straight lines are made irrelevant by a plateau's precipices and river courses are unreliable guides for travel. In pragmatic terms, this landscape presented unparalleled difficulties for travel and for the tasks of surveying. As Hayden noted in his *Ninth Annual Report*, "The great trouble in working was lack of water. The parties were often obliged to ride out ten, fifteen, and even twenty miles from the rivers to make a station and back again for camp, because outside of the rivers themselves there was no water at all."[32] The *New York Times* was more blunt, describing the area in which the surveyors would be working as a "sterile fastness."[33] Members of the Survey saw the environment as hostile; although it intrigued them in a scientific sense, they never saw it as beautiful or picturesque or inspiring. When the 1875 field season ended, Hayden's men were happy to be rid of an area they saw, in Jackson's words, as "without a single interesting or redeeming feature, except the vestige of the long-forgotten race who once peopled its plains and canyons."[34]

Yet the work of the Hayden Survey, almost unwittingly, created a new desert plateau aesthetic, which, in the twentieth century, gave rise to its own visual and literary culture as well as institutional expression in the national park system. Jackson's photographs, by the simple act of making known to a wider public what had never before been imagined, helped popularize the distinctive features of the canyon and plateau country. As was the case with Yellowstone, photography proved that the strange and exotic landscapes of the Four Corners region were real. By linking the scenic views of the Colorado basin with the material remnants of the region's ancient civilizations, the Hayden Survey laid the foundation for the modern concept of wilderness, an ideal in which people are mere visitors, not inhabitants of a particular locale.[35]

The events of the Hayden Survey's 1875 summer field season were, on occasion, dramatic. But the majority of time was spent traveling across dry plateaus and along meager riverbeds, performing the mundane routines of camp life and familiar scientific tasks. The work could be physically demanding, although nothing beyond what a healthy young man could do without any special equipment or experience. The greatest demands on Hayden's men were patient observation; precision in making and recording measurements in hot, dry conditions; and tolerance for extended weeks of camp life. Yet within these ordinary—and occasionally extraordinary—activities we can see at work the transformative tensions between older ideas and practices and emerging new ways of imagining and constructing the world. It is not only the scientific work that these men performed, it is also how they went about that work and the ways in which they described themselves, the vast landscape through which they moved, and the people they encountered that tell us about a world in transition. These records, then, allow us to see within the routines of daily life and work, the great transformative currents of change at play in the late nineteenth century. Sometimes consciously, but often without self-perception, these men were making the world different.

# CHAPTER I

# An "Outfit of Special Character"

## Denver to Los Pinos Indian Agency

### JUNE 7–JULY 27

PREPARATIONS FOR THE HAYDEN SURVEY'S 1875 FIELD season began at its headquarters in Washington, D.C., on the top two floors of a large office building on the corner of Pennsylvania Avenue and Eleventh Street. *New York Times* correspondent Cuthbert Mills, who was to accompany the Survey that season, visited the busy offices in April to learn more about the "outfit of special character" destined for the trip west. He declared the Survey men he met that day to be "just the sort of fellows one would most desire for comrades in a mountain expedition." Mills found the Survey offices busy. William Henry Jackson was sorting images from his trip to Mesa Verde the previous year, and William Henry Holmes was preparing maps from the 1874 work. This activity reflected Hayden's commitment to quick publication of the Survey's work, but processing the information from one field season was also critical to preparing for efficient deployment of the divisions for the future undertaking. This year-round effort, distinctive to the Hayden Survey, was one of the keys to Hayden's success.

With a rapidity and comfort unthinkable only a few years before, the Hayden scientists left their East Coast homes and traveled by train to the bustling western city of Denver. A. C. Peale, who came from Philadelphia, had shopped with his mother in New York City on May 27 and, after passing through Niagara, Detroit, and Kansas City, reached Denver by June 2. As in previous seasons, the Hayden scientists rendezvoused with their western counterparts, the packers and cooks, at a camp outside Denver. For a week, everyone engaged in a flurry of activity, sorting equipment and supplies for each of the Survey's divisions. Then, to the delight of the city's residents, the whole expedition marched through the streets, separating at the edge of town toward their differing routes over the Rockies and on to their months-long labors in southwestern Colorado. The Gardner and Gannett Divisions were headed toward the Los Pinos Indian Agency, a journey that would take them nearly a month.

## GETTING ORGANIZED IN DENVER

The eastern scientists met in Denver, where the Hayden Survey maintained an office. They spent a week riding back and forth between camp and town, where they shopped for last-minute necessities; the packers and cooks were busy at the camp six miles away on Clear Creek, where the men from the separate divisions organized supplies, checked equipment, and prepared the mules for the long journey over the Rockies to western Colorado. F. V. Hayden did not arrive in Colorado until later in the summer, so it was James T. Gardner who supervised the preparations. A. C. Peale, about to embark on his fifth field season with the Hayden Survey, recorded the comings and goings in the concise, matter-of-fact tone of someone who had been through it all before. Cuthbert Mills, about to begin his first trip with the Survey, was more taken up by the excitement of the pending travel and the hustle and bustle of preparations. In the first of more than a dozen articles he would post to the *New York Times* over the coming months, Mills shared with his readers the challenges of getting men and mules on the road.

### A. C. Peale ❋ Denver, Colorado Territory, June 2

Had a good breakfast at Wallace this morning and a miserable dinner at Hugo. Spent the day reading Wilkie Collins' "Moonstone." We got to Denver about half past five o'clock and went to Charpiots and found Gannett and all the boys except Bechler and Chitt there. Aldrich is here. I came with Gannett to the boarding house he stays at and am in the room with him at Mrs. Powers. . . . Sent postals to Mother and Ellie.

June 3rd. Spent most of the day at the office and shopping. Saw Mrs. Jackson, who has not been well, and drove her from the office of her sister's, Mrs. Chalfant. Afterwards went to camp in a carriage with Jackson. Saw Judge and all the old men. Atkinson, Gannett's assistant, is in camp.

June 4th. Spent the day in Denver, shopping most of the time. Gannett was out at camp. This afternoon I wrote to Mother, to Ellie, Ed Hubly and to Taggart. Bechler came tonight. Wrote to Dr. Hayden.

June 5th. Spent the day in town finishing shopping. Wrote to Uncle John. This evening we had a dance here at the house but I did not go down. I called on Mrs. Jackson but did not see her, as she was not well enough to come downstairs. Chittenden came in tonight. Had my trunk brought to the office today.

Sunday, June 6th. Camp No. 1. Clear Creek. This morning dawned cold and wet, spoiling the plans of the ladies at the boarding house, who had intended paying us a visit at camp. It was cold enough for a fire. We went to the office, where I changed clothes and packed my trunk. I wrote to Emilie, to Dr. Mills and to Fred Jackson.

Billy, my mule, was sent in, and I rode to camp with Jackson and Holmes. Jackson is the only one who did not stay out. We will all leave in the morning. Adams came from the east tonight. He is the last one to come, except the Dr.

*Peale Diary, June 2–6, 1875, Howell Papers.*

### *Cuthbert Mills* ✾ *Camp Hayden near Denver, June 5*

That bewildering confusion in which the survey expedition seemed involved a few days ago has disappeared. Order reigns and system appears. The six messes into which the survey corps is divided according to the plans for this season are set off, each with its own cook, its tables and its tents, and instead of one general camp, there are half a dozen separate ones. The work of selection, repair, refurnishing, and provisioning has been going on busily for the past two days, and on Monday our little army of thirty-five or forty men and eighty odd animals will pull up stakes and start for the mountains. We shall

Clear Creek was a favorite starting and ending point for the Survey because of its close proximity to Denver with all of its amenities, including the railroad. Designated as Camp Hayden, this site was active for only a few weeks at a time. *Courtesy F. M. Fryxell Collection, American Heritage Center, University of Wyoming, Neg. #10165.*

probably all travel together the first day; our line of march will carry the whole cavalcade through the principal street of Denver. After that each division commander will take the route previously assigned to him.

The selection and apportionment of the mules and horses was done yesterday afternoon under Mr. Gardner's direction. There were a few new arrivals among them, but the herd was in the main composed of old acquaintances, which had been in the service of the survey for several years. Nine mules out of ten seem to have all the stubborn perversity of the ass, with the spirit of the horse; very few become thoroughly tractable under favorable conditions, and in this country, the conditions are extremely unfavorable for domestication, either of horses or mules. When not in use they run at large on the prairie, kept together by mounted herdsmen; in the winter they run loose. Very little consideration is shown them, a kick in the ribs being the most common method of starting. Under this system they are all pretty wild and catching them for use is lively work, as we find it.

When time for selection came, the herd was driven into an old barnyard enclosed by crumbling adobe walls which are dignified with the name of corral and nearly all the camp followed. The packers were provided with halters and ropes, and two or three who could use them, carried lariats. The afternoon was a broiling hot one and the cloud of dust soon raised by the rushing and trampling of the frightened animals became almost choking. Accompanied by the stock-master, Mr. Gardner looked over the herd and indicated each animal to be caught. Then commenced a lively chase. Round and round the corral went the whole lot, kicking, jumping, and snorting, while half a dozen men and everybody in turn, tried to separate the particular animal required, to allow the lariat man to make his throw.

. . . When all of the herd had been caught and apportioned off, the fitting of the aparejos commenced. An aparejo, as everybody knows, is simply two great leather cushions stuffed with hay which are slung across the mule and act as pads on which the load is packed. . . . I saw a fine, spirited animal brought up to have the aparejo fitted and it stood perfectly still until the "cinching" commenced. Then when two powerful men commenced with knee and arm to draw tight and tighter the broad band which holds the aparejo on, it protested. To say it kicked would be mild. For a few moments it seemed to be all legs. The packers let go everything and jumped around lively. Then they tied up one foreleg and commenced again, and still on three legs it bucked and jumped, reared and fell over backward, and it was only after ten minutes' hard work, when the animal lay on the ground almost exhausted, that the cinching was completed. Instead of a sleek and shapely mule it appeared then to have a stomach like an hour-glass. All the mules were not so vigorous in their protests as this one, but it was probably not because they disliked their treatment the less. Of course the riding animals are not subjected to this rough usage. There is no occasion for it. They are selected for their good walking powers, a walk being the usual marching pace in the mountains, and freedom from bucking tendencies. Every man in the party has his own riding mule, and the choice of these is a matter of some moment. When a man gets a good one he generally tries to stick to it.

*"The Western Surveys,"* New York Times, *June 13, 1875.*[1]

*Cuthbert Mills* ⁑ *Camp One, south of Denver, June 7*

With a punctuality not surpassed by that of the best regulated armies, the Hayden Expedition broke camp this morning and soon after breakfast the whole force was on the move. . . . It was about 4 o'clock when the earliest risers began to emerge from their tents to call out those who were still sleeping. By two's and three's these also came out, shaking themselves and pulling their coats more closely around them for the morning was chilly. Every one fell to work and for the next three hours the glade presented a scene of picturesque and lively activity. There were ninety animals to be packed or saddled, and all the immense variety of articles necessary for a five-month's journey through the mountains to be stowed away fit for packing.

While the small army of packers were fitting on the apparatus and packing on that portion of the general cargo which had been made ready—the mules meanwhile protesting with voice and feet, and the men in much the same way—other members of the force were striking their tents, rolling them up, strapping their blankets, selecting the most indispensable articles of clothing for their war bags and saddle pockets, examining rifles and pistols, saddling their riding animals, or possibly taking a wash in the stream as a cooler preparatory to the march. The last articles to be packed were the mess kits, which the cooks had been busily washing and getting together since breakfast. Several shouted "Good mornings" from the end of the glade, giving notice that Mr. Jackson's division was the first to go.

It was 8 o'clock when the little train began to file out of the grove. The other packers redoubled their exertions to make ready and shortly Mr. Gardner's and Mr. Holmes' divisions followed the first departures. There was a general handshaking and bidding of adieus with the members of the remaining divisions, which were to go different ways then at last we found ourselves fairly on the road. Our line of march led us directly south through Denver. When we reached the ridge which overlooks the town, there was Mr. Jackson's party and several gentlemen who had come out from Denver to meet us, awaiting our arrival. A general halt was called, the united trains brought up together, and in good shape the whole body filed down the hill, across the Platte [River] bridge, and up through the principal street of the town. It was a beautiful, sunny morning. Our fellows were in the highest spirits, the mules behaved astonishingly well, the townspeople exhibited the greatest good feeling, and everyone seemed to feel that our march through Denver was a great success.

*"The Hayden Survey: Breaking Camp,"* New York Times, *June 20, 1875.*

## The Gardner Division Heads to Western Colorado

With preparations completed, divisions organized, and supplies packed, the various groups headed west along different routes toward the Four Corners region, where their primary work would begin. Jackson and Holmes were headed for the La Plata Mountains, with plans to make photographs and establish triangulation stations along the way. (The westward travel of these divisions is described in chapter 2.) The Gardner and Gannett Divisions started for a planned rendezvous at the Los Pinos Agency on the Ute Reservation by late June. Gardner himself remained behind to finish some tasks in Denver and then left for the Trinidad coalfields. He spent most of June there, engaged in a private survey of coal and iron resources on lands owned by backers of the Denver & Rio Grande Railroad. He rejoined his crew at the Los Pinos Agency. Cuthbert Mills reported the progress of the Gardner Division as it moved westward from Denver. Robert Adams also posted on the group's progress to the *Philadelphia Inquirer* and the *Rocky Mountain News*.

### *Cuthbert Mills* ❋ *June 7*

Leaving the pretty little town behind us—and Denver is as pretty a town as one can find in the country—we struck into the Plum Tree Creek road en route for Colorado Springs. A railroad runs down to this place, which is rapidly becoming a fashionable summer resort, but transportation is so costly that for this and other good reasons it was thought advisable to march there rather than to take the railroad. Our division (Mr. Gardner's) was under orders to march the whole distance; the others were to turn off some miles down and cross the country to the east, pursuing the routes assigned to them.

We marched about fifteen or sixteen miles close beside the railroad line, and between three and four [o'clock] turned aside into a gulch and camped beside a dry creek. On the opposite side of it was a small frame house of the roughest description. Here we obtained water which, being from a well, tasted strongly of the alkali with which the soil is impregnated. With some difficulty we also obtained milk at ten cents a quart. The settler had not much to spare. I asked him how his crops had faired. He said the grasshoppers had eaten almost everything he had put in.

*"The Hayden Survey: Breaking Camp,"* New York Times, *June 20, 1875.*

### Robert Adams ✳ On route from Denver, [n.d.]

It is nearly two weeks since we broke camp at Denver and the parties are by this time scattered in all directions. It will therefore be impossible for me to follow their doings, except such reports as we may from time to time receive, so I will take up the route of our party, viz., the geographical division, under Mr. Gardner. Leaving Denver, we followed the river Platte south along the main road to Colorado Springs. Good ranches lined the way on each side, and the miles of fences and passing trains told us we were still in the land of civilization. The pack animals, too, fretted under their newly-imposed burdens, and our skillful packers were kept busy in tightening their loads. A night's sleep in the open air of Colorado refreshes one after the greatest fatigue; half past four in the morning found us up with good appetites and ready for the march.

This second day's ride furnished new beauties in scenery. Crossing the divide we left the waters of the Platte and followed those of Plum Creek. Leaving the road with my companion, we made a detour to the right, passing through Pleasant Park, the home of Mr. Perry, President of the Kansas Pacific Railroad. He has, indeed, chosen a lovely spot. Shut in by foothills with the new peaks crowning the wall, this protected valley is covered with verdure and flowers. Large boulders of red and white sandstone rise, solitary and grand, through the park, while the full-blooded Alderneys and Durhams, grazing on the banks of the mountain stream or resting under the shade of the forest pine, lend a domestic character to the wildness of the landscape.

The park is several miles long; we rode through enraptured with its beauties, looking back with regret as we turned towards the dusty road to rejoin the pack train.

On this day's ride we were overtaken by a Ute Indian on his way to the reservation. We were much amused by the sudden galloping up of a new member of the survey to join us for protection, especially as he confided to us later that he thought the Indian was an escaped lunatic, never having seen the noble red man in his native garb before. The supposed lunatic, however, proved himself to be of sane mind. Requesting a chew of tobacco, he returned the whole plug to his pocket instead of giving it to the owner. The mistake is not an unnatural one, for the dress of an Indian who frequents settlements is a strange mixture of civilized hat, shirt, shoes, and rifle, with a savage amount of paint, feathers, and buckskin leggings, with a tremendous amount of fringe down the sides of the same.

The third and fourth day's ride was mainly over a vast plain occupied with sheep ranches, with lazy Mexicans herding the drove, basking all day in the sun until we entered the pass to Monument Park. This is one of the places of interest adjacent to Colorado's famous resort of Manitou.[2] As we met the carriages filled with people dressed a la mode, we felt more like tourists than explorers; some of the party might have been detected arranging their neckties, etc., with an effort to spruce up, but alas! Our already blistered faces and burnt hands betrayed we were but mule whackers after all. . . .

"Hayden's Expedition," Philadelphia Inquirer, *June 29, 1875.*[3]

*Correspondent with the*
Rocky Mountain News ❊ *Poncha Pass, June 23*

The easy marches that Mr. Gardner's party have made in getting from Denver to the [Colorado] Springs and from there to this place, have not hurt the stock at all, though they carried full packs. Our mules, benefited by the rest they have had here where we are awaiting Mr. Gardner's orders before resuming the march to Saguache, are as fat as a roll of butter, and Shepard Madera, our boss packer, is happy at the sight of them. We usually call him Shep. He is one of those packers that a mule is proud to be cinched by. He can pack a mule with anyone, balance his packs to a half ounce, pull a rope like a locomotive, make the flakiest of biscuits, quote Shakespeare, and stand on his head. These are accomplishments which everyone will acknowledge to be rarely combined in one individual.

He never loses his temper except when the stock wanders more than five miles from camp. That is the limit of his forbearance. They did that a morning or so ago. Shep's "pard," I scarcely like to give his name because he is a modern young fellow who would blush to see it in print but it is Clarence Kelsey, had gone on a hunt after the stock and was away so long that Shep became alarmed and started out, too. Scarcely had he got over the hill when the whole herd came tearing up the canyon as if a certain nameless gentleman himself were after them. But it was only Kelsey. About two hours later, Shep came limping into camp, walking with the help of a big stick. His boots were new and hurt him while his stockings had been worn into holes by his tramp. Under these circumstances it will be conceded that a man might be excused for displaying some little temper, but Shep did not. He simply sat down and spent the following twenty minutes or half an hour in betting his bottom dollar, his boots, his life, and various other articles usually supposed to be necessary to one's comfort and convenience, that each night hereafter he would tie every adjective mule in the herd neck-and-heels and then see if they would go on any more five mile rambles.

*"The Hayden Survey,"* Rocky Mountain News, *June 27, 1875.*[4]

### Cuthbert Mills ✳ Saguache, July 7

When one stands at the head of such a valley as the San Luis and looks south to where it meets the sky as the ocean does, and on either hand views the distant ranges of mountains which bound it, cloud-capped, rugged, and inexpressibly magnificent, the observer is impressed with the grandeur of the scene. Let him look down at his feet and he will see that the spot he stands on is a dry, fine gravel like the shingle on the sea beach in which a few blades of gray grass seem struggling for life. He will travel all day and find the soil nearly the same. He must so arrange his marches that each evening shall find him at the edge of some of the rare streams which water the valley; there he may find food for his stock.

Here a "proud mule" has its gear being secured with a diamond hitch by Shep Madera *(right)*. Beneath the load is an aparejo, or pack saddle, with stuffing that was adjustable for the comfort of the animal and that prevented slippage and injury. *Courtesy Hayden Party Photofile, American Heritage Center, University of Wyoming.*

The country has for many years been settled by ranchmen, but a ranch requires miles of ground for the cattle to range over. As the constantly coming tide of immigration brings in more land-hungry men, the limits of the ranches are gradually being narrowed. As unfavorable as the soil seems, farming must eventually take the place of grazing. Here, the immigrant farmer is now coming, who must irrigate every foot of the soil he puts a plow into. Let him go south and he must do the same. But south and southwest he is going. It is evident that the ideal picture of the Western pioneer with which we have been so long familiar must be changed. It is no longer the stalwart, bare-armed man, leaning contemplatively on his axe beside the felled tree in the forest clearing with the log hut in the background. Now it is the same individual on a sandy plain, resting on his spade and considering the line on which he shall run his irrigating ditch, while an adobe house takes the place of the well-known log cabin. The wealth of this region lies in its cattle and mines.

This town [Saguache] derives its main subsistence from the cattle trade with over a million dollars' worth of cattle owned in the section which is tributary to it.[5] It is a typical western town as things are now and is only thirteen months old. About eighteen months ago, two men who owned the land put their heads together and started the town. They set up a weekly paper and a very creditable looking paper it is. They used it to advertise the great advantages of the town of Saguache, and by the exercise of a great deal of energy and no little shrewdness, they disposed of the town lots and brought in settlers.

About one half of the hundred houses in the place are adobe. This is a word which sounds well, and in its usual translation of "sun-dried brick," it sounds well, too. But in plain English adobe is mud and mud it stands confessed, after a house built of it has been beaten upon by a few rain and snow storms. It is, however, the cheapest material of which houses can be built in this almost treeless country so certainly it speaks well for the energy of the people here that they have done so much for a place which had no mining excitement or any extraneous aid to start it. Mr. [Otto] Mears, one of the originators of the town, and owner of the land, the main store-keeper for this region, and the oldest settler, claims that he does a business of $140,000 a year and that there is "a heap of money in the town."[6] I hope there is, and that the little town increases as fast as its inhabitants' desire for they certainly have treated us in the heartiest way.

*"The Hayden Expedition: From Poncha Pass to Saguache,"*
New York Times, *July 18, 1875.*

## THE GANNETT DIVISION MOVES TO
## LOS PINOS INDIAN AGENCY

Henry Gannett and his crew in the Western (Grand River) Division had left Denver at the same time as Gardner's Primary Triangulation crew and followed roughly the same route to the rendezvous at Los Pinos. As A. C. Peale described in his diary, the trip was uneventful as men and mules grew accustomed to the routines of travel. Moving ever further from the comforts of Denver, the crew enjoyed fresh foods, good meals, and leisurely evenings at camp, knowing that these would become increasingly scarce. At Los Pinos, the Hayden crews had their first substantial encounter with the Indians on whose territory they would soon be surveying. Peale's diary, filled with observations of Ute families at the agency as they were issued provisions, hints at the unease both sides felt about what lay ahead.

### A. C. Peale ✴ North Fork of South Platte, June 10

Platte near Slaght's Ranch. The aparejos needing refilling Gannett decided not to move camp this morning. We bought hay at the ranch and the packers were occupied almost all day in putting it in the aparejos. I tried fishing this morning but did not succeed in getting even a bite. About noon I went down to the ranch and read the latest Denver papers. The afternoon I spent reading "M'liss." Steve joined us this evening. He says Gardner and Aldrich left for Colorado Springs yesterday.

Friday, June 11th. Camp No. 5. South Park on branch of Michigan Creek. We broke camp this morning about 8 o'clock and had to leave one of our mules at Slaghts, it being too lame to travel, having been injured while being shod, before we left Denver. . . . It has been cool and pleasant travelling today. Last night was cold.

Monday, June 14th. Camp No. 8. Trout Creek. Got away from camp this morning rather later than usual (8:30 A.M.). . . . Gannett and Atkinson left camp before the train to do some hunting. They had not been gone long when Atkinson's mule came back without him. Shortly after, Atkinson came back on foot. He had seen a deer & fired at it while holding the bridle. The mule scared and upset Atkinson. When we started I found he had left the barometer, so I carried it and after travelling about two miles met him coming back for it. It has been very windy and those riding behind the train today were coated with dust. I went fishing after we camped but was unsuccessful although I had several bites. Judge caught one fish.

Saturday, June 19th. Camp No. 12. Saguache Town. Holman and I reached the town about a quarter after eleven, Gannett and Atkinson coming in soon after. We found Steve here with the mail. I had five

letters, two each from Emilie and Mother and one from Dr. Hayden.
. . . Mr. Aldrich passed through here a few days ago but we do not
know where he went although probably to Del Norte. Gannett had
a postal from Jackson telling us that our dry plates are here. He was
in Canyon City the 14th. Saguache is going downhill. It is not nearly
as lively as it was last fall.

Sunday, June 20th. Camp No. 13. Saguache Creek. We left Saguache this morning about half past eight, Holman and I riding ahead.
We stopped at the Rock Cliff dairy, a short distance above camp
and waited until Gannett and Atkinson came up. We lunched on
biscuit, fresh milk, and buttermilk. A German keeps the place and
it is the nicest dairy I have ever seen. We brought milk and butter to
camp, and will make arrangements to have butter sent to us during
the season. Before dinner most of the boys took a bath in the creek.

Tuesday, June 22nd. Camp No. 15. Los Pinos Creek above the
Agency. Gannett, Holman, Atkinson and I came in ahead of the
train, reaching the Agency about 11 o'clock. Gannett and I took dinner
with Mr. and Mrs. Bond.[7] Our supplies are here; Gannett separated
them into three piles, one for ourselves, one for Steve, and the third
for Gardner. We spent most of the afternoon at the Doctor's office
getting a vocabulary of the Ute language, as far as he has made it out.
Shavano, the war chief of the Utes, was at the agency, and does not
want us to go to the Uncompahgre without permission from Ouray.
When he learned that Gannett is going to see Ouray he was satisfied. It has been showery all afternoon, the first rain we have had this
season. After we came to camp, I wrote to Mother and to Emilie so
they can be mailed in the morning early.

Wednesday, June 23rd. Camp No. 15. Los Pinos Creek near Agency.
Gannett, Mr. [Henry F.] Bond and Dr. Mack went down the creek to
see Ouray about our getting permission to go on their reservation. The
talk was not very satisfactory. Ouray said he would not be responsible
if there was any trouble. He was told that we were ordered to go in and
if there was any trouble he would have to be responsible. He seemed
to be offended that he had not been notified from Washington as he
had been about the survey of the boundaries of the reservation, which
is to be carried on this summer. . . . Gannett has decided to wait until
Mr. Gardner comes here.

Thursday, June 24th. Camp No. 15. Los Pinos Creek near Agency. I remained in camp all day; most of the boys are going in to the Agency to separate supplies, and bring them to camp. I spent the morning getting my things ready for work. I put buckskin on my working breeches. I finished my letter to the Press and wrote some to Mother, and spent the rest of the afternoon reading. Some of our supplies were brought to camp in a wagon. Dr. Mack came out with Gannett and took supper with us. The Indians say we must not go on the reservation.

Friday, June 25th. Camp No. 15. Los Pinos Creek near Agency. Dr. Mack stayed with us all night and took breakfast, after which he and Gannett went to the Agency, the doctor riding my mule. I spent the day in camp reading most of the time in *Harper's Magazine*. . . . Gardner has not yet arrived, nor can we hear where he is.

Tuesday, June 29th. Camp No. 15. Los Pinos Creek near Agency. I spent the day in camp reading. Had a shower this afternoon. No news of Gardner yet.

Wednesday, June 30th. Camp No. 15. Los Pinos near Agency. We heard that Gardner's party had been seen at Poncha Pass waiting for Gardner, who left them at Colorado Springs saying he would join them in eight days. He was waiting on General Palmer and Ex Gov. Hunt. The party had been in camp over a week and did not know where Gardner was.

Thursday, July 1st. Camp No. 15. Los Pinos Creek near Agency. This being issue day at the Agency most all the boys went down. Provisions are issued every ten days. The Indians began to come in about 11 o'clock and by one all were at the Agency. They came in groups, dressed in their best. The bright colored blankets made them very picturesque. Scarlet, magenta, blue, green and striped Navajo blankets gave variety to the costumes. One old man had a suit of broadcloth, rather rusty, and a dilapidated beaver hat with the nap all worn off. It looked as though it had been "sat on" for several months. Another was resplendent in a military coat with huge epaulets and red sash. He wore a military hat. His uniform degenerated toward his heels. As long as his head alone showed he made rather a good appearance.

Some of the bucks have a broad piece of flannel trailing behind from beneath their blankets, like a tail.

Ouray does not mingle with the vulgar herd, the work falling on the other chiefs. He is too dignified to take part. His squaw brought up his ponies while we were at the Agency. She has to do a great deal of work. I saw Shavano, Piah, Sapinero, Guero and ever so many other Indians. They all seemed very friendly.

The beef was given out first alive (on the hoof). Some escaped and there was a great deal of excitement as the Indians chased them, shooting as they ran. The Indians shot the remainder in the corral. One of them was not dead when the Indians jumped over the fence and they tortured it in the most barbarous manner, hacking at it with hatchets and knives. The cattle for the chiefs were killed separately. The meat was divided and then the flour was issued.

The squaws were ranged in semicircles about the door of the storehouse, squatting on the ground, while Shavano distributed tickets among them. When the flour, etc. was given out there was a crowd of black heads like a lot of mops, below which was a mass of bright colors of the shawls on the backs of the squaws. It reminded me of a soup house in an eastern city. . . .

Gannett has decided to move on Saturday. Mr. Bond, Shavano, and another Indian will go with us as far as the Uncompahgre Valley. Steve will travel with us a few days. We had showers this afternoon. Couracaute wore a military uniform.

Friday, July 2. Camp No. 15. Los Pinos near Agency. I spent the morning in camp writing letters to Mother and Emilie. Our supplies were brought out in a wagon and packs arranged for a start tomorrow.

*Peale Diary, June 10–July 2, 1875, Howell Papers.*


## THE GARDNER DIVISION
## AT LOS PINOS INDIAN AGENCY

As Peale's diary suggests, relations with the Utes were tense and posed a potential problem for the Hayden survey crews. This group of people, who, until recently, had been generally friendly with the U.S. military and others involved with westward expansion, were now becoming restless. Their lands were under assault by miners, cattlemen, and other vanguards of encroachment, fostering suspicion. Robert Adams tried to place the situation facing the Hayden Survey that summer in

Piah *(right)* and other warriors at the Los Pinos Agency, 1874. Three of the five men wear peace medals and carry new Winchester Model 1873 repeating rifles. Each has a blanket that was worn in different ways for various occasions. *Courtesy National Anthropological Archives, Smithsonian Institution, MS 4605 (01603609).*

context for readers of the *Philadelphia Inquirer.* Cuthbert Mills also described life at the agency for the *New York Times.*

James Gardner, who had field responsibility for all the Hayden crews, had spent most of June separate from the other divisions, pursuing his own project. He finally rejoined his men at Los Pinos in early July to perform one of his main tasks—conferring with Chief Ouray. His crew, and that headed by Gannett, had not yet begun their work on lands still part of the Ute Reservation or only recently ceded under the Brunot Agreement. Like his counterpart, Gardner also had a lively encounter with Ouray about surveying in the La Sal Mountains, since the government had specified that as spokesperson and leader of the Utes, Ouray would be held accountable for any problems. Ouray realized he had very little control over an amalgam of Utes, Paiutes, Jicarilla Apaches, and Navajos, who had remained independent of various tribal agencies. All that Ouray could do was to caution and advise. Gardner reported to F. V. Hayden on his July 11 meeting with Ouray later in the year, when he returned to Denver. By that time, exactly what Gardner hoped his June visit with Ouray would prevent had, in fact, happened.

*James Gardner* ✳ *Denver, September 18*

Dear Sir [F. V. Hayden], On the 11th of July, of this year, I had an interview with Ouray, head chief of the Utes at the Los Pinos Agency, in the presence of Mr. Henry F. Bond, the agent. Ouray, convinced that we were sent to the reservation by an express act of congress to collect such information as the government needed and without which the respective rights and relations of the whites and Indians could never be properly adjusted, promised full protection to our parties. He then asked our routes of travel. It was all satisfactory until I spoke of going to the Sierra La Sal. Then he said that was not good; that the Indians there were robbers; that they never came into any reservations, either of the Utes or Pah Utes, but lived by depredations in Utah and by trade with the Navajos; that they were in the habit of killing one or two men found alone and stealing a few head of stock over in the direction of Salt Lake, and then retreating across innumerable and almost impossible canyons to their mountains. He said nothing of their trading with the Utes, at this time, nor did he speak of any Utes being among them, and from everything said, I inferred that they were Pah Utes. He said the band was small and would not probably dare to attack seven armed men, but that we must watch our mules well. He also said that they were farming in the valleys on the east and west side of the mountains alternate years, and that this year they ought to be on the east side of the range.

*"The Old Man of the Mountains,"* Rocky Mountain News,
*September 22, 1875.*[8]

## Robert Adams ✳ Los Pinos Agency, August 1

The Utes are one of the most powerful of the southern tribes who as a nation are friendly to the whites. This amicable feeling is owed partly to their intercourse for a long period with the Mexicans and also to a terrible chastisement by the soldiers and volunteers inflicted upon them in the Arkansas Valley about 12 years ago. This was in punishment for their attack upon Pueblo, [Colorado], situated on that river, then only a trading post unable to defend itself.[9] This led to the establishment of Fort Lyon which has been maintained as a military post ever since.

Ouray, their chief, is a very intelligent man and has raised himself solely by his ability, for strange to say, he is not a full-blooded Ute, as his mother belonged to the Navajo tribe.[10] He was brought up by Major [Lafayette] Head at Conejos and speaks Spanish fluently, as do most of the tribe. Their reservation comprises fifteen thousand acres, and occupies the western portion of Colorado. Most of it is a mountainous region, abounding in game, but some fine valleys lie within its limit, capable of cultivation. To labor, however, the Utes, like all other Indians, are not inclined. The government supplies them liberally with rations and there is plenty of game and so they are not to blame. Ouray controls most of the nation with unbounded influence and as long as his counsels prevail there is no danger of the present peaceful relations being broken.

Crossing the divide we entered into a beautiful valley through which flows Cochetopa Creek at the upper end of which lies the agency. We could not but realize the different relations existing between the government and these Indians with those in the north by the appearance of the few peaceful buildings comprising the agent's house and the necessary store and workshops. We contrasted this scene with that of our approach to the Crow Agency in Montana four years ago. There was a huge fortification, square in shape, with bastions projecting at the corners, the buildings all within the enclosure and massive oaken gates that dropped like a portcullis at sundown, after which none were allowed to enter. Indeed as we rode across the broad plain upon which it lies, we were strongly reminded of a Norman keep, so formidable was its appearance and so angular were its outlines.

We camped on the stream; as our tents arose amid the surrounding lodges, the whiteness of our canvas contrasted strongly with the yellow smoked skins of the neighboring tepees. We were soon inundated with visitors whose olfactory nerves can scent a meal from a great distance, but we dared not extend hospitality to one without danger of being fairly eaten out of tent and camp by all. After dinner we called upon the Reverend Mr. Bond, who is the agent at Los Pinos for the Southern Utes, and were kindly received. I cannot help expressing our great appreciation for the many hospitalities received at the hands of he and wife during the three days of our stay. We learned from Mr. Bond that the Indians objected to our entering their reservation for the purpose of exploration. After the Black Hills experience [with the Sioux] they were scarcely to be blamed, fearing that, if treasure or arable land were found, they would soon be driven from their homes.

It is proper to state, in this connection, one of the great advantages of our survey. Had the government possessed one of our geological maps of that section, no doubt could have arisen as to the nature of the country and thousands of dollars and many lives would have been saved in determining the question. We accordingly repaired to Ouray's residence, which consists of an adobe house, when Mr. Gardner was not long in satisfying him of the value of our survey, both in laying down the limits of the reservation, hitherto not done, and in obtaining a good map of the country and a thorough knowledge of the resources of it. The visit was particularly enjoyed by the writer, since he and Ouray were old friends, having met in Denver two years ago, when he had the chief and a dozen braves photographed for the [sentence incomplete]. At this point we had a very merry time in coaxing some of the warriors to unbend sufficiently to allow the camera, with its dangerous looking projectile, to be pointed at their martial breasts.

We then returned to camp, but sleep was almost impossible, owing to a wretched howling kept up all night long in a neighboring lodge. This was explained to us next morning by Dr. Mack, the resident surgeon, to be the cries of the medicine man to cure a dying client, who believed if the sufferer fell asleep he would never awake. He thus employed this method of curing by denying the exhausted man of all repose. The doctor could do nothing, his services being declined, or rather his directions not attended to, the Indians giving preference to their own school of treatment. The medicine man is held in great repute by the Indians, not only in the healing art but in all questions of state and prophecy; opposed to the civilization of the whites as destructive of their power, they are our bitter enemies and often influence the Indians beyond the control of the chiefs, and are at the bottom of many an outbreak.

The next day, Sunday, presented one of the most picturesque scenes. It was the tenth day since the last issue of rations so the noble red men came pouring in to receive their allowance, oblivious of the fact that it was a day of rest for the pale face. They came galloping over the hills from every direction, their ponies prancing, and feathers waving with the brilliant colors of their Navajo blankets adding to the beauty of the scene. The squaws followed more slowly with their papooses slung in their blankets behind or securely strapped in the barbarous wicker baskets [cradleboards] in which they incase them. A few older children were tied on to ponies, taking their first riding lessons, laughing and shouting with delight as they galloped along, whipping their horses with their quirts to go faster. On learning no grub was to be obtained, they contented themselves in passing the day in horse racing on a neighboring plateau. Single pairs or up to a dozen at a time indulged in trials of speed, ceasing only with the setting of the sun.

Then followed a howling even louder than during the previous night, resembling the Harvard cheer of "rah, rah, rah," only in a more monotonous tone. This proceeded from a large tepee, brilliantly lighted, and was soon recognized as the cries accompanying their gambling and continued revelry. Their method consists of two pieces of bone, one black and the other white, which are hid in the hands behind the back. The closed hands are then held up to the front, the opposite Indian guessing which fist contains the black bone. If correct, he wins and the holder then pays one counter and passes the bones to the winner, who in turn hides the bones for another to guess. Each player has ten sticks for counters and when these are exhausted, he loses his stake which generally consists of a blanket or pony, but sometimes even his squaw. A white man who once lived with the Indians made the Snake tribe nearly bankrupt by having a double set of bones up each sleeve attached to rubber strings.[11] Of course they never guessed right, as he would instantly let that bone fly up his sleeve and show the other. He was finally detected and drummed out of camp.

The Utes, like all Indians, are great gamblers and many a warrior is unhorsed and unarmed, staking the things he prizes most in life to his devouring passion. The game lasted long into the night, as we could tell by the unceasing "Rah! Rah! Rah!" of the participants. The issue next day was a sight as odd as it was interesting. Double the number of Indians came riding in arrayed in all sorts of costumes and riding various animals, sometimes a whole family on one horse, father and squaw, with papoose slung behind. One chief, Chorianty, was dressed in the uniform of a major-general, epaulettes and all. The most comical was a huge "buck" mounted on a small burro, a Mexican donkey, and carrying a large cotton umbrella opened above his head. For what earthly purpose mortal could not tell, as it was a cloudy day, so provided protection against neither rain nor sun.

Our ideal of the Indian was realized by the appearance of the second chief, Sapinero, who is tall of stature, finely developed physically, and whose carriage is so full of dignity he seems every inch a chief. His countenance has a calm repose about it that impresses one with a look of wisdom backed by a depth of feeling that would be terrible were the passions aroused. His dress was simply gorgeous, his blankets and leggings covered with broad bands of the finest beadwork, for which his squaw is famous. He was the only Indian of the hundreds assembled who fulfilled the portraits as drawn by Catlin or Cooper thirty years ago. The squaws among the Indians do all the work, so consequently the flour and bacon were delivered to them. They carried whole sacks and lashed them to the horses. Their physique is finely developed, being much more muscular than the men who are of light frame and generally very lean until an advanced age. They take but little exercise, except on horseback, and to one's surprise, are very chilly, continually seeking the fire, which makes it hard to understand how they stand exposure so well.

The utmost good humor prevailed; a continued chattering kept up all the while. One ancient squaw of immense proportions seemed the butt of all the witticisms, but from the roars of laughter that followed her retorts she was evidently able to hold her own against all comers. The scene changed to one of great hilarity when it came to the issue of sheep. The flock had been driven into the corral, when some of the men, but more boys, entered with their lariats to lasso them. The animals ran around the enclosure frightened to death, and when caught, struggled frantically to get free. Many a hard tussle took place between the smallest of the boys and the sheep; the strength was about equal and as they rolled about, shouts of applause arose from the spectators who had climbed up all around the fence. A more comical scene could not be imagined; it far surpassed any circus. The Indians were soon engaged in butchering the captured sheep, eating certain of the entrails raw. Most of the Indians were enveloped in the far-famed Navajo blankets, one of which the writer has coveted for a long time. They are woven by a neighboring tribe to the Utes, who trade for them and prize them highly. They are very heavy, of brilliant colors, and woven so closely that they hold water.

The red men proved to be sharp bargainers, as I found to my cost, and have entirely lost faith in the reported impositions of the white traders. One chief demanded a pony for his blanket; it was hard to make him understand that we were so poor that we rode mules, an animal despised by the braves. I finally succeeded in swapping for two, but gave their full value in greenbacks. We watched an Indian purchasing his outfit at the trading store. He wanted canvas to cover his tepee, quoted the prices at Saguache and Denver, and beat about until he got a bargain. They now began to scatter in all directions, the horses ridden by the squaws laden with flour and bacon, the sheep hanging at the sides, while the men pranced about on their ponies in all their glory. Suddenly half a dozen started running with wild yells, but it was some time before we learned the object of their chase. It proved to be a jack rabbit they were endeavoring to run down, but he eluded them and escaped. This ended the events, and with the parting of light they disappeared over the range to close one of the most interesting days of our trip.

*"Hayden's Survey: Indians—Los Pinos Agency,"*
Philadelphia Inquirer, *August 30, 1875.*

# CHAPTER 2

# *"Grand and Beautiful Scenery"*
## Denver to Parrott City
### JUNE 7–JULY 27

W ILLIAM HENRY JACKSON SET OUT FROM DENVER ON
June 7, traveling through Colorado Springs, Canon City,
Mosca Pass, San Luis Valley, Del Norte, and Antelope Park, with a
two-week side trip to the Lake Mining District and Lake San Cristobal.[1] The Photographic Division took this different route toward
southwest Colorado to fulfill its special assignment of photographing
particular scenic vistas. Jackson had brought with him a large-format
camera. As he would later write about working at 13,000- to 15,000-
foot altitudes, "such cross-tacking and zigzagging, puffing and blowing was never had." Add to this challenge, problems associated with
working with a 20" by 24" camera in inclement weather—rain, snow,
and cold temperatures—and one can sense some of the challenges
the men faced.

Upon completing this work, Jackson intended to replenish his supplies in the La Plata Mining District before heading toward the Hopi
mesas. Parrott City had been opened the year before, so the Hayden
Survey established a supply depot at the newly created town founded
by Capt. John Moss and named after financier Tiburcia Parrott of San
Francisco. Both men held hope that rich silver deposits were located
there. Though that dream had vanished within ten years, at the time
of the Survey, rampant speculation still fed this growing community
and encouraged Hayden to use it as the base of operations.

Charles Aldrich was responsible for transporting the heavy wagons
loaded with supplies to that point. At forty-seven, he was one of the

oldest men in the field that year and had little experience in freighting in the southern Rockies. He was, however, an accomplished journalist, and his dispatches to the *Daily Inter-Ocean* were a good example of late-nineteenth-century writing. He wrote with an unrestrained enthusiasm for capitalism's expansion, confidence in a racial and ethnic order predicated on white superiority, and an unquenchable thirst for the drama and ruggedness of the West. His route took him to Conejos, Colorado, just above the New Mexico boundary. It proved a difficult task.

When Jackson arrived at the appointed destination in late July, no supplies had yet appeared. Aldrich brought the wagons in a few days later, just in time for Jackson to reorganize and begin his journey. William H. Holmes was also waiting for Aldrich. He and his crew, who were to survey the San Juan River region, had left Denver in June, along with the other parties, but had traveled a different route. Like Jackson, Holmes had only a few days at Parrott City to resupply before heading south to his assigned region. Though they worked separately on their journeys westward, Jackson and Holmes were engaged in the same process of making art and science serve each other, especially by making visible to a popular audience the geologic information produced by the Survey. Knowledge was the Hayden Survey's product, paid for by tax dollars; art, in the form of photography, painting, and cartography, was an important medium for communicating that knowledge. Jackson and Holmes traveled together to the banks of the San Juan River in southeastern Utah, then parted company, each to his various assignments.

## Capturing Colorado Scenery

### *William Henry Jackson* ✳ Pioneer Photographer

The main purpose of my 1875 expedition was to follow up my work among the cliff ruins in '74 by another trip to the Southwest. . . . I could not, however, pass through the mountainous San Juan region again without paying particular attention to its outstanding scenic features. On my first trip I had used only a 5×8 camera, but I had been so deeply impressed with the snow-clad peaks, rugged canyons, and lovely lakes and valleys that I thought so small a picture wholly inadequate to their proper representation. My ambition ran to something larger even than the 11×14 plates of '73 and I finally decided upon a 20×24 outfit as the extreme limit as to size which I could safely venture.

When one realizes what this meant—not only the packing of so large a camera (not the compact, folding ones of today) with the necessary plates and chemicals over hazardous mountain trails but also the difficulties in manipulation of wet plates magnified many times—it is a wonder to me even now that I had the temerity to undertake it. Nowadays bromide papers furnish ready means of enlargement to almost any extent from small negatives. In the seventies, however, such papers were not in general use and large photographs were made from equally large negatives. I have mentioned elsewhere that there were no ready-made dry plates at this time and also no prepared printing papers; the photographer purchased plain paper and sensitized it himself as required.

My first try-out of the large camera was not made until we were well up on the Rio Grande on our way to Baker Park [Colorado]. Making a detour over to the Lake Fork of the Gunnison, we pitched camp on the shoreline of the beautiful Lake San Cristobal. Here we set up the dark tent, and after some unexpected mishaps, I finally got a satisfactory negative.

The next subject was to be a close-up view of Uncompahgre Mountain, one of the highest on the northern flank of the San Juan group. Taking Bill Whan [packer] to assist with the two pack mules, we began climbing the foothills about two miles below Lake City. It was a stiff climb and Old Mag [a favorite pack mule] had a hard time of it with her bulky, top-heavy pack. At one place, in attempting to get by a tree that obstructed the trail, she lost her balance, and falling backwards off the trail, was saved from destruction by lodging against other trees. On the steep hillside it seemed impossible at first to get her up without incurring the danger of rolling farther down the mountain, but while I checked any tendency that way by a firm hold on the halter strap, Bill finally got the lash ropes loosened, the camera carried to where it could be repacked, and Maggie on her feet again with no greater damage than delay. It was demure Old Mag that always came in for the hardest knocks because of her assignment to photographic work.

We made a camp at timber line about noon and after a hasty lunch, staked out our animals securely, as we thought, and then went off with our guns to prospect for viewpoints and incidentally to bag some game. I finally found a location for a near view of the peak to which we could take the pack mule. This was at an elevation of about 11,000 feet, so that its whole height of 14,286 feet did not seem so very much higher. Returning late in the afternoon to our timberline camp, I found that Bill had brought in a fine mountain sheep; but as our animals in the meantime had pulled up stakes and vamoosed, he had gone in pursuit. I followed their trail half way down the mountain and then, concluding that both Bill and the stock had gone all the way to the lake camp, I went back to my lonely bivouac to await their return. After getting supper, I built a big fire, hung the sheep well out of the reach of prowling animals, and rolled up in my blanket for a good sleep.

Bill was back with our mules and horses before I was through with breakfast. The morning, however, was cloudy and by the time we had reached our view location a troublesome wind was blowing across the high plateaus. The dark tent was set up, plate prepared, and an exposure made, but without success, for the wind shook the camera so that I got only a blurred image due mainly to the long exposure required, as instantaneous work with wet plates was impossible.

With a storm impending, we cached the apparatus under the rocks and retreated to our timberline camp. A long dreary afternoon of drizzling rain and fog dragged along while we waited for a change in the weather. This was followed by a bright, clear morning that promised good work—and a celebration as well, for it was the Fourth of July. Anxious to take advantage of early morning conditions, I went on ahead to set up dark tent and camera while Bill followed later with the animals. There was time for but one exposure; the wind was rising and before we had finished packing up, clouds were drifting over the peak with intermittent flurries of snow. With our main object accomplished in securing a good negative, we made quick time in getting down to our lakeside camp. . . .

No more large negatives were made until after our return from the far southwest limits of our trip among the old ruins. From Baker Park,

Sultan Mountain was photographed, although we had to wait several days with tent and camera set up for rains to cease. Then Mag was called upon again to make the hard climb over the 13,000 foot pass to the San Miguel for larger negatives of Trout Lake, as the smaller photographs of our former trip failed to do justice to this region. We spent a day locating a high waterfall, said to be in the canyon below the lake. We came upon one which, though rather picturesque, did not measure up to the descriptions we had been given. Just as I had finished making a large negative of it, one of the packers reported that he had found another fall, larger and much finer than the one just photographed. Going down the canyon, I found it so much better that I decided I must have a view of it.

The day was waning and we must hurry. While I was cleaning off and preparing a plate, all the others joined in getting the camera down into the gorge and up to the falls. I followed later with the plate holder strapped on my back. I had to go nearly half a mile and then make a precipitous descent of some four hundred feet down into the gorge in which the falls is located, and then follow upstream over the rocks to a favorable point of view. The exposure was made all right, but as a result of the effort to get down and back in the shortest possible time, when I opened my plate holder in the dark tent I found that the plate had slipped from the corners and, rubbing against the back of the holder, was completely ruined. I developed it, however, and found the exposure all right. This was about the longest time I had ever had a plate in transit from sensitizing to development. The back of the plate had been thickly covered with wet paper and the holder wrapped in wet towels. My satisfaction in noting how well the plate kept was some compensation for the failure of the picture itself.

*Jackson and Driggs,* Pioneer Photographer, *217–24.*

## The San Juan Division Makes Its Way to Parrott City

William H. Holmes and the crew of the San Juan Division arrived at the designated location of the Hayden supply depot soon after Jackson, but not before they had struggled with their own weather issues

Jackson's self-portrait as a "pioneer photographer" in the Colorado Rockies does not capture the difficulties he faced using glass plates, sensitive chemicals, a small portable canvas tent for a darkroom, and bulky packing materials. Given the circumstances, his results were phenomenal. *Courtesy L. Tom Perry Special Collections, Harold B. Lee Library, Brigham Young University, Provo, Utah, W. H. Jackson, #155.9G9.*

and rough trails. Holmes made his way westward, keeping Hayden informed of progress along the way. Major stopping places on their route included Pueblo, Del Norte, the Los Pinos River, the Piedra, and the Animas River, thence to the supply station at Parrott City. On a mundane level, Holmes was pleased, at one point, to swap a couple of old mules for better stock. His admiration for the toughness of these animals is expressed through the experience of one in particular: "Old 'Joe' managed to topple off the trail the other day and turned a two hundred feet summersault down the mountain. He came up safely on his feet, however, and at the same moment brayed such a bray as made the echoes 'reverberate from a thousand hills.' He was not hurt in the least."

### W. H. Holmes ✳ "My Dear Sir," Pueblo, Colorado, June 13

Our [mule] train reached this place yesterday morning. We are camped in a grove in south Pueblo—less than one hundred yards from Lieut. Marshall's camp.[2] I came in ahead—on Saturday—in order to get the articles sent from Denver by rail in good shape for packing. I have forwarded the bulk of our first six weeks' provision to Del Norte by fast freight. Shall pick it up as we pass by. This secures light loads for our mules for the first two weeks. It seemed necessary to carry five or six weeks' provisions from the start in order that we might not run short before the stores shipped to the Mancos Camp [Parrott City] should reach that point.

Our drive from Denver to this place was not as pleasant as a picnicking party might desire. For two days in crossing the divide we encountered fierce cold winds which parched our faces fearfully and gave us sore eyes also. The change from office to saddle was almost too sudden, but we are nicely hardened now.

Met Mr. Gardner here on Saturday. He seemed to be making a little trip with Gen. [William Jackson] Palmer and at the same time keeping an eye on the various outfits.[3] We march with Wilson for five days yet. Our party—Chittenden's & mine—have not made a miss or had a hitch yet. I hope that good luck will still attend us.

He—Chittenden—is considerably dissatisfied with the unequal mention of our names—in all the accounts of the organization of the party and is anxious that in the progress of the work in which he bears so prominent a part, there shall be a more equal distribution of the credit. He does not wish to appear a mere appendage to my party, but desires an independent and separate recognition. I think, myself, that this is only just. It is with him not only a matter of price but a question of position in his profession—in other words of bread and butter. He has written to Mr. Gardner about it, and doubtless he, Mr. G., will do all that can be done to make the thing more equal. There is really no difficulty between Mr. Chittenden and myself. I think we shall get on quite pleasantly.

*Holmes to Hayden, June 13, 1875, RG 57, Howell Papers.*

### W. H. Holmes ❊ "My Dear Doctor," *Camp on the La Plata, June 29*

We are at last through—in good time and good order. Got in a full day's work today and are now camped just below the placer mines of Capt. Moss. I wrote you last from Del Norte—or perhaps San Juan City. We camped about ten miles above the latter place, on the 23d. On the 24th we crossed the divide from the Rio Grande to Los Pinos Creek. On the 25th, 26th & 27th we had a hard pull. This route was recommended by Mr. Wilson and hence adopted, I believe, by Mr. Gardner. It is certainly a very hard one—at least to follow from Mr. Wilson's instructions—since he was unable to follow it all of the way himself and his advice led us out of the way about one good day's travel.

From the Pinos we crossed into the Piedra, thence by a very hard route back into the Pinos. We afterward found that the Canyon of the Pinos, which we were instructed thus to avoid, has really a trail through it. From the Pinos we crossed into the Florida and yesterday crossed the Animas—a very large stream—said to have but one ford throughout the whole valley. We have had unhoped for good luck. Through canyons, over mountains, and across torrents we have passed in safety, and now if we can "stave" off the Utes, we are bound to succeed to the end.

I saw Capt. Moss yesterday and he has promised to go with us down to the Ute encampment some twenty miles below, to inform them that our party is not the one whose duty it is to run that *obnoxious line*. He says that they are determined to prevent—by any means—fair or foul—the running of the southern line of the Animas purchase, and that our party will be taken for the one said to be on its way west for that purpose. The Captain is a man of considerable influence among them and I hope will be able to convince them that it will do them no good to molest us.

*Holmes to Hayden, June 29, 1875, RG 57, Howell Papers.*


## MOVING SUPPLIES TO PARROTT CITY

The supplies expected at Parrott City had been delayed by bad weather and the general vicissitudes of transporting heavy wagons across rugged country. Charles Aldrich, "naturalist" and reporter, received the task of accompanying the logistical support from Denver by train to Pueblo then Canon City, the final stop on the rail line, before riding overland to rendezvous with the supply train at Conejos. On behalf of the Survey, John Moss had arranged for supplies to be sent north from Albuquerque to Conejos. Aldrich and some Mexican drivers took the wagons to the new mining camp of Parrott City, first traveling south, west, and finally north, taking them through the heart of southern Colorado's Hispanic communities.[4] He made extensive observations along the way, pointing out that the Animas Valley by this time was thickly settled and overgrazed by livestock, and that what feed was left was being eaten by a scourge of grasshoppers.


### *Charles Aldrich* ✹ *Conejos, Colorado, June 20*

During the past week I have journeyed from Pueblo to this strange, remote town, by rail to Canon City and from that point up the valley of the Arkansas, over Poncha Pass, down San Luis Park, on horseback, roughing it, sleeping on the ground and living on the usual camp fare. The first night I caught "something of a cold in my head," but that soon passed off, and on the whole I have "enjoyed" it. There is a world of grand and beautiful scenery along the entire route, too much, in fact, to be minutely particularized.

As you pass along, even at the slow pace of a Texas pony, the scene is constantly changing. New mountains are appearing before you on either hand, while those you have passed are reaching into the dim blue distance. Fresh vistas open wherever you look. If I was very tired as I turned into my camp bed, I attributed some portion of my weariness to this constant strain upon the attention. But one must expect all this, unless he is fortunate enough to have leisure and wealth in abundance. Such favored people can "do" these mountains in an elegant and quiet way, to which the mass of us must remain strangers. There need, however, be no envy in any direction for all sorts of people get along in all sorts of ways out here and each goes and comes in just such style as he can afford. If you should see a rough-looking fellow with a slouched hat and buckskin patches on his coat and pants, riding a mule and driving a *burro* or Mexican donkey to carry his baggage, camp bed, and cooking utensils, it would not be safe to wager your last dollar that he was not a graduate of one of our first colleges, for you would stand an equal chance to lose it. Really, appearances go for less in this country than in any other where civilization prevails.

But as I was saying, I came from Pueblo to Canon City on the Denver and Rio Grande narrow-gauge railway which has been so loudly praised by newspaper people who stray out this way. This road extends from Denver to Pueblo, and thence up to the base of the mountains, where the bright little town of Canon City has been judiciously located. Like all other unfinished railroads, it is now standing still, but I judge that this is only temporary. Its president, General Palmer, is earnestly at work seeking out the resources of the country beyond its present termini and looking up practical routes with a view to further extensions in the not very distant future. Last week he visited Trinidad with an eminent American scientist for the purpose of examining the heavy coal deposits of that vicinity. Various routes into the mountains have also been looked up. I believe that, as soon as the times improve, possibly sooner, this very useful enterprise will be extended in more than one direction.[5] These mountain passes can be surmounted by narrow-gauge locomotives so it is only a question of time that they will be. . . .

We are speedily whirled into Canon City, a thriving town which is destined to enjoy a rapid growth. It is noteworthy from being near one of the finest canyons in the Territory, from possessing quarries of exceedingly beautiful stone, several mineral and hot springs, rich mines of coal,

A curse to the Utes, a boon to entrepreneurs, and a loud voice in Washington, D.C., miners like these threaded throughout the Colorado Rockies, seeking wealth in some of the most impossible of places. This exploratory mining camp suggests the simplicity yet ruggedness of the venture in 1875. *Courtesy U.S. Geological Survey, W. H. Jackson Photo 0566.*

a thriving population mostly of Eastern people, and many other items, saying nothing of the territorial penitentiary. The mountain scenery is very fine. I consider it one of the very few towns I have seen of late which has room for an addition to its legitimate business facilities. . . .

We nooned at Saguache (they call it Sah-Watch), where we had an excellent "square meal" which was duly appreciated after so many days of camp fare. This town is built largely of adobe brick and pine and poplar logs, and looks as though it had been hastily flung together and almost as hastily abandoned. It is an outfitting point for San Juan miners and is now in the height of its dullest season, as everybody who can get away from these towns is off prospecting in the mountains. A fine looking and well-edited paper is published here, but I cannot see how its publisher manages to keep it alive in so sparsely-settled a region, for really, Saguache looks very much as though it "had been."

Del Norte has enjoyed a rapid growth and has a prosperous look, though extremely dull just now. Everybody, almost, has gone to the mines. It is located on a narrow flat, bordering the south bend of the Rio Grande, the town plat extending up and down a mile or more. Some fine brick business houses have been built and others are in progress, but the universal adobe and poplar and pine logs seem to be the main resources for building materials. Many adobe buildings with neat brick fronts have been erected. A United States land office has been opened within a few weeks, though but little of the adjacent territory has been surveyed. The town has brilliant mining and railroad prospects ahead and seems to me to be the best business point in all of the valley that lies in Colorado. It now has a very heavy trade in wool, a single firm having just shipped away 100,000 pounds.

Between here and Del Norte there is some good grazing country, a few valley ranches, where the hand of industry is making the desert productive, but the region is generally a barren waste where sandstorms are of frequent occurrence. The Rio Grande crosses over from below Del Norte to the eastern side of the valley, and its long, low line of timber is visible most of the way from the higher level of the road. We frequently saw the "mirage of the desert"—the phenomena being that of a succession of lakes constantly coming into view and as constantly fading away. In one place the trees beyond seemed actually mirrored in the surface of the phantom water. There are many small streams, filled, they say, with trout coming down from the western mountains, each one of which is settled down to the river though the land is still un-surveyed. There are some Americans, but the people are for the most part Mexicans, who live in the huddled plazas or in isolated adobe cabins. I will say something of these plazas when I have seen more of them.

Yesterday I reached Conejos which is altogether the strangest place I have ever seen. Strange to me for the simple reason that it is an adobe-built Mexican town. It is situated on each side of the river of the same name, another of these impetuous, crazy streams which has not yet settled down to steadiness since its leaps and tumbles down the mountains. With but very few exceptions the population is Mexican. All the buildings except a private edifice and a new brick flour mill are made of adobe.

The principal citizen of the town is Major Lafayette Head, who came here a long time ago from Missouri as an Indian agent.[6] He married a Mexican lady of much culture and intelligence and has resided here ever since. All his life an active business man, he has acquired a competence and is looked up to as the father of the town. His residence, which is comfortable, commodious, and pleasant, is altogether a unique affair. It faces north, is one story high, about 20 feet wide, and 288 feet long! The walls are very thick and the windows and doors resemble the embrasures of a fort. A verandah runs along the entire front upon which the doors and windows open. The rooms are probably ten feet high and the roof is supported by large pine logs which have been smoothly planed. The ceiling overhead, resting upon these logs, is simply unpainted pine boards. The room answering for the parlor is forty or fifty feet long, contains two beds, a lounge or two, tables, chairs, etc., and the walls are decorated with pictures.

Major Head was a friend of Kit Carson and he has the last photograph of that famous border hero with his autograph on the margin. Mrs. [Maria Juanita Martinez] Head informed me that Kit seldom wrote his name and hence his autograph is a great rarity. The picture is highly prized. The floors are covered with coarse woolen matting, doubtless an indigenous production. The house and its furnishings are not altogether Mexican, but a mixture of both American and Mexican notions of taste and comfort. A yard forty feet wide extends along the front of the house and is enclosed with a plain adobe wall. This space is partly given up to shade trees and partly devoted to the purposes of gardening. On the north side of the house is a large open court which must be nearly an acre in extent, with continuation of the building round nearly its entire extent. On the west side of the house, the adobe walk extends to the Major's new flouring mill, enclosing also another new brick edifice which is his business office. The house and grounds are models of neatness and order and I found the abode of solid comfort and good cheer while I remained. In former years Major Head had much to do with the Indians and was not only useful to the government in its dealing with them, but very influential with them. After an active and useful life, he seems to be enjoying its well-earned results in a most dignified and rational manner, possessing in an unusual degree the love and respect of all who know him.

The population is almost wholly Catholic and is ministered unto by three Jesuit fathers who came from Italy. The establishment also includes several lay fathers or brothers of the same order, I believe. The church is a huge one-storied adobe structure in the shape of a cross. It stands just across the square from the residence of Major Head. In its rear is a small cemetery enclosed with a heavy adobe wall, while on the south side is an open court surrounded by large unfinished buildings, which, when completed, are intended for a convent for the Sisters of Charity, who are expected to take charge of a school for the education of the children in the vicinity. The residence of the fathers stands some twenty-five rods west of the church, and is a very large, commodious, and comfortable adobe structure, though it is yet unfinished.

Aside from being their residence, it also contains a small chapel. The church is adorned with a large number of pictures, such as are usually seen in Catholic churches. Nearly everything in the way of the internal adornment of the church has been improvised here on the ground, far from railroads and large towns and is, of course, more or less cheap, rough, and unpolished, for the Mexican has not yet risen to be much of an artisan. Taken as a whole it is not unpleasant and speaks much for the zeal and energy of the people and the fathers who preside over and instruct them. However people may regard the Catholics, it is evident enough to me that by no other instrumentality could this rough border population be influenced, instructed, or controlled. It was evident enough to me that these very learned Jesuit fathers were doing a noble, useful, and praiseworthy work. Father Peironne [Peron?], who is at the head of affairs here, kindly showed me through their various buildings, explaining their purposes and hopes with regard to the singular community whose religious interests have been committed to his keeping.

Last season these religious houses, as well as the home of Major Head, were photographed by either the artist of the Hayden or Wheeler expeditions, and I suppose may be seen in most of the stores where stereoscopic pictures are for sale. They are certainly great novelties in the way of architecture, whether you see them by the aid of the stereoscope or here upon the ground. On the other side of the river from where I am stopping, there is a large collection of these adobe buildings, in some of which several families reside, a few stores, all built from the same materials and in the same way. The adobe bricks, which are a mixture of mud and gravel, are eighteen inches long, nine inches wide, and three inches thick. They "layup" very fast and there is so little rain here that they last almost as well as bricks which have been burned. If a wall suffers an abrasion it is very easily repaired. Where the effort is made, these houses are kept clean and neat and they are invariably dry and comfortable. Considerable building is in progress here, principally by the Mexicans and Americans who have intermarried with them, and who will doubtless control the business interests of the town for many years to come.

A queer feature of most of these houses is the little conical adobe ovens which generally stand nearby. They are about the size of an old-fashioned dog-kennel which they much resemble. They are heated with dry wood and "run" very much as were the old brick or stone ovens in the days of our great-grandmothers. Another is the fireplaces which are generally in one corner of the rooms. They are deep and narrow and are easily made in the walls and of the plastic material as the house is going up. Those which I have seen and which seem to have been much used would appear to have been very durable. On the whole, adobe is a success in this quarter of the world, cheap, efficient, durable, and universal; but to me it is a decided novelty.

*"Among the Canons: An Inter-Ocean Correspondent with the Hayden Expedition in Colorado,"* Chicago Daily Inter-Ocean, *July 3, 1875.*[7]

*Charles Aldrich* ✻ *Tierra Amarilla, New Mexico, July 1*

We soon had to descend the famous "Big Hill"—steep, rugged, rocky, the worst descent I ever saw that could be called a road. It was necessary to chain the wagon wheels and even then it seemed that the stout vehicle must be dashed in pieces.[8] But we passed safely down, *facilis descensus Averni*, and were very soon toiling over the hot, yielding, blistering sands of the Ojo Caliente country.[9] Not a drop of water or a tuft of grass, only scrubby piñon trees and sagebrush. Previous floods had washed deep gullies in the sandy soil, but it was now only so much suffocating dust. The heavy wagon wheels sunk six or eight inches into the dusty road and how our poor animals, which were almost famishing and hourly losing their strength, ever drew them

An example of what Aldrich called "a queer Catholic church" made from sun-dried adobe in a distinctly Hispanic American style. This Jackson photograph of the Church of San Miguel in Santa Fe is representative of those found in almost every early Spanish and Mexican community in southern Colorado and New Mexico. *Courtesy Bob Blair.*

through I can hardly conceive. The last three or four miles we had to travel in the bed of a dry creek, large enough to carry the waters of the Platte, but as dry as a lime-burner's wig, and the sun pouring his heated rays upon our heads.

Finally at 2 P.M., we came to an irrigating ditch filled with very warm water taken from the Ojo Caliente Creek. Our horses were frantic with thirst. . . . [line missing] start, and we lay there a couple of hours, by which time we had satisfied their thirst without injury or danger. We went on three or four miles, camping at the mouth of the canyon up which lies the road to Rito. It was but ten miles to the latter place, but heavens! What a road! Sand, sand, nothing but sand, and worse by a great deal than we had found it the day before. For two-thirds of the way up the bed of one of those large dry creeks or rivers, it was necessary to put all eight of the animals before one of the wagons and haul it a mile at a time. No water had been seen there since the spring floods and the hot sand was in many places a foot deep.

I have seldom, if ever, seen so uncomfortable or discouraging a day. There was no grass and we had to make another "dry camp" at noon. But we toiled slowly on until night and just as the shadows were falling, we reached a comfortable camping place on the banks of the Rito, which is here only one remove from a dry creek, but a different affair a short distance above. I am glad I have seen the Ojo Caliente country, but I don't care to see it again. Such drought, desolation, and sandy barrenness, I had never dreamed of before. Now, "I know how it is myself," for I think I never wished for a drink of good, cool water with such keen earnestness in all my life before.

These words, Ojo Caliente, simply mean hot springs, as I have previously stated. A creek, a river, by that name comes down from the mountains above, but it is a humbug. Its bed must be 1,500 feet wide, but the stream was shrunk to a small brook when we passed. On the east side is a Mexican plaza, the adobe residences of eight or ten of these families "to the manor born." Near the center of population stands another of these queer Catholic churches. It is an adobe structure, perhaps eighty feet long, fifteen or twenty feet high, and thirty feet wide. Its one window is simply an affair with wooden bars or grates and without glass. Its great front doors, fastened with a huge padlock, are the coarse work of a Mexican carpenter who had only an ax and saw to work with, and both, doubtless, very dull. A little yard in front is surrounded with an adobe wall within which there are a few graves.

In the center stands a huge, rough, wooden cross. In one corner of this yard there are four or five of these large crosses made of timbers, eight inches thick and probably sixteen feet long. These are borne on the shoulders of the Penitents, or *Penitentes*, an order of devotees in the Catholic Church.[10] It is their custom, on certain holy days, to do penance publicly for their sins. One of the means of wiping out the ugly scores which have been run up against them is to bear these great, rough, heavy crosses through the streets. They will weigh about two hundred pounds; a stout man can easily worry himself very much in carrying one of them two or three miles. They also lacerate their backs with knives or flints and then whip themselves with scourges made of the Mexican soap-weed.[11] This is a tough, textile plant, with long-pointed, spiny leaves. Some of these old crosses have been borne by these Penitentes over the shoulder, as the Savior is represented to have carried His in some of the old pictures, until the lower end, dragging on the ground, has been worn off to a regular "slant."

On the 24th of last December, they went through the form of crucifying a man by binding him to one of these crosses. A hole was dug in the ground, the cross raised, and kept in an upright position for more than half an hour. There is a story here that on one of these occasions the poor Penitente was crucified so long in this way that he died before he was taken down, but of course, I cannot vouch for its truth. While bearing these crosses, even in the coolest weather, the Penitentes are clad in nothing but thin cotton drawers. They prostrate themselves every few steps with their naked, lacerated backs, with scourges made of the gentle soap-weed, and sing or recite prayers in mumbling crooning tones. It is stated that the Catholic priests do not endorse this most preposterous and outrageous folly, but I am inclined to think they do for the simple reason that they could stop it with a word. They are learned men, the Jesuits in particular being among the most cultured of our race, and they ought to cease encouraging such mockeries. If they do not, let them speak out. Much of their work, their organized chants, their schools, the preservation of good order among these rough, half-civilized people, is in the highest degree praiseworthy, but these mock martyrdoms are very ridiculous.

But to recur to the church of Ojo Caliente. It seems to be of great age for an adobe structure and to be pervaded by "a flavor of mild decay." It is cracked on one side from the roof to the ground and the wall around the little front yard leans inwardly and has been much worn away where the sheep or small boys have climbed over it. An old bell, green with verdigris, and which might have come to the country with Carter, moves in a little aperture in the wall which rises above the roof in front.[12] It is reached by a rough ladder on the outside of the building and the faithful would seem to be called together by beating it with a club.

The hot springs [that] come out of the rocks on the west side of the river are said to be very efficacious in curing rheumatism as well as a certain nameless malady which is quite common in France.[13] There are two baths, one in the natural rocks, the other made of boards. The last is quite too hot for comfort, though two or three patients were just coming out as I was shown through. The water from the other spring is quite pleasant to the taste and would seem to be strongly impregnated with soda and iron. These springs, as a resort for patients, do not seem to wax fat to their owners just now, but one of these days may enjoy more popularity. It is all an invalid's life is worth to reach them.

From the divide above Rito we had a pleasant view in front and rear. Back of us stretched the sand hills of Ojo Caliente, while in front lay the broad expanse of the Rito Valley which is several miles in extent. The hills were covered with a heavy growth of pine, suggestive of a different country from the dreary barrens over which we had dragged our weary way during the past two days. As night fell, we made our camp and found that welcome rest which both ourselves and our weary animals so much needed.

The plaza Rito was about a mile above our camp so we made a brief halt in passing through the next morning. It is a village of four hundred inhabitants and has a few stores and quite a fine looking Catholic church. We called upon the Reverend Father Valezy, I believe his name is, a native of France. He was exceedingly kind and pleasant, refreshing us with a glass of excellent native wine and showing our party through his church. This was a large adobe edifice with very heavy walls, neatly whitewashed and painted inside, and abounding with a great amount of carving and paintings by native artists. The great round beams which support the flat roof are ornamented at each end by a bracket elaborately carved and painted in two or three colors. There are two large wooden structures in the form of screens on the large panels of which are painted in a coarse, rough way, the principal characters of the New Testament history. On the wall back of the altar, those rude old artists had painted many portraits and scenes also from sacred history. All of this ornamental work is of exceeding crudity, but it is nevertheless received with much favor and awe by the half-civilized communicants of this church. This reverend father, who seems to be an excellent and useful man, attends to the

spiritual wants of quite a number of places, large and small, informing us that he was at home but a very small portion of the time. He
came out of France eleven years ago and crossed the plains when the
Indians were still very hostile and troublesome. He endured much
privation and hardship in getting through, and at one time was two
days without food.

> "*The Canon Country: An* Inter-Ocean *Correspondent with the Hayden Expedition
> in Colorado*," Chicago Daily Inter-Ocean, *July 15, 1875.*

## *Charles Aldrich* ❋ *Parrott City, Colorado, August 4*

If the last letter in which I wrote of my journeying reached the readers
of the *Inter-Ocean*, it informed them that our little party was waiting
on the banks of the San Juan River for the subsidence of a flood, and
for sundry repairs for our wagons, for which latter we had sent back
to the plaza of Tierra Amarilla, a distance of fifty miles. It is one of
the most palpable evils of traveling in these regions, far from towns
or even of isolated habitations that the breaking of the simplest part
of a wagon becomes almost a calamity. Few of my readers "in God's
country" would deem the breaking of a wagon tongue or axletree or
the collapsing of "the hounds" as anything but a very trivial affair,
but if they were traveling in the Rocky Mountains fifty miles from
even a clumsy Mexican blacksmith, such an event would assume a
very different phase.[14]

Our two Mexican drivers were about used up by their severe labors
in that constant deluge of rain, one being quite ill and the other
suffering from an injury to one of his feet and both very homesick.
Neither would go home to hurry up the "ex" without the other, and
so we let them both go. But it was several days before the new drivers arrived, and in the meantime, I started back to Tierra Amarilla
to find that they had been twenty-four hours on the road. When I
overtook the little train it had been traveling two days. The river had
been safely crossed and some of the most terrible portions of the
weary way passed over.

But I must tell about the disagreeable night I had when I was lost
in the mountains! The trail to Tierra Amarilla was very plain and
easily followed until I arrived within twenty miles of that point. From

thence there are so many trails, made mostly by the nomadic herds-men that they become a labyrinth which no one but an expert can unravel. When I arrived in Willow Canyon, I saw half a mile from the trail a shepherd with a great flock of sheep and goats, so I went at once to his camp for the purpose of securing a guide over to the plaza. I found an elderly man and two boys, whose only house was the spreading branches of a cedar tree, very comfortable when the sun is shining warm and bright, but quite as bad as out-of-doors when the cold rains are falling. But then, when the weather is beautiful, there is nothing a shepherd likes better, and when the weather is foul, he can-not bestir himself to provide anything better. By dint of signs and half a dozen words of broken Spanish which I had treasured up, I made them understand what I wanted. Neither of the boys, muchachos, knew the way and so the adult greaser offered to pilot me through for a trifling reward. I hurried him off as speedily as possible for I was more than anxious to get through that night and start on the return trip early the next morning.

We were not more than twenty miles from the plaza. The weather was charming and it seemed altogether an easy ride, as it was only 3 P.M. But my guide, as I afterward learned, had never been to Tierra Amarilla. He knew "the lay of the country," however, pretty well and no doubt thought he could go straight through. He soon left the trail for a straight cut across sundry divides, which he gave me to under-stand would save me much time. But dusk came upon us when we were still some miles out and instead of going straight forward my guide swung round to the left and kept on traveling and traveling, possibly in a circle. He finally became discouraged and gave it up with the remark: "Me no sabe commeno Tierra Amarilla."

It crept through my brain just at that particular moment that I was lost in the Rocky Mountains in company with a scalawag of a Mexican who had purposely led me far from the road and who would probably cut my throat for two-and-sixpence if he believed I had that much about me! We came out here having heard most ridiculously false stories all the way about our fellow citizens of Spanish-Aztec descent, until we believed them to be a nest of thieves and assassins. But I determined to make the best I could of this queer plight so for a time worked hard to find the road. I heard various sounds, which I thought came over the reaches from the distant plaza, but they died away without throwing any light upon the problem.

At one time in ascending an elevation, I thought I saw a short distance ahead of me a large wall tent. I hastened forward but it faded away as I approached, proving to be a portion of the sky as seen through an opening in a thicket of cedar trees! Finally, we came to the base of a high mountain which in the dim haze seemed not only difficult of ascent but to extend far up and down the country. Lighting a match, my watch informed me that it was already 11 o'clock. I was sorry it was not still later. It had begun to rain and there was nothing left for us but to camp and remain there until daylight. I unsaddled my horse, hobbled him with my leather belt, and made my guide understand that we must have a rousing big fire. If it was to be my last night on this terrestrial ball, I was bound to keep warm. So he gathered a great heap of pine knots and limbs, piled them against a low stub, and set them on fire. We then lay down to rest, though I did not intend to close my eyes that night. I verily believed that the greaser intended to kill me before morning and I intended that he should find me wide awake when the pinch came.

So I set myself to watching him and I believed that he closely watched me. He lay so that a shadow fell upon his face, though I could see that he could observe every motion I made without any movement on his part. I beat him at this little game, however, for I put my hat down over my eyes so that I could see any motion he might make without changing my position. I got up frequently and replenished the fire and walked about to keep awake, went to see my little horse and talked to him, though the night was the longest I had ever seen. During the day I had discharged all the shots in my revolver but two in killing a big rattlesnake. I repented myself bitterly for this act, for I had no more ammunition with me!

I did not intend to sleep, but I guess I must have dropped off into a doze very near morning for I sprang up with a start to find that daylight was broad on the mountain. A couple of magpies were holding an animated discussion in the branches of the tall pine above my head and that terrible "greaser man" was snoring heavily a dozen feet away! My throat had not been cut, and I smiled at my ridiculous fears, as the reader may if he chooses. But it is one thing to have such an adventure and quite another to laugh at the absurd fancies of somebody else. Waking my old guide, we climbed the mountain just as the sun brightened the valley beyond, and the mystery was unraveled. We were on a spur of a mountain a little northwest of Tierra Amarilla. The beautiful valley of the Rio Chama lay at our feet with its cultivated fields. Bandit Peak was off to the right, while straight in front were the high rocks northwest of Tierra Amarilla of which I have heretofore written. We speedily descended to our camp, saddled our horses, and in less than half an hour were on the trail to the plaza, where we arrived in good time for breakfast. I transacted some little business affairs, slept two or three hours, and late in the afternoon, started on the return trip.

*"Mountain Life: The Perils and Privations of an 'Inter-Ocean' Correspondent in Southwest Colorado," Chicago Daily Inter-Ocean, August 28, 1875.*

⁂　　⁂　　⁂

From the settled Hispanic frontier communities based on agriculture and livestock to the more primitive mining camps of southwestern Colorado, Aldrich provides a travelogue pregnant with possibility. In many respects, Frederick Jackson Turner's famous essay, "The Significance of the Frontier in American History," outlines the various stages of development that the Survey people encountered. Aldrich's description of the mining camps with their boom and bust, ebb and flow of hopeful participants and the ever-present thought of getting rich quickly was part of that experience. His classic example of "boosterism" has a clear ring of credibility—everything from a geological explanation to the testimony of experienced miners fresh from the goldfields of California and Nevada to an eyewitness account to another option of silver if not gold. Readers are swept into the possibilities, for one cannot go wrong; it is just a matter of where and when wealth will be uncovered.

### *Charles Aldrich ⁂ Parrott City, Colorado, August 14*

This incipient city is located just where the little Rio de la Plata comes out of the mountains. It consists at the present writing of one rough board house, about 12 × 20 [feet], a log house of considerably more area, a log blacksmith shop eighteen or twenty feet square, with a pole and dirt roof over the forge, and a modest little tent in which the writer hereof is temporarily sojourning. That is all there is at present of the city, though two or three large log houses are to be erected and finished during the next month. The board house first mentioned, with cracks an inch wide between the boards, is the headquarters of Captain John Moss, of whom I shall have occasion to speak in another portion of this letter. It was built of boards which were "elaborated" from pine logs with what is called a "whipsaw." I have not seen one yet, but it is a saw propelled by one or two strong men; it must be a slow and tedious process of manufacturing lumber, but it is the only one yet in vogue in this distant region. Instead of a shingled roof, the house is covered with "shakes," a species of shingle of about double the usual length simply split from the logs. But the town or city has done well enough so far, considering its distance from shore. A whole quarter section has been laid out in lots and the adjacent bluffs bristle with streets and avenues with all sorts of appropriate names. Though it is little more as yet than a "stake town," I am of the decided opinion that a busy, bustling little city is to spring up in this vicinity, here or immediately hereabouts, but most probably where the commencement has been made. What is to make this city, build it up and keep it growing will be evident before I finish this letter. . . .

It has been known for many years past to miners who have occasionally passed through or briefly sojourned in this valley that gold was so abundant that "the color" or "a prospect" could be had almost anywhere. It has also been believed that much of the gold known to exist in placers down on the lower San Juan came originally from the La Plata Mountains. But not until during the past two or three summers has there been any systematic prospecting in the upper part of this valley, where of course, the richest deposits must exist. About three years ago Captain John Moss, an old Californian, and, I may also add, a cosmopolitan for he has traveled in many parts of the world, came here and settled, and after him and with him several Nevada and California miners, also in search of "fresh fields and pastures new." These gentlemen have spent their summers here hard at work, wintering in various other localities where "grub" was more indigenous.

Until the present summer their labor has been mainly that of prospecting for gold, making claims, and generally preparing for extended

Jackson's diary on July 23, 1875, tells how the photographer found Boren "hard at work on his river claim. This was the last day in which to complete his assessments work. [There were] lots of miners about waiting and ready to jump any one of his claims if the opportunity afforded so he was taking no chances." *Courtesy Scotts Bluff National Monument,* SCBL *1006.*

operations in the future. They have found gold dust almost everywhere. In some of the old times, almost or entirely geologically old, this little river ran in channels which are now on the opposite side of a great mesa 500 to 800 feet high. In these old channels the prospects are said to be very fine. But the main placer or river claims have been located from say a couple of miles above Boren's Gulch down a distance of ten or fifteen miles along the present river valley. In all this extent, the valley often widening out from half a mile to one or two miles, I think the territory has been claimed and located.

The mining laws are very liberal in their present scope, allowing a man to claim twenty acres and hold it until twenty days after water has been brought to the vicinity in a ditch. Of course many of these, probably most of them, have been located on speculation and if the claimants are not lucky enough to sell, they will lose them when the ditch is complete. The higher up the river one goes the coarser the gold becomes, until you reach Boren's Gulch, some five miles from here. Above that locality there is some gold, but the main drift of all the gold of the valley would seem to have been derived from that gulch.

All this golden current must hence come down from one or more of the richest and most extensive gold lodes in this country; but up to this time no one has been able to find it, though scores of experienced and inexperienced miners have looked for it day after day. Claims have been made in its vicinity, at haphazard, in the hope of blundering or stumbling into its possession. Standing at Boren's cabin, you look up the granite slope, across acres and hundreds of feet of debris, to crags and cliffs, far away above the timberline, but seeming very near at hand, almost, in fact, within gunshot, and between you and that far summit this rich gold lode unmistakably exists; and it is from there that has come most of the gold dust which the little river has so widely diffused through the long valley below and carried into the San Juan. . . .

Every pan full of soil, even upon the top of the ground, gives one or more colors. The bed rock has been reached only on one side of the gulch, whence it slopes south and east being covered with coarse and fine sand and gravel solidly cemented together with clay. In a little prospecting here, Mr. Boren found several nuggets of pure gold, the largest of which weighed twenty-seven and one-half pennyweights. I saw this beautiful specimen and several others before they were taken off by Captain Moss to exhibit to the capitalists of Nevada and California, who he is anxious to enlist with him in his operations here.

I was at the gulch Saturday when Messrs. Boren and Findley washed out a few handfuls of gravel at my request. They worked at great disadvantage for they had to take this gravel from under the water. Gold would, of course, sink to the bottom of the rough bedrock whence it could not be brought up with a shovel. But every pan exhibited fine colors and from one we took a bright little nugget. In fact the residuum of black sand seemed filled with gold dust, which, with the present means for mining, they are unable to save. A few days before a quantity of earth containing two or three cubic yards was washed out in their rough sluice-boxes and gave them $36 worth of gold. . . .

But great interest has seemed to center in "The Bar," which is a broad mesa or plain extending five miles below the point where the ditch first strikes it just above town. To the eye this bar looks like a great natural meadow, fit to be cut up into a dozen or twenty farms, but it is composed of earthy debris, gravel, and boulders washed down from the mountains. In some places the bedrock is known to be not over fifteen feet below the surface, while in others it is very likely to sink as low as 100 feet. Gold dust is found in the grass roots and the dirt thrown up by the gophers and squirrels and the old miners who have gained their experience in Nevada and California are of the opinion that more and more gold will be washed out until the bedrock is reached, and upon that they expect to find very large amounts of this precious metal. . . .

But I believe my readers will be more interested in their promise of the precious metals than of aught else, and on this point I have the word of old, experienced miners that no new district ever discovered in this country has given such splendid indications of unlimited wealth from the same amount of investigation. Last spring a shaft was sunk twenty feet on the bar, seven miles below Boren's Gulch, and the earth "panned out" every six inches. . . .

Until six or eight weeks ago the principal interest in these new mining regions had centered in the placer mines along the river and "the bar," but it "leaked out" that certain parties here had, for a year or more, known of the existence of silver-bearing lodes in the mountains two to six miles to the north. In a twinkling almost, the placers were nearly abandoned and everybody rushed away up the canyon to make his everlasting fortune in the discovery of a silver mine! Up to this time I should judge that 150 have been located, and more are being discovered almost daily. In fact, the hills for many miles up the valley, how far no one can tell, are full of these leads or lodes. I was up at Boren's Gulch on Friday, when in passing along the base of one of the hills we saw a dozen of these exposures of silver ore in not to exceed one-fourth of a mile! Those nearest each other were not over thirty feet apart! These lodes vary much in thickness. Some are not over a few inches, while they come up to five or eight feet. It is believed that where the "bed rock" of the river is exposed in the course of the placer mining, some of the richest and best silver lodes will be brought to light.

*"A New El Dorado: Recent Discoveries of Mineral Wealth in Southwestern Colorado,"*
Chicago Daily Inter-Ocean, *September 1, 1875.*

# CHAPTER 3

# "The View from the Top"

## Parrott City to the San Juan River

### JULY 27–AUGUST 8

JACKSON AND HOLMES SHARED THE INITIAL PART OF THEIR trip after leaving Parrot City. Holmes started with thirty days' provisions on July 27, while Jackson and Aldrich waited one more day for the mail before departing. Destination for all—"Ute Peak," known today as Sleeping Ute Mountain.[1] Jackson took the opportunity to recruit an additional member to his crew. He had hoped that John Moss would accompany the Photographic Division to Arizona, but the entrepreneur had other business, so he recommended instead a seasoned frontiersman named Harry Lee.

Even in his haste to catch up to Holmes's main party, Aldrich took time to note that, in the Mancos Valley, there was "no end to the hay that might be cut; no end to the livestock that might be reared and fattened," but that water was the key to the usefulness of the entire region. He and Jackson also mentioned the many Ancestral Puebloan ruins along the way. The interest was so great that even after many days in the saddle, some of the men had the energy and interest for a short five-mile side trip into New Mexico to visit today's Aztec Ruins—which Holmes said "formed the grandest pile I have yet seen." Interestingly, the "dead" Indians held more fascination than the living ones, although Holmes had picked up two Ute companions, who would provide real assistance during his travel.

### *Charles Aldrich* ✻ *Parrott City, August 1*

During last week Mr. Jackson, photographer of the Hayden survey, remained here, waiting chiefly for the mail, which only comes once a week, and even then is very uncertain. Before he was ready to leave, Mr. W. H. Holmes, the artist-geologist, came in with his party and stayed two or three days, both divisions, however, moving southwesterly together on Tuesday last. The mail not coming as was anticipated, on Tuesday evening, the 29th, Mr. Jackson stayed over another day in order get whatever that uncertain vehicle of intelligence should bring for the two parties. Messrs. Jackson and Holmes had very kindly invited me to go down with them as far as Ute Mountain, nearly fifty miles, where it was expected that both parties would find more or less work to do, and in the vicinity of which there are many interesting ruins. I was exceedingly pleased with the rare opportunity, but not a little chagrined to see one of the precious days wasted by the delay of the mail carrier. But you cannot help these things out here, and so we could only wait his slow progress. He finally came on Wednesday evening, twenty-four hours behind time, and, worse than all, only brought about one-fourth of the mail which was reasonably due us. Of newspapers, we received next to none at all, only two or three weeklies, and the news they contained was mostly older than our bacon.

*"Prehistoric Ruins: The Hayden Survey in Southwestern Colorado,"*
Chicago Daily Inter-Ocean, *August 21, 1875.*

### *William H. Holmes* ✻ *July 28*

Left Mancos Camp with the intention of marching about fifteen miles, but found no water until we reached the base of the peak, a distance of thirty-five miles. We reached (Ute Chief) Narraguinip's Camp at about five o'clock.[2] "How-de-do" pointed out a spring to us—a very weak and obscure one—the only water in the neighborhood. Without the Indians we should probably have had a dry camp.

July 29th.—Jackson and Aldrich did not come. The mail is probably late. Chitty and Bandy go across the canyon to make a station. I rode out on a skirmish, passed up to the immediate base of Ute Peak, and thence back toward the Mesa Verde. I came upon a group of ruins within a mile of camp at the head of a shallow side canyon of McElmo. The main ruin is of a great treble walled tower that stands amidst a cluster of irregular apartments—some sixty or eighty—and is certainly of great interest. There is, also, on the brink of the cliff the base of a small tower and on a lower level, one wall of a two-story house. At the base of the bluff and on the neighboring points are groups of shapeless piles of ruins; depressions surrounded by raised walls from two to five feet high. No evidence of hewn stone or well-built walls.

In returning to camp from this place, I met Mr. Aldrich and Mr. Barber, who had gone to visit the ruins of Aztec Springs. Jackson and Aldrich had reached camp safely in the middle of the afternoon. Accompanied these gentlemen to the ruins, five miles south of camp and on the head waters of Arroyo Creek. These ruins form the grandest pile that I have yet seen. I estimate them to cover 480,000 feet of ground to an average depth of four or five feet. They are located on a green spot some 1½ or 2 miles from the base of the Mesa Verde and are built of the sandstone of the mesa and of the locality lime-sand stone, which outcrops in different parts of the plain. There have been two main structures, the western one being probably the most important. The building has been rectangular; the walls running pretty nearly with the points of the compass; they are still about fifteen feet high and are fairly covered with the immense mass of debris from the fallen parts. Originally they could not have been less than thirty or forty feet in height. The wall is double, there being a space of about seven feet between the inner and outer walls. Partitions cut this space into rooms. The enclosed part is divided into three apartments. The depression in which there was formerly a spring is under the south wall. The house and spring have been partially or entirely enclosed by a connected line of houses or fortifications of which the plan will give a good idea.

The eastern or lower house had the double wall only on the north side. This part still stands some twelve feet high and is built of well-dressed stone. The walls on the east, south, and west are small and stand now only two or three feet high without much debris. Near the center of the enclosure is a circular basin which seems to have been a water tank. There appears to be no out houses to this structure. There is a great deal of broken pottery, but no tools or indications of roads.

*Holmes Field Notes, July 28, 1875, Howell Papers.*

## *Charles Aldrich* ✳ *La Plata Mountains, August 1*

[W]e left camp about 5 P.M. for the Mancos River, which runs parallel to the La Plata, in a generally southerly course, about fifteen miles away. This ride was a very pleasant one. We had some difficult hills to descend, but between here and the valley of that stream there is some very beautiful country. On the left a range of green but abrupt hills run all the way round one circuitous trail, which constantly bears to the right. To the right of us rose the grand peaks and crags of the La Plata Mountains, which are soon to be the theater of a mining industry which will set hundreds of men nearly crazy. Their altitude has not yet been definitely ascertained, but snow lingers in the ravines near their summits, and they go far above the timber line. I hope to climb one of them before this month ends. Nearly all the way over the trail leads through fine groves of pine, which one of these days will be in demand in these mining gulches and upon the ranches. We passed over hundreds of acres of the choicest grass that ever grew, deep and rank and green, and then rotted upon the ground. No end to the hay that might be cut; no end to the livestock that might be reared or fattened. But these things will come along, and at no distant day. Wherever there are such deposits of mineral wealth as there are in the valleys and mountains hereabouts, the coming farmer will thrive even better than the miner, save in those infrequent instances where one finds a silver mine. . . . The sun had gone down and the shades and chill of the evening had descended upon us as we led our horses down the last steep hill which encloses the beautiful valley of the Rio Mancos.

Just as it was fairly dark we reined up in front of the [cabin of] the only white resident of this valley Mr. James Radcliffe, one of the most pronounced type of Rocky Mountain pioneers. How long he has been in this region I know not; possibly, however, nearly his whole life, for he is booked up in all the ways of "roughing it," and there are few phases of border life with which he is not familiar. He is a merry bachelor about forty years of age, does his own housekeeping and attends his ranch, which last he avers he would rather own than the richest lead on the La Plata! He is master of the situation, cooks a trout in a most appetizing style, makes a cup of coffee almost as good as you find at the Palmer House, and generally elaborates the eatables in such a way that "Jim's Ranch" is a most welcome place to all who travel in these deserted wilds.

A capital story-teller, with rich and varied experiences of wild Western life, it was a rare treat to sit at his table and spend an evening with this merry-hearted "hermit of the Rio Mancos." He was perfectly contented with his lot, idolized his ranch, which he deemed equal to the Garden of Eden, and looked forward with the clearest faith to "the good time coming" and not very far distant, when these valleys shall again teem with an industrious population, as industrious, but how much more enlightened than their predecessors, whose only monuments are the ruins of which I shall presently speak.

The valley is really very beautiful. It is walled in by high mountains, but the soil is excellent, the timber abundant and very fine, the grass everywhere better than any I have seen. Just below the house two noisy branches of the Mancos unite, to form one of the noisiest little rivers, both full of delicious mountain trout, that I have yet seen. Jackson and I made our bed together on the adobe floor, for each man out here literally takes up his own bed when he walks or rides away, and in the present instance we could only carry a limited portion. So all combined our resources in this line, and were soon lulled to sleep by the never-ceasing music of these bounding streams, which pursue their course a few rods distant.

Of course we were up early, for we did not know how far ahead of us the teams would be, and all were anxious to catch up with them as soon as possible. Camps have to be made wherever it is convenient to find water, a most uncertain article when you get away from these tedious streams which come bounding and tumbling down from the lofty, snow-clad mountain. Jim "flew around" and got our breakfast very quickly, so that we were off by 6 A.M. Our course was down the valley of the Mancos for six or eight miles, passing the mouth of its famous canyon, which is so celebrated for its prehistoric ruins. We then crossed a divide which took us over into a valley that is probably drained into the McElmo, whenever there is any fluid to run that way. The trail leads along westerly several miles from the northern limit of the Mesa Verde, that beautiful upland plain which my friend Chittenden so graphically described in some of his notes that I sent to the *Inter-Ocean.*

This plain is 1,000 to 1,500 feet above the valley. It is covered with dark green pines, piñons and cedars, while for the first two hundred to three hundred feet from the top the rocks have been worn into perpendicular precipices. . . . Gulches have been worn into these rocky masses, leaving bold castellated projections, which, from their regularity, look like huge piles of masonry. The Mesa Verde is forty to sixty miles square, sloping southward and eastward, and in addition to being cut through by the valleys of the La Plata and Mancos, it is "seamed and gashed" with canyons until it becomes a perfect labyrinth. The name, I believe, simply means "Green Plain" [Green Tableland or mesa]. It is a beautiful region where you can look out from an elevation over its vast sea of pines, or survey its slopes and palisades from a distance below, but a rough and difficult [terrain] to travel through. As we crossed the divide the valley widened. To the north and west lay extended a wonderful pine-clad region stretching an indefinite distance, but cut up with gulches and canyons so as to be almost impassable.

Ute Mountain occupied the foreground, a huge trachyte cone, rising above same lesser hills, to the height of 10,500 feet above the level of the sea. A grassy valley extends round the northern side of the Mesa Verde, and between it and the peak, to the Mancos, which emerges from its canyon on its way to its junction with the San Juan. A vast extent of country is before you, widening out into far distances, but for the most part dry as a desert. There is some grass in the lowest depressions, occasional groups of cedars and piñons, but many, many miles of the universal and most monotonous sagebrush. But we traveled rapidly, too much hurried to give any attention to the ruins which we could see every few miles, and at noon came up with our friends, who were camped on the northwest side of the mountain, and in one of the smaller canyons at the head of the McElmo. The camp was in a beautiful place, near a small spring which came out of the rocks, but where water was woefully scarce and very poor. On a little mesa in front of the camp were a number of foundations of the houses of the old prehistoric race, but we cared little to look at these when we could find those near at hand in which the masonry was still standing.

*"Prehistoric Ruins,"* Chicago Daily Inter-Ocean, *August 21, 1875.*

❉        ❉        ❉

Accompanied by Aldrich, the surveyors climbed Ute Mountain to make a station and to view the canyon and plateau country they would soon be entering. All seemed to appreciate that the changing quality of the landscape posed greater challenges. While one group enjoyed the scenic vista, Jackson ventured ten miles down McElmo Canyon in search of a better source of water.[3] After climbing Sleeping Ute Mountain, Aldrich left Jackson and Holmes to return to his duties at the La Plata supply depot. The two divisions traveled together for a few more days before separating. The first entry below by Aldrich provides an excellent description of the mapping process of party members following their ascent of 4,250-foot Sleeping Ute Mountain.

*Charles Aldrich* ❉ *Working on Ute Mountain*

When I got to the summit, Chittenden had his tripod and plane-table in position, and was rapidly sketching the materials for his map of the surrounding country. This topographic work consumed most of the day for the field of vision extended all the way from seventy-five to two hundred miles! Streams, water courses, and elevations were sketched, and the bearings and directions of all prominent points noted, so that these maps become marvels of accuracy. The preliminary map is fastened upon the plane-table, and it is then an easy matter to make all lines and angles mathematically correct. Streams may not always be laid down correctly in all their tortuous courses through a canyon country so nearly impassable, but they are mapped with sufficient accuracy for all practical purposes. Mountains, peaks, and other marked features, are, of course, correctly established.

But the view from the top of the mountain is one of the grandest I have ever seen. Not so high by 3,000 to 4,000 feet as some of the more noted, it still overlooks a very wide scope of low and comparatively level country. Facing the east you behold the La Plata Mountains and the valley which I have mentioned as lying between the foothills and the northern abutments of the Mesa Verde, widening out to the south until it reaches the Mancos and San Juan Rivers; south and west you can trace the valley of the latter as far as the eye can reach, a thread of "living green" in the midst of yellow, sandy barrens; westward, through the smoky haze, you see far into Utah, where the glass brings out a whole battalion of buttes and stone columns in the midst of a region in which you discern little or no vegetation to relieve the monotony of the desert waste; northward, as far as vision can reach, you see a pine-clad region, threaded by canyons too intricate and tortuous to be traced whither to their sources or their lower termini. . . .

The view over Mesa Verde is especially grand, but turn which way you will, there are lengthened vistas each possessing its marked and distinctive features. We spent most of the day on the summit. Mr. Holmes sketched the cliffs, exposures, escarpments, and long reaches of the Mesa Verde, and Chittenden worked out his topography with occasional assistance from Brandigee, who is a skillful botanist of much repute, aside from his present vocation of assistant topographer. When the work was done, a column of rock was piled up to the height of five or six feet, and a record of our visit deposited in it. This is the first time that an exploring party had ever ascended Ute Mountain, but during this month two others are to perform the task, that of Professor Gardner of the Hayden survey, and one of Lieutenant Wheeler's divisions. . . .

There was a scarcity of water which was very annoying. The animals had so nearly exhausted the supply that we had not a gill to spare to wash our hands and faces after a day of dust and sweat. What we could get was strongly impregnated with alkali, roily, and unfit to drink. But with the aid of citric acid, it allayed thirst. That night Jackson and Holmes determined to start early down the McElmo, marching due to the San Juan, which was forty miles away if water was not sooner found. Some Utes who were camped in the vicinity told them they would find a supply in "tanks," holes in the rocks or ground, on the "Hovenweep" some twenty-five miles distant, so this was made the objective point of Friday's [July 31] march.[4] We lay down to rest in the open air in a mild temperature and beneath the clear starlight, but I slept very little. Our animals were noisily searching for water and various other annoyances banished sleep. I was, therefore, very glad when Jackson roused the camp at 3 A.M. We had our breakfast before daylight came and at 5 A.M. I [Aldrich] bade my friends, who were also ready to move, "good-by and God speed," and left on my long ride back to this camp [Parrott City]. They had to start on their march without water for their animals, and with barely enough to prepare their breakfast and fill their canteens.

*"Prehistoric Ruins,"* Chicago Daily Inter-Ocean, *August 21, 1875.*

## *Charles Aldrich ❋ August 23, 1875*

While at this place [the mouth of McElmo Canyon], one of Jackson's packers found the skull and part of the skeleton of a man a few rods from camp. Further search revealed a Navajo blanket concealed under a rock upon which there were unmistakable blood stains. The skull, without doubt, was that of an Indian and so we had less solicitude concerning its owner than would have been the case had we supposed a white man had been slain in that lonely, secluded place. Old "How-de-do," a Ute well known hereabouts, was camped near us and he said the skull was that of an Indian of his own tribe, though he gave us no further account of it.

Speaking of the Indians, I saw while in this camp an instance of maternal solicitude and affection rather distancing anything of the kind that has ever come immediately under my own observation. Old Mrs. "How-de-do" has a fat little daughter, over whose head perhaps ten summers have merrily sped their way. This family all came regularly to our camp at meal time to be fed and it is a matter of pure policy to indulge these worthless nomads to that extent for they might otherwise make it unpleasant for those who travel this way. While they were waiting for the second or third table one day this little girl laid her head in her mother's lap, a very natural thing, of course, for little girls to do. The old matron, with a decent gravity which well became her wrinkles and her years, at once began "looking the head" of her little Minnehaha. Whenever she found a specimen of animated nature and they were very plentiful, she eliminated it from those raven locks and put it in her mouth with a delicious smack of the lips, which you might imagine to have been a kiss if you hadn't been looking in that direction. I kept no count, but I should guess that old Mrs. "How-de-do" pulverized a hundred or more of these well-fed lice while we were eating our dinner.

Starting out in the early morning, I intended to visit the ruined tower which Mr. Holmes had sketched, but somehow I missed it when I struck off to the left to get into the trail. He told me, however, that it was a round structure, evidently for defensive purposes, very symmetrical, the walls still standing twelve feet high, and that it was fifty feet in diameter with double or triple walls. There were also some cedar windows, caps, and sills still in fair preservation. I much regretted that I did not find it, but I know that I was not in a mood to make a long search and that I did not go far enough to reach it. But six or eight miles ahead I found another of those towers which I had seen off at a distance when we were hurrying along to find the parties. It is situated on a branch of the McElmo which affords no water at this time. The stream bends northwardly and runs around a half circle one third of a mile across. This semi-circular tract is considerably elevated above the surrounding country and it is the site of a dozen or twenty of those houses, some of which are quite large. One must have been forty by sixty feet square and the depression in the debris would indicate that it contained eight rooms, large and small. None of the wall is visible, it being now a pile of stony rubbish about ten feet high. All of the other buildings were of lesser dimensions.

I saw here more fragments of pottery than in any other locality I have yet visited. Bushels of them might be gathered. Half a mile farther on my way I saw a building on the opposite side of the creek, of which a side and wall of bright yellow sandstone were still standing. I tried to reach it when I discovered a very novel feature in this little canyon. Its rocky walls were apparently from six to fifteen feet high and it seemed easy enough to find a depression where I could ride across. But I found that it had been very much filled up with mud earth similar to the soil of the adjacent valley, the worn-down materials of the mountains. In this now dried mud, a gully had been worn to the depth of fifteen or twenty feet, impassable alike for man or horse! I could reach the river only by making a detour of a mile or more and so I left it unvisited.

Plodding along I passed two graves which are referred to this old race. Somebody had attempted to dig out the bones of the occupants, but had evidently given up the job, after going some two or three feet. When they buried their dead they put flat stones up and down the sides and ends of the grave, filling the center with earth. These stones projecting above the ground and enclosing a rough, longitudinal square reveal the places where the Indians are not hostile in southwest Colorado. Rumors have been published to the effect that some of Dr. Hayden's party in southwest Colorado had been, or were likely to be interfered with by the Utes. Mr. Gannett met with some detention and threats off north of us which I think must have been adjusted long ago; but the only danger down this way lays in the fact that the lazy Utes may starve the parties out by begging their provisions! No other trouble seems possible or probable. A few days ago there was a large camp of the Utes with their ponies and goats, three or four miles below us in this valley and they were here for something to eat all day long, but they have, very happily for us, all left for other regions.

"*Prehistoric Ruins,*" Chicago Daily Inter-Ocean, *August 23, 1875.*

❋    ❋    ❋

Holmes and Jackson next started their travels to Hovenweep and eventually the San Juan River. (Jackson and E. A. Barber left behind a good description of the ruins and what the exploring parties found in them, too detailed to be discussed here.) Then, on August 3, Jackson and Barber parted company with Holmes's division and continued to travel down the San Juan River, with the Hopi mesas in Arizona as their primary destination for this leg of their trip. Holmes, on the other hand, eventually headed south into New Mexico.

### *W. H. Holmes* ❋ *July 31*

This morning we said good-bye to Narraguinip and How-de-do, who with their family, boarded with us for three days, and started down the McElmo, expecting to have to march to the San Juan thirty or thirty-five miles away. These Indians have been quite useful to us but they eat like fury. Passed by their corn fields, some damp patches in which they have planted a little corn, less than an acre in all. It grows in clusters, a hundred [?] stalks in a hill; will soon be in silk if the dry weather does not cut it off. Jackson and Harry rode on ahead to look for water; found some at the Ruined Castle or Hovenweep, by noon; thither we followed. . . .

August 4—Moved 14 miles down the San Juan, camped within a few miles of our western line—109° 30'. Passed by the mouth of the

Rio Montezuma, a deep valley with a dry bed but many cottonwoods. Met an outfit of Indians consisting of four men and five squaws. The two younger fellows were impudent "devil-may-care" fellows. The two older were quieter and more polite. The oldest was a tall slender man of, say fifty years, with a sober composed countenance and a mouth of ungodly width. He shook hands and called me "Mi amigo" ("my friend") and said also that they were Navajos. They drove some twenty or thirty sheep and goats and indicated that their "wickiup" would be made at the junction of Montezuma and the San Juan. My outfit soon came up and I took them to camp, four miles below the Montezuma. Chitty had crossed at the wagon trail ford and was making a station south of the river. The Indians advised him to "piqua" (get out) up the river but Chitty didn't pike.

The night following was destined to be one of unusual excitement to our party. I was awakened at ten or eleven o'clock by a confusion of sounds and the excited inquiries by Chitty and others as to who that could be yelling on the south side of the river. At the same moment my ear caught the hoarse yell of someone in the greatest excitement. I was on my feet in an instant, and shouted in reply. It was Tom [Cooper, a packer]. He was yelling, talking, and swearing, in the most desperate manner. I could only make out that something very disastrous was happening and that our help was instantly needed. We seized our rifles and hurried forth to meet him in the darkness and soon learned that we had possibly escaped a disaster indeed.

Early in the night as Tom happened to be lying awake in his tent, he noticed that there seemed to be some rather unusual disturbance among the animals and presently that the bell began to tinkle as if the bell horse were trotting or running.[5] The herd was evidently moving down the valley. He was up in a minute and after them. Steadily they advanced, perseveringly he followed, but found it very difficult to get closer to them. He suspected nothing wrong only that they had been frightened by a coyote or wolf, in which case they would certainly soon stop. Already he had chased them two miles over gulches and rock, through weeds and bushes and brush. Would they ever halt? The perspiration was putting him blind and his wind was nearly gone. Suddenly the noise ceased and the bell was silent. He could only keep on toward where the last sounds were heard.

To his utter amazement he discovered the herd just ahead of him, rounded up in a close bunch and standing quite still. He passed around above them to turn them back. He came within a few feet of them. There was the white face of Old Baldy the bell horse moving, but no bell. It suddenly dawned on him that these strange movements were not made by their own will, but under the guidance of some band of Indian desperadoes. The explanation was perfect. His hair stood on end; his flesh crept, for he was utterly defenseless. He had only his hat rolled up in his hand to stand for a pistol. He still continued to move forward, however, and was in the act of speaking to the nearest horse when a flash of lightning revealed the crouching forms of two savages almost within the reach of his hand.

They caught sight of him at the same moment and were so struck with amazement that they thought only of flight. With a bound they sprang upon their ponies and were off like a shot. Tom, doubtless somewhat unnerved, did not take to flight, but jumping upon the nearest horse started the herd up the valley and then lit out for camp uttering the most fearful yells at every jump. The redskins, as they flew down the valley and over the rolling hills, must have felt their blood curdle at the terrible sounds. Certainly they did not stop until many miles intervened between them and the scene of their undoing. In half an hour our animals were all safe in camp and we were congratulating ourselves on having escaped the misfortune of being set afoot in a desert two hundred miles from the nearest habitation.

On the following morning [August 5] we rode out to the scene of the mutual surprise and there found the bell, which had been cut from the horse's neck, a pair of hobbles the removing of which had caused the delay that saved our mules, and a pair of fine rawhide lariats dropped by the thieves in their sudden flight. All about were moccasin tracks. We took the pains to follow them back and discovered that these two had walked all the way from their camp four miles above, Indian file, and that their ponies had been brought around to them by a circuitous trail through the hills. Tom and John [no last name given] rode up to the Indian camp soon after, while Chitty and I went upon the mesas above to do our day's work. The boys were determined to raise quite a noise in the "wickiup" of the supposed guilty red men, but felt inclined to give up the idea when they discovered—instead of the four men seen yesterday—eight fierce looking devils grunting over a pipe and looking forbidding enough in their sullen stoic mood. They were neither communicative nor polite and the two boys came away impressed with the notion, as Tom put it, that they were determined to give us another deal yet. The audacity of the thieving pirates went ahead of anything we had ever heard of.

August 6. Not only did they stay all night boldly in the camp to which we had tracked them, but at noon rode coolly down to our camp, dismounted, and seated themselves in a half circle in the middle of camp and proceeded to scrutinize every object in the outfit, to beg this and pretend to wish to "swap" for that. They were probably looking for their lost lariats. One old scamp had the audacity to nudge me with his elbow and order me to bring a pail of "agua" (water). We treated them as coolly as possible, kept our rifles within reach, and held such manner of powwow with them as we could. Traded some matches for some arrows and gave them some bread to eat. We watched them so closely that they failed to steal anything and saw them depart with a feeling of great relief.

These fellows came more nearly up to my notion of what fiends of hell ought to be than any mortals I have seen. We mounted double guard for the night, determined to protect ourselves to the utmost. I think I recognized two of the Indians as the same we met on the 25th of July between the Mancos camp and La Plata mines. The party has doubtless been following us since that time and will perhaps be lying in wait for us until we get out of this southeast corner. They are cowardly scamps who would not care to harm us if it were liable to endanger themselves. They know that we sleep and eat and work by our needle guns and they move with great caution in consequence.

August 7th. Moved camp nine miles up the San Juan to the ford about halfway between the mouths of Montezuma and McElmo [Creeks]. No Indians in sight. They had moved out on the 6th. Perhaps they were hiding in the cottonwood groves below. The valley at the mouth of which the mules were recovered seems probably to have been the one ascended by Capt. [John N.] Macomb in 1860 [1859].[6] A trail follows it six miles to its source thence northward across the sage mesa. We named the stream Recapture Creek.

*Holmes, Field Notes, July 31–August 2, 1875, Howell Papers.*

# CHAPTER 4

# *"Making Stations"*
## Los Pinos to La Sal Mountains
### JULY 3–AUGUST 14

O N JULY 3, AFTER TEN DAYS AT THE UTE RESERVATION Agency, Gannett moved his crew north up the Uncompahgre Valley. For the next month, his men worked on "making stations," sometimes two and three times a day, as they traveled the land on or near various river drainages. Moving along the Uncompahgre, San Miguel, Dolores, Grand (Colorado), and back to the Uncompahgre River kept them generally in mountainous terrain covered with timber and watered by frost, rain, and hail. Their travels provided real contrast to the weather and geography they had encountered while mapping farther south. Part of their route crisscrossed a trail blazed by Lt. John Williams Gunnison in 1853 as he worked on identifying a possible railroad route to the Pacific Ocean. In October of that year, Pahvant Indians had killed Gunnison and seven other men while they were camped on Sevier Lake in west-central Utah.

At this point, Gannett had had only peaceful relations with the Utes frequenting the area in which he worked. Agent Bond and Shavano, riding in a buggy, accompanied the surveyors to the site of the new agency. Everyone joined in to study the lay of the land and to identify the best place for a ditch to bring water for a future sawmill that would cut boards for construction. A week later, the surveyors left the agent and soon ran into a Ute encampment of thirty-six lodges, where they were greeted by "every dog in the village," but were treated kindly. The surveyors continued to follow broad Indian trails threading over much of the terrain, and so it was not surprising that two weeks later, they chanced upon another group that had just broken camp on the Grand River. On July 25, A. C. Peale noted, "We all left camp with the train this morning and followed the trail of the Indians who camped near our campgrounds. Just as we came to the edge of a bluff we met a lot of Indian boys who were badly scared when they saw us and commenced yelling to those behind. There was a large crowd and a young buck who spoke tolerably good English came up and shook hands with all of our party. They said they were going to the Navajo country and had buckskins to swap. They wanted to trade a beaver skin for powder. When they found we had none, they wanted Gannett's knife for it or his shirt. They all begged for matches."[1] Soon the two groups parted company.

On July 31, Gannett's survey crew reached the junction of the Grand and Gunnison Rivers, the point previously designated for a field supply camp, thus ending a relatively uneventful month of surveying.

### The Primary Triangulation Division Begins Work

While Gannett and his crew spent July in their assigned area, Gardner's group, responsible for primary triangulation, had begun their work on the Dolores River. They had arrived at the Los Pinos Agency only days after Gannett's departure. Like his predecessor, Gardner had a lively encounter with Ouray about surveying in the La Sal Mountains, since the government had specified that, as spokesperson and leader of the Utes, Ouray would be held accountable for any problems. Ouray also realized that he had very little control over this amalgam of Utes, Paiutes, Jicarilla Apaches, and Navajos, who had remained independent of various tribal agencies. All that he could do was to caution and advise.

### *Cuthbert Mills* ✳ *Camp Fifteen, Los Pinos Agency, Colorado, Sunday, July 11*

If these letters were devoted solely to the personal adventures of our little division of the Hayden expedition, I should certainly expatiate in this on the pleasures of the outdoor life in the rainy season. I might tell how it feels to march in the rain, to camp in it, to eat one's supper at a table in the open field with a driving thunderstorm in progress, and lastly, how very enjoyable it is, and suggestive of sweet dreams of rheumatism, to take one's blankets pretty well soaked in the extremities and generally damp and sticky. This has been our experience during the past few days and we have the pleasure of hearing that this month is the opening one of the rainy season which will probably last until the fall when the rain changes to snow.

Under these circumstances I am greatly inclined to consign to eternal perdition the man who made my poncho blanket just four inches too short, whereby I get "the full of me boot," as one of our packers expressed it, whenever I walk in a storm. The ordinary poncho is a covering only fit for use in the saddle. It will protect the wearer very well while there, and is large enough to cover his rifle if he has it slung from his saddlebow, but for walking, a long rubber coat is certainly the best protection and any one intending to make a trip through the mountains would do well to have both blanket and coat. It is, however, quite possible to keep out of the rainy region. At Saguache it rained steadily nearly all the time we were there (about thirty-six hours), but it was evident that such a fall was unusual. Many of the tenants of the adobe houses set to work throwing more earth on the roofs which is a rough-and-ready way they have of mending them.

A resident informed us that in three years before there had been no such continuous rain. Saguache is in the San Luis Valley or a little off from it among the foothills. The wet season there is a short one, rain usually only coming in showers during the latter part of July and the beginning of August, but in the Los Pinos Valley where we are camped, the season is much longer because of the high ridges which enclose it, and, apparently, capture every damp cloud which comes around. Irrigation here would not perhaps be necessary and for most crops would certainly be useless for there is frost at night every month of the year. The agent has made one or two attempts to raise oats and potatoes which he considered sufficiently hardy to stand the climate, but he has been successful with neither.

The only use to which the land can be put is grazing and then the cattle have to be fed in the winter because of the deep snow. Raising cattle under these circumstances does not pay, it being the universal

custom in other parts of the territory to have the cattle "winter out";
but an attempt will be made this winter by Mr. Mears of Saguache,
the Indian trader, who had hundreds of cattle in the valley, to have
them winter out. If there be only a light fall of snow, the experiment
may be successful, but should there be a deep fall he runs the risk of
losing half his herd. Other persons than Mr. Mears are not sanguine
of the success of his experiment. Anyone unacquainted with the cli-
matic peculiarities of the region, looking at the valley as it appears
now, might jump to the conclusion that it only needed to be settled
to turn it into rich farms. The grass is good, there is abundance of
water in the creek, rains are abundant, there is plenty of wood in the
surrounding hills, and a good wagon road to Saguache and the settlements. What more could the most enthusiastic land agent require for
descriptive purposes? But I asked a resident of the Agency what crops
could be raised and he said "grass, and in a garden, spinach."

The boundary line of the Indian reservation is ten miles west of this
point, and of late, it has been discovered by someone that the Agency
is too far east for the convenience of the Indians or else that the Los
Pinos Valley will do for cattle ranching and the Agency is to be
moved a hundred miles west. A decent looking frame building for the
agent's residence, some log houses scattered around for the men who
work here, a log building with a cupola converted from its original
purpose of a schoolhouse to store provisions, with some stables and
other outbuildings, completes the "outfit" of the Los Pinos Agency.
Their removal would not appear likely to involve any ruinous expense.

The loosely-arranged outpost is possible because the Utes are not
a powerful or a troublesome tribe and Ouray, their principle chief,
lives here and keeps them in good order. He has an adobe house of
our good-sized rooms, is rich in ponies and other Indian wealth,
altogether is a good sort of fellow, and has always been friendly to
the whites. He did, however, make some little fuss, it appears, about
Mr. Gannett's party, over the divisions of the survey working on the
reservation. But after some powwowing between him and the agent
and some lesser chiefs, all objections were withdrawn and when we
arrived Mr. Gannett had started. The doctor here told us that for a
few days there was quite an excitement among the Utes, who usually
feel sore about something which the government has or has not done

and it appeared for a time that the survey of the reservation would have to be given up.

This tribe, however, has to be on their good behavior, as their fate, if the government withdrew the weekly rations, would be speedy extinction by starvation. There is not enough game in the country to keep them alive and if their reservation is anything like this valley, it is hard to see how they could support themselves by agriculture even if they were willing to, which they are not. Dr. Mack said that indigestion in various forms was common trouble among them and he attributed it to the fact of their getting their food without working for it. Every ten days they come to the agency and draw rations, which is served out on the same scale as army rations and with these the men retire to their lodges and do little or nothing until next issue when they come up for more and so on the year round.

I confess it gave me a little surprise to find that hundreds of able-bodied men were daily fed and clothed by the government without doing a stroke of work in return, but I suppose it's all right. It would appear, however, that they have to do a little sometimes. We have been wondering what the constant bang banging of guns which we heard all round the valley was for; the problem was solved by morning by the sight of an Indian on the hunt for prairie dogs with which, it seems, they extend their supplies of food until ration day. There are not a great number of lodges about the agency at this time, most of the tribe being off in the hills, but their number is increasing, and Ouray has sent out to gather up the scattered warriors because of the rumors that a large party of Sioux have left their reservation and are coming down here to thrash the Utes for stealing four hundred of their ponies last summer. The fellows in the lodges about a mile off have soothed us to sleep the past two nights with the chant of their war songs, which, in full war paint and feathers, they have been singing against the time when the Sioux may come down.

This sounds very well; but if what I hear of the two tribes be true, should the Sioux really succeed in getting so far south as this point, there would be such a getting up and dusting among the Ute tribe as has not been seen for many a long day. But it is not at all probable that this will happen for the Sioux have too many enemies, both white and Indian, to trust themselves so far from their own country. Ouray,

This Ute encampment located in Cochetopa Pass, 1874, illustrates the flexible mobility available for a hunting and gathering lifestyle. The tepees, made of buffalo or deer hides, were quick to set up and take down, warm in the winter and cool in the summer—with sides opened for air circulation—and highly transportable. Goats, unlike sheep, travel quickly, do not require herding, and serve as a ready food source on the trail. *Courtesy Scotts Bluff National Monument, SCBL 3074.*

however, says they could do it if they were determined to come here, by traveling on foot in small parties at night, gathering at some point previously agreed upon. There has been some trouble among the Utes and settlers in the Animas country, southwest of here both parties claiming the land. A company of the Fifth Cavalry passed yesterday on their way back. They could not get to the place by this route and were coming out and going down south to try it from that direction.

We were treated this morning to the sight of cavalry of another sort, the Indians riding in from a large camp they have about three miles back on the road. They have been coming in parties of three to a dozen, and as our camp is on their road to the agency, many of them have stopped and had a talk or stared at us silently. To the usual inquiry where we come from, we reply that we are Washington, which implies that we are a government party. One of them who spoke English pretty well remarked that "Washington was slow man," a reference to their Congressional trouble. Mr. Adams recognized an old Denver acquaintance in one of the chiefs and they had a powwow in his tent. The chief had a watch which had stopped two days ago and we set it right for him; he showed us cartes-de-visite [small photographs] of himself, his brother, and his family, which he had taken in Denver.

Most of the men were armed with rifles and revolvers, but a few had only the bow and quiver of iron-headed arrows. The man who made the remark about Washington carried a beautiful little fawn in front of him on the saddle. I stroked its little head and said it was pretty to which he replied, "Yes, very pretty," and told me he had caught it. One of them took up my carbine, and said, inquiringly, "Winchester?" Mr. Pearson, who stood by him, I think, mainly to see he did not steal anything, said, "No, Springfield." "Springfield," repeated the Indian, shaking his head; "No bueno" (good). This was a mistake of the worthy son of the forest of which I am quite sure he would be convinced if he were about 250 yards off and somebody was looking at him over the sights of it.

Like a great many other things our Indians looked best at a distance. As they came galloping over the hill with their bright scarlet blankets loosely hung around them and their feathers and beaded trappings fluttering in the wind, they looked picturesque enough; but nearer acquaintance disenchanted us, and we speedily tired of their society. As for our boss packer, Shep Madera, a farmer, trapper, and hunter, who suffered a good deal at the hands of the noble red men, he cannot endure the sight of them and appears to be unconsciously feeling around for a six-shooter whenever one approaches the camp. I grieve to state that they have shown so little respect for the Sabbath day as to have employed it in horse racing and, of course, betting, for they are born gamblers. Tomorrow we shall probably see the whole tribe in force when they come in for their rations.

From this point our route lies entirely in the wilderness beyond the region of post offices and roads. Hitherto we have never been entirely beyond the settlements, except, perhaps, on our last day's march, from Saguache Creek to this place. From the frontier town our road was through the Cochetopa Pass over the Pacific and Atlantic divide. Los

Pinos lies fourteen miles west of the divide so that now we may say we have fairly crossed the main range of the Rocky Mountains. We made the distance from Saguache here in two marches, one of eighteen miles, the second of twenty-five, and very trying on men and animals this long march proved to be. A brisk ride on horseback for that distance is easy enough, but to follow the monotonous walk of a pack train for eight or nine hours without a stop and on a mule is more wearisome than anyone who has not had the pleasure of doing it can have an idea of.

Monday, July 12—Not an Indian in sight, but better than all, just as we were finishing breakfast there came a real Indian hello—a "Ya-o-o-o!"—from the direction of the Agency. The next moment a little man in knee boots and buckskin suit came in sight, walking briskly toward the camp. A loud shout in answering welcome greeted our long-delayed chief and in another moment we were shaking hands with Mr. Gardner and pouring out a flood of inquiries. As we surmised, his letters and dispatches to us while in Poncha Pass had miscarried and are now probably in the Dead Letter Office in Washington. A letter which one of the party had written to a Denver paper was the means of finding us. Mr. Gardner has been working hard in the coalfields around Pueblo and only finished his report on them two days ago. Though very tired, there is to be no delay and tomorrow we start. The packing of our supplies will keep us busy all today.

*"The Hayden Survey—Beyond the Settlements,"* New York Times, *July 27, 1875.*

### Cuthbert Mills ✳ Camp Twenty—on Ohio Creek, Colorado, Saturday, July 17

Our start from the agency was made on Tuesday afternoon. Monday had been entirely occupied in preparations for the two months' journey, so when the train filed up the valley on the way out, the load which each mule carried was sufficiently weighty to draw its attention very closely to the trail. Our destination was a peak in the Elk Range, about sixty miles north by west, and Mr. Gardner's calculation was that in three days a convenient spot could be reached from which to make the ascent of the mountain.[2]

Traveling among the hills, however, is apt to be uncertain. We did not arrive at this place until the morning of the fourth day. The first day's march seemed to be all up hill and our camp that evening was at an elevation, as shown by the barometer, of 9,500 feet. The remains of rudely-constructed wigwams, sets of tepee poles, fragments of hides, burnt bones, and other debris of an encampment gave evidence that it was a favorite camping ground of the Indians. A family party of them passed us early next morning, just as we had finished breakfast, and the brave laughed heartily at the sight of Charpiot quietly seated beside the mess kit washing dishes. There was something extremely funny to him in a big muscular man doing such squaw's work. Very soon after our start we passed our first party of returning miners who looked with much interest at the well-appointed pack train; truly their own outfit of scrubby mules and shaggy little donkeys appeared a very shabby affair beside it.

This day's march was enlivened by one of the mules running away. Something scared him and he was careening wildly over the hill, head and tail up, and the packs flying in all directions before anyone very well knew what the matter was. When caught it was found that the pack saddle was broken. This looked a little serious but Shep Madera, who is always equal to the emergency, rigged up something on which the pack could be held with his own riding saddle. He had to ride bareback in consequence, and as I wanted to learn that accomplishment, I offered to lend him my own riding mule for a time. To this he agreed and with many cautions to hold on tightly and offers to see my body carefully conveyed east if anything happened, I vaulted on the little spitfire he rode, and with full confidence, clapped spurs to its sides and started full speed down the steep slope. Never are stirrups so necessary as when riding downhill and never did I feel them to be more so than in that brief ride without them.

At the third jump of the little brute, I was on his shoulders, every succeeding one threw me where I ought not to have been, and in fact, I have only a vague idea of where I did or did not get to on that mule. From behind and above came the sounds of screaming laughter, but before me I saw a slope which seemed like the roof of a house and down which I felt sure the mule and its rider must roll together. Yet Providence befriended the distressed. In one brief instant, when thrown into momentary equilibrium, my hand instinctively tightened on the reins, I turned my fiery steed, headed him along the side of the hill, and triumphantly joined the train still on his back and with no worse damage to my neck than a severe crick. After this experience and fortified by many congratulations, I felt confident enough to go anywhere on anything. About an hour after, in crossing a miry spot, my charger made an unexpected jump which conveyed him in one direction and me considerably in another. I thought I had had enough of bareback riding which is not comfortable anyway. . . .

Looking at such a scene as this valley [Ohio] presents, so rich in its fertility and in its aspect so grand, one feels something like a twinge of conscience at having said a word unfavorable of a territory in which such a spot can be found. Yet a little reflection will convince anyone acquainted with Colorado what its first settlers must have found, when they came, many valleys as beautiful as this, which after a few years of occupation by cattle ranches, presented a very different appearance. Even the Arkansas Valley, that picture of dry desolation, ten years ago, an old resident informed me, was green with a growth of grass knee deep which is now all eaten and trampled out by cattle.

If ranches were established along Ohio Creek, the first settlers would probably make fortunes if they had a few favorable winters; but in a few years, the immense herds would reduce these green slopes to the same gray sterility that marks the great San Luis Valley. As the land, unlike that valley, is unfitted by its high elevation for agricultural purposes, every succeeding year would see it growing poorer and less able to sustain the numbers of cattle feeding upon it. Crowding cattle on a range appears to have nearly the same exhaustive effect as the old southern system of cotton planting where every few years the land had to be abandoned till it regained its fertility by lying fallow. The Ohio Creek Valley will retain its beauty just as long as it remains untouched.

*"The Hayden Survey: Los Pinos to Ohio Creek Valley,"*
New York Times, *August 27, 1875.*

\#      \#      \#

Following a series of Indian and game trails to accomplish several critical triangulations over the next week and a half, the party camped in the Elk Mountain Range then moved south. As they did so, they faced the problems of getting lost in a seemingly impenetrable forest and an encounter with bears. In the first instance, there were mistakes that taught lessons about wood lore; in the second, one wonders about the wisdom of chasing after bears through the brush with pistols.

### Cuthbert Mills ✳ August 29

At 7:15 the train was on its way and about ten [A.M.] we came in sight of a large camp of Indians and passed through it. Mr. Gardner was ahead and having a friendly chat with the chief, but as they were Indians, of course, the guns, pistols, rifles, knives, and other deadly instruments in the party were slung in the most carelessly conspicuous positions as we neared the camp. The only difficulty we experienced in getting through was from the fright of the mules, the scare they always take at the sight of Indians or probably their gaudy trappings being supplemented on this occasion by the barking and snapping of numberless dogs. This was a camp of friendly Utes on their way to the White River Agency. With most of them we exchanged the customary salutation, "How! How!" Parenthetically I may say here, as an interesting illustration of Indian character, that in their social chat the old chief, who spoke a mixture of Spanish and English, became quite communicative with Mr. Gardner.

He told him, among other things, that he had three wives. The first, an aged female, "sabed stars," which meant probably, that she told fortunes and was wise in counsel; the second, a younger woman, "sabed pie," meaning that she was a good housekeeper and could set an excellent table; the third, a buxom girl of eighteen, "she was very nice." I am unable to explain what he meant by this last. A brave with his family accompanied us for some distance on our way but parted company where we finally left the trail we had been following so long and struck away in a direction from which even the faint evidence of human occupation offered by a trail was absent. It was, however, a beautiful country of broad grassy meadows and gently-sloping ridges, well watered, and it looked good for game.

Now the luck which we did have was not good at all. Between us and [Station] Forty-five lay a wide bottom, traversed by the creek we were camped on, and beyond this a great mountain ridge, heavily timbered, which had to be climbed and descended on the other side before the desired camping ground could be reached. It could not be said that we started well, as two mules got mired at the first attempt to cross the creek and the instruments which one of them carried were soused in the muddy water. But we pried out the unlucky animals, crossed in another place, started afresh, and soon got up in the timber.

We remained in it till nearly 4 o'clock that afternoon, then making a last drive for its lower edge, reached it and camped there, the most fagged out and ragged lot of men and mules to be found in the country. For anyone who has had experience with mountain spruce forests, it will not be hard to conceive what difficulties attended the attempt to carry the train through this one. To understand how thick the fallen timber lay on the ridge, take a double handful of parlor matches and throw them on a table; the confused heaps in which they will scatter will give a fair idea of the quantity and disposition of the timber we had to climb over; now imagine that half of these logs lay with the dried, sharp branches sticking up all along them like a *cheval de frise*, for a spruce, unlike the aspen, rots at the bottom and falls with all its branches on it; that many were broken in their fall and lay with ragged ends pointing up in the tall grass and weeds like snags in a river; and that this was in a forest so dense that the earth was in deep shadow—a forest thick with underbrush and on a steep slope seamed by numerous canyons cut by little mountain streams, which here and there were dammed and made horrible bog-holes—and then consider what a heavily loaded pack train would have to encounter in forcing a passage through such a terrible maze.

As a matter of fact, we did not get through, but were nearly seven hours trying to do it, and to crown all, had a great fright by losing Mr. Gardner's assistant, young Pearson. Of this rather alarming episode of the day's adventures I was the innocent cause. Some trouble with the saddle had caused me to fall a considerable distance behind the main train, but as this was not uncommon in riding through rough country, I jogged along after it without a thought that my absence had even been noticed or in fact any particular thought at all. About half a mile or more had been passed slowly over for swarms of ferocious horse flies plagued my little animal terribly and I heard Pearson shouting from some invisible spot up the hill ahead, asking if I had the trail. Now, as to my having the trail, it was something I never bothered about, because it was useless. No one so inexperienced could follow such a thing unless it was in wet sand, but I had discovered that a mule can nose out a trail like a foxhound following a fresh scent. Some are better than others at the work, but all can do it; therefore, I had ceased to concern myself about trails and expected my mule to attend to it in the same way that I expected him to carry me.

But when the inquiry was made I looked down, and the trail there happening to be very distinct in the weeds and grass, replied that there was one as good as a wagon road. In a minute or two the shouting was renewed in tones of great urgency for me to hurry on; rather alarmed, I drove my mule as hard as he could go in the direction from which the shouting proceeded. This brought me into a little opening, and entering it on one side, Pearson dashed in on the other with an excited inquiry if I saw any mule tracks ahead. Of course there were none as I had left the trail, whereupon he exclaimed, "My God! I am lost and so are you," and almost in an instant dashed out of sight into the timber to the right. So incoherently had he spoken that I understood the exclamation to be that some of the mules were lost, and for a minute or two searched around for tracks. Then recollecting the absurdity of attempting such work, turned up to the left, began working up to where the train had probably gone, and in a few minutes sighted Mr. Gardner and Adams who had come out into another opening to look for the lost ones. It was then explained that Pearson had turned back to find me and had evidently lost himself in doing it. Think of being lost in such a trackless wilderness as this!

Old and experienced mountaineers have been known to go almost wild with terror at such an accident and here was a young man to whom the whole country and all about it was entirely novel, probably at that moment frantically urging his fleet and powerful mule in a direction in which every step carried him further and further from safety. There appeared no other course than to go back, make camp, and organize a systematic search. Luckily, we had to turn back at this point, for no practicable road could be found ahead. The end of it was that in an hour or so, to the great relief of everyone, the lost was found. On his return he said that when he first sighted me, the train was not far ahead, but I came along so slowly that it disappeared, which it would soon do in that thick timber, and then he lost himself and for some time was beside himself with fright. The death-like pallor

Gardner poses in front of a studio Rocky Mountain backdrop. Unlike many adventurers from the East, he lived up to the image he portrayed. Cool under pressure, wise enough to listen and respect those with firsthand experience, he was a competent leader in the field and trusted by those who followed. *Courtesy James Gardner Photofile, American Heritage Center, University of Wyoming.*

of a face ordinarily ruddy and sunburned gave good evidence of the truth of this statement.

The blame for the affair rested on the one, and it certainly was not our chief, who never would have made such a blunder, who sent back on the blindest kind of a trail a mere novice in woodcraft, who had apparently not yet learned the full value of the animal he rode. When the young fellow had recovered his wits, however, he had very sensibly made his way back to the last stream the train had crossed as the best landmark from which to regain the trail and it was there that Mr. Gardner found him. It may very easily be supposed that we drew a breath of deep relief on resuming the march with the company all complete

It was then about 12 o'clock and for three hours more we struggled through this tangled wood, and then finally abandoning all idea of crossing the mountain by that way, turned down it and camped in the open at its foot. The damage of that day's march, the worse we have had, was various. Some of the instruments got wet and one leg of the theodolite tripod was fractured; the bread pan got a large dent in its side, and the handle of the frying pan was broken off short; some of the mules scratched themselves on spiky logs and the backs of others had sores rubbed on them by the packs; a bottle of valuable liniment for the cure of such things was broken and smelled dreadfully; Adams had half the front of his navy shirt torn out; Kelsey and I lost the only pipes we possessed; Pearson lost himself, and our chief and guide lost a little of his temper. As for the sheet-anchor of the train, our indefatigable Shep Madera, he could not very well drop anything he wore without the loss becoming too plainly apparent to be permanent; but he badly damaged his left hand in hitting on the nose of a mule which insisted on jamming on to him in a mud hole, into which he had jumped to the assistance of another mule, fast there by all four legs, stuck in like long spikes. On the whole, however, we came out of the scrape pretty well and Sunday came very opportunely to give all parties a day of well-earned rest. . . .

I have said that some of the country we have been marching through this week looked good for game. The evidence we had that it was a game country was given at camp Wednesday evening and furnished the most agreeable excitement of the journey. Four bears, two old ones and two cubs, walked down from the timber and out into the meadow where we were. Of course they selected the worst possible moment for their visit. It was just after supper; Charpiot was washing his dishes; Mr. Gardner had gone up into the timber in search for a trail; Kelsey was off rounding up the stock for the night; Pearson, cleaning his rifle, had just taken it all to pieces and nothing was ready to give the visitors a becoming reception.

The first one to notice their presence was Adams, who with the exclamation, "Good heavens, boys, there's a bear," seized his rifle and fired two shots at her in rapid succession. The sound of the firing and sudden confusion in the camp turned me toward it at top speed for I had wandered off some little way, while Shep Madera came running out with my rifle in one hand, holding out the other for cartridges. Hurriedly giving him a handful, I looked in the direction he turned to go and saw, with some secret satisfaction I confess, a large cinnamon, not grizzly, bear walking with two cubs near the edge of the timber about a hundred and fifty yards off. At that moment the huge beast reared up on its hind legs, gave a clumsy lurch forward, and started on a run for the brush with Shep and Adams in hot pursuit, firing as they went.

She had the advantage, however, and by the time her pursuers had reached the timber, neither mother nor cubs were anywhere to be found. Vainly was the brush beaten around and poked into; not a sign of them was to be seen or even the way they had gone and Shep had already started to return to camp when he came tearing back with the report that another bear, bigger than the last, was feeding some distance off in plain view. Excitement went to its highest pitch. Pearson had put his rifle together and joined us. I had borrowed Adams' navy revolver, having first gone into the hunt with the only thing left me, a little pocket pistol. Adams had his heavy-bore rifle and Shep still my carbine. It was lent to him in the hope that we should witness the knocking out of the brains of any bear he drew bead on. Not only were the shots he fired of no apparent effect, but when, with blood in our eyes, we were stealthily crawling upon our game ready for that bear or any dozen like him, his was the voice which constantly whispered protests against any nearer approach and expressed the cheerful conviction that if any were made, "Some of you boys will get chawed up."

It was not, probably, from any want of courage for he has worn the buckskins of the hunter and trapper for years, but he doubtless did not put much faith in ours. He knew it is generally only wasting cartridges to shoot from seventy-five yards and it proved so in this case. At the sound of the three rifles which cracked at him, the bear jumped around, probably slightly wounded, took one look at us and then put for the brush in the liveliest manner as the other had done. Up sprang the hunters and followed, but the brush was thick and high, and they paused, angry and baffled, at its edge. Here Shep was right in preventing any advance, for it is the awkward habit of a wounded bear when he takes to the brush to lie down in his tracks and to spring suddenly up face to face with his pursuer. Such an interview might have ended unpleasantly for us.

The silent pause was broken by a crackling of branches and instantly every ear was strained in anxious expectation. The crackling continued, the sound coming our way. "Look out, boys," said Shep, stepping back and bringing his weapon up. "He's going to show fight." In another moment along came the bear near us, but indistinct in the thick under-brush and gathering shadows of the evening. There was no fight in him, not a bit of it. He was running as hard as he could go. Crack! Bang! Crack! Crack! went every rifle and pistol. Still the bear ran. "Don't go into the brush, I tell you," shouted our mentor, as a forward movement was made. "Give me my pistol," cried Adams, at a white heat of excitement, "I can fight any dash-blanked bear in the country."

"Go it, Adams. Let him have it," responded another equally excited one of the party. "Then go in and be clawed," said Shep, desperately, and into the brush he went and the rest with him. But while all were ready to run the risk of being clawed by a bear, none cared to be shredded to pieces by bramble bushes and a very short passage through them was enough. The bear got away, of course, while the hunters, after lingering some time longer, slowly returned to camp, very hot, very vexed, and much crestfallen, and there received a lesson in bear hunting from Mr. Gardner, the point of it being that you should always go sufficiently close to a bear to shoot into a vital part, and invariably keep perfectly cool. In our bear hunt we had done neither.

*"The Hayden Survey: Making Station Forty-Five,"*
New York Times, *August 29, 1875.*

## Gardner and Gannett Divisions
## Meet and Join Forces

Following the experience with the bears, a three-day march across increasingly arid lands brought the party to the junction of the Grand and Gunnison Rivers, site of the tentative supply camp to be emplaced by Gannett's party. With eager anticipation, Gardner's men had set out over the now desert tableland, only to arrive and find that there was no supply camp and that the Gunnison could not effectively be crossed where they had hoped. After determining that no one from Gannett's division had been there, Gardner decided to continue moving to locate the missing group, obtain supplies, and then move toward the La Sal Mountains. The party broke camp and began the move to establish contact. Cuthbert Mills, traveling with Gardner, explains what happened next.

*Cuthbert Mills* ❊ *Camp Thirty, on the Dolores,*
*West Colorado, Friday, August 6*

There is no grumbling about orders in the field. They only have to be obeyed. The train was out again on the dry plain next morning early, making for a different point of the river, some old trails leading that way seeming to indicate that there had been or were fords there. Distances are as deceptive on the desert as on the ocean. It is easy to mistake a floating object which may be a bottle for a log or a boat, or vice versa; and as easy to mistake the dust raised by a coyote for that raised by a band of horsemen. So when Shep Madera, about half an hour after the start, drew attention to a small puff of dust on the face of the plain in the far distance to our left, all anyone could do was to watch it and wait.

Just outside the shadow of a bluff, a puff of dust no bigger than would be thrown up by a rifle bullet striking the ground appeared, but it was something which in this section of country would not be well to disregard. In ten minutes the cloud had slightly increased in size and Shep, now thoroughly aroused, dashed ahead and pointed it out to Mr. Gardner, for he had been so intent on the trail or something as not to have noticed it. A halt was called and the mysterious cloud carefully examined through a field glass. As far as could then be made out, it was raised by a horse or horses, then, that it was a single horseman, but who could it be riding alone in such a country? Indian or white man? A white man by his riding, so Shep gave his verdict. This was while still to the naked eye there was only a black speck in the cloud.

Ten minutes more and the horseman could be discovered amid the flying dust coming toward us as if life or death depended on his speed. Two or three minutes more, and while Mr. Gardner rode out to meet him, we recognized in this flying horseman no other than Mr. Gannett, the head of the other division of the survey doing topographical work in this section. He came with no alarming intelligence of hostile Indians or equally dangerous horse thieves, but to leave a letter, enclosed in a yeast can and stuck on a pole at the place where the supply camp was to have been. Mr. Gardner had said he should be there on a certain day and his calculations were so correct that, had not Mr. Gannett ridden as hard as he had, they would have missed by a few hours. It appeared that the river had been so swollen by the rains when the supply train reached it, that no way of crossing it could be found; and further, it was discovered that a much better and shorter way to the Sierra La Sal could be taken over the plateau and through the canyons than by following down the river.

The two heads consulted long and then agreed that it was better for them to go through the dangerous section with combined forces. Probably they felt that the stock, really about the only thing they had any anxiety about, would be safer from "hickory [Jicarilla] Apaches" and renegade Utes when there were thirteen men to guard them rather than two much smaller and widely-separated parties. This decision relieved us of the desert march and the lively shaking up which we should have had in looking out for nightly visits from those "heap bad Utes," of which we had been warned by old Ouray at the agency. Of course the stock will have to be guarded at night, but as these braves never attack a party without first acquainting themselves with its strength, they will probably keep at a respectful distance when they get that information about ours.

In pursuance of the change of plans, the Gardner party turned its course, marched back some six miles up the Grand, struck the trail of the Gannett party, which had gone on while its head came on his solitary ride, forded the stream where it was broad and shallow, and then drove fifteen miles more over a horribly stony plateau, and camped four miles behind the other party in a box canyon. The sagebrush was so thick here that one had to search around for a place to spread a blanket. The soil was a red dust which sent up a choking cloud of impalpable powder at the slightest movement, the only water obtainable was in a muddy hole and tasted horribly of iron, and there was scarcely a mouthful of anything for the mules, while some of them ran off and our meal was spoiled by having to get up and chase them.

I shall never forget the first box canyon I ever got into as a most interesting sight and a detestable camping ground. Yesterday we took up the chase of the Gannett party, followed through the canyon, found it gradually expanded into a noble valley, and caught them as they went into camp at one of the widest and most beautiful parts of it. There was a grand reunion of seventeen men, including the supply train party, and a general comparing of notes, and among those who indulged in it, a mutual and immediate anxiety about tobacco. But alas! Both parties had thought alike; the Gannett men that they could get some from the Gardner boys because they had run out themselves; the Gardner men that they could get what they wanted from the others because their own was exhausted. The combined result did not produce much beyond a groan of despair.

"*The Hayden Survey: Colorado Deserts and Canons,*"
New York Times, *August 30, 1875.*

### *James T. Gardner* ✳ *La Plata River Mining Camp, August 22*

On Wednesday, August 4th I met Mr. Gannett, as I had hoped, on the Gunnison River, near its junction with the Grand. Owing to high water, he had taken the responsibility of changing the plan previously approved by us of putting the supply camp at the junction of the Grand and Gunnison Rivers and had pushed it westward with his own train on the Dolores River. I followed and overtook them in one day, within eighteen miles of the Dolores. This point being on the Ute reservation, Mr. Gannett considered it safe for a supply camp. I had, however, been informed by Ouray that the Indians in the Sierra La Sal Mountains, which lie in Utah about thirteen miles west of the Colorado line, were likely to steal stock if they got a good chance. He said that a party of seven armed men would be safe in the region, but they must watch their animals carefully, and if one man was caught out alone he might not be safe. In short, these Sierra La Sal Indians were represented to me as sneak thieves who would bear much watching.

For the sake of making it easier on the night guard, and having enough men to supply escort to the topographers, I had determined that if I could meet Mr. Gannett, I would unite the two parties for the survey of the country west of the Dolores. This was accordingly done August 7th, when we left Mr. Gannett's supply camp on the Rio Dolores. He left there Messrs. Holman and Dallas, and sent back Hovey and Babcock for more provisions. (For reasons which you will understand, I preferred not to interfere with any of Mr. Gannett's plans, except where it appeared absolutely necessary.) I, therefore, made no objection to his change of position of the supply camp. This plan was his own and was partially carried out before we met. After the two parties had joined, I, of course, took general charge of the whole and all responsibility for all movements.

The scientific party now consisted of seven men, viz: James T. Gardner, Henry Gannett, A. C. Peale, Robert Adams, W. R. Atkinson, Cuthbert Mills, Frank Pearson; the employees, six in all, were Shep Madera, Clarence Kelsey, Jacque Charpiot, Benj. Northington, Charles McCreary, and Judge Porter, thirteen in all. Seven were armed with rifles, the remainder with revolvers. During the march, the men with rifles rode in front and rear, and in camp, a guard, regularly relieved at stated times, watched the animals, all except the cooks taking their turn.

"*Professor Gardner's Report*," Chicago Daily Inter-Ocean, *September 8, 1875.*

### Cuthbert Mills ✳ September 9, 1875

The topography of this region, as viewed from the summit of the Sierra La Sal, is very peculiar. These mountains and the Sierra Abajo, forty miles south of them, appear as islands rising from an elevated, plateau country, which, as far as the area of upheaval extends, is much broken into hogbacks. Beyond and below this, almost as far as the eye can reach, lies a vast desert of sedimentary rock mainly light and dark

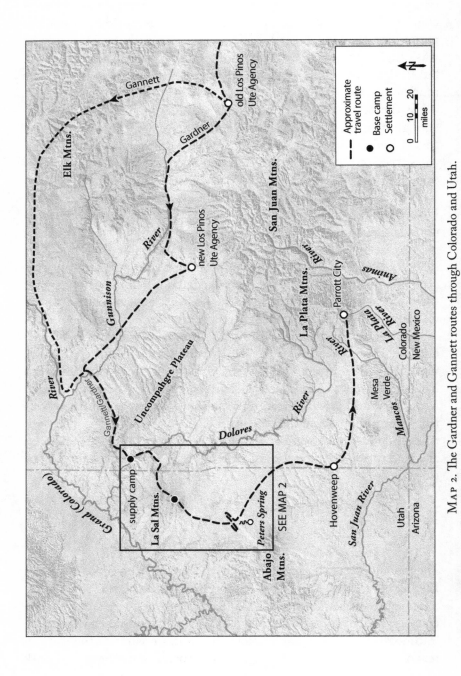

MAP 2. The Gardner and Gannett routes through Colorado and Utah.
Map by Ben Pease, based on a map by Winston Hurst. *Copyright © 2016, University of Oklahoma Press.*

red sandstone and seamed from end to end with those water-worn passage-ways called box canyons. Immediately on the slopes of the mountains there are good grass, good timber, and abundance of cool, fresh streams. The scenery is almost of pastoral beauty. Directly the water reaches the lower canyon region it runs among soft rocks, over salt and mineral beds, and becomes muddy and impure, and many of the streams sink out of sight in sandy, arid valleys. Nearly the whole of this canyon region is a burning, death-like desert in which nothing thrives but sagebrush and piñon pine. No man can live there, not even the Indian, but many fly to it as a safe sanctuary. They live on the edge of the mountain slopes and only descend to the lower portions when pursued or pursuing. The unlucky traveler they catch there is like to fare ill. If he escapes their hands, he may perish of hunger and thirst, hopelessly lost in the innumerable canyons and valleys. . . .

It will be easily seen that such a region presents nothing which is ever likely to attract any other inhabitants to it than it has now; but to these it offers all they most need. Being on the boundary lines of the ranges of three tribes, the Utes, the Paiutes, and the Navajos, the most desperate rascals from each congregate there for mutual protection and plunder when they dare not openly appear anywhere else. They acknowledge no authority but that of their own chiefs—murderers and robbers every one. The several bands number respectively from seven to twenty and are probably about as poor and desperate a set as mountain brigands usually are. There is not much doubt, however, that some of them occasionally come into the agencies and under cover draw rations and trade there, for of the band which paid their attentions to us, two at least, were recognized as having been at the Cochetopa Agency some weeks before. Their regular trading is done with the Navajo tribe south from whom they obtain arms, ammunition, and horses in exchange for the proceeds of their hunting expeditions—either of game or men. Ouray had warned both Mr. Gannett and Mr. Gardner of the character of these men, but at the same time expressed the opinion that they would not attempt to do more than steal our stock and that a party of seven men was quite safe.

When the two divisions joined, making a force of thirteen, any ideas of danger which might have been before entertained were dismissed. The only precautions taken were to set guards over the stock every night. This was begun the first night we left the supply camp on the Dolores, Aug. 7. The march was nothing new to the old members of the survey. They had all of them done their share of it in what was regarded as far more dangerous country than the Sierra La Sal and never had more than an occasional false alarm to vary the monotony of the night. Neither had we on this occasion, though while occupying our most elevated camp on the mountain slope we could look down upon an Indian encampment [of nine lodges] pitched in the valley to the east of us.

*"The Hayden Survey: What the Sierra La Sal Indians Did for It,"*
New York Times, *September 9, 1875.*

### *James T. Gardner ⁕ La Sal Mountains, August 11*

During the first few days no fresh Indian signs were seen, though we were continually scouting. When, at last, we marched to the south end of the range to climb the highest peak, which is a station of the primary triangulation, we found fresh signs, and I took the train far up through the woods to a little sheltered basin, directly under the peak and 9,500 feet in altitude. The position was admirably situated for concealment or defense. Two thousand feet below, to the east of us six or eight miles, we discovered an Indian camp of nine lodges. This was August 11th. These were just about on the line between Utah and Colorado.

*"Ute Warriors: A Band of Renegade Redskins Attack the Hayden Party,"*
Rocky Mountain News, *September 5, 1875.*[3]

CHAPTER 5

# Vestiges of Bygone Ages
## San Juan River to Hopi Mesas
### AUGUST 3—29

THE PHOTOGRAPHIC DIVISION UNDER JACKSON AND
Holmes's San Juan Division parted company on August 3 in
the corner of southeastern Utah near Montezuma Creek. Holmes's
primary task—establishing triangulation stations—would take him
into all four territories. During an uneventful two-and-a-half weeks,
he surveyed in the corners of southwestern Colorado, southeastern
Utah, northwestern New Mexico, and northeastern Arizona. Holmes
made extensive field notes on the geology of the area, triangulated
points in the Carrizo Mountains, and further explored Anasazi ruins.[1]
His notes, written under extreme field conditions, are detailed, techni-
cal observation of the region's geology and so are not included here.
Readers interested in this aspect of the survey will find his final
reports most useful. Holmes concluded his work without difficulty
by late August and returned to Parrott City, anxious to hear news of
the other Hayden divisions.

Jackson's experience, on the other hand, provides a rich study in
various Indian cultures of the time, as well as some interesting events,
and so is the focus of this chapter. As he headed south along the San
Juan River on the second phase of his fieldwork, the object was less
about scenery and more about the ancient Indian populations that had
left an amazing variety of ruins in the cliffs and canyons. Jackson's
destination was the Arizona mesas inhabited by the Hopis, or Moquis,
as nineteenth-century Euro-Americans called them. Was there a link
between these modern Indians and the ancient inhabitants of the

spectacular ruins? Jackson, supported by contemporary speculation, set out to determine how closely these American Indians paralleled the culture of the Ancestral Puebloan.

E. A. Barber shared with his readers of the *New York Herald* a current theory that started with the Toltecs, an "industrious, harmless, peaceful people," who lived and prospered in Mexico until the twelfth century. Then a "fierce, barbarous, and uncultured" race called the Aztecs conquered and enslaved the Toltecs for a short time before disappearing. How and why the Aztecs disappeared, Barber does not say. In fact, their "disappearance" is surprising, given the extensive Spanish accounts of the conquests of the Aztecs in the early 1500s, but the important piece in our narrative is the connecting link of the Hopis to the Toltecs. To Barber, what happened in Mexico with the Aztecs parallels what occurred in the Four Corners region in the deserted ruins built in a defensive posture to protect the Hopis. The Utes become the "fall guys" once again as Barber connects the physical remains from the past with what he sees in the present. Today there is no proof to substantiate much, if any of this, but these beliefs do help one to understand the thinking of the nineteenth-century mind in the beginning days of anthropological and archaeological theory.

### E. A. Barber ❋ Southeastern Utah, August 3

Until lately, there seemed to be a wide gap in time between those ancient races and the Indian race of today. The connecting link seems to be the modern Moquis, who most undoubtedly descended from the builders of the ancient ruins we are now investigating, and they, in their turn, were in all probability remnants of the subjugated Toltec race, escaped from bondage.[2] The builders of these ruins seem to have come from the south and built northward and were then driven back, step by step; for generally the lowermost ruins are the most perfectly preserved and evidently the most recent, becoming more complicated as their creators retired southward.[3] For a time this scattered people seem to have regained their freedom, prospered and multiplied, spreading their towns and secreted communities throughout most all of the canyons of the tributaries of the San Juan, and thence west as far as the Colorado River.

But presently another foe, as relentless and persecuting as the Aztecs, appeared on the scene. These were the ancient Ute Indians, who were a strong, bloody tribe, inhabiting a section of country north of the San Juan. We have this fact from the traditions, both of the present Utes and the Moquis; and, although mere Indian traditions are not data on which to base facts, still they help to establish truths when taken in connection with other facts which are indisputable. All the Utes at the present day will tell the traveler through this country that these ruins are "Moquitch" remains. We made it a point to ask the questions whenever we had the opportunity and invariably received the same reply. Showing a party of Utes one day a collection of pottery which we had gathered, we inquired of them whether it was Ute pottery, and were answered "Moquitch," with a point of the finger southward.[4] As we were digging in one of the old graves at another time, a Ute passed by, who informed us that it was a "Moquitch cache." We have been repeatedly told that the walls of houses in the vicinity were those of "Moquitch" houses and it is certain that this idea prevails among the Navajo Indians as well as the Utes—that the Moqui tribe once inhabited all this country many, many years ago, beyond the recollections of their grandfathers.

The Ute traditions, which have been handed down from one generation to the next for centuries, give accounts of a war with this race long ago, in which the Moquis were driven from the country. We know that between three and four centuries ago the seven Moqui towns occupied their present positions on the mesas of Arizona, and we therefore conclude that these ruins possess a still greater antiquity. It is quite certain that the present Moqui towns were not built until after the tribe had been driven south and took their last stand there, where they have since remained undisturbed for many hundreds of years.

In regard to the antiquity of the ruins, a great diversity of opinions exists. Some writers give them an antiquity of nearly a thousand years, while others set them down as being not far from three hundred. It is most probable, however, that they have been standing, as near as it is possible to conjecture from the external evidence which they present, for a time in the neighborhood of five hundred or six hundred years. Many of the crumbled mounds of stone and clay could not possibly have become decomposed to such an extent as we find them in a less time by the ordinary action of the elements, and especially in such a dry, equable atmosphere as characterizes the whole ruin country. Whatever the genealogy or origin of these people, there can be not the shade of a doubt that they were the ancestors of those present inoffensive industrious tribes living in New Mexico and Arizona known as the Pueblo, Moqui and . . . We will have an opportunity of comparing wherein the two people were similar and of determining whether they were not identical—that is, whether the ancient race was the ancestral stock of the Pueblo, Moquis, and Zunis, for the three tribes are nearly related and what is proved regarding one will apply to all.

"*Ancient America: Races of Men Flourishing Here a Thousand Years Ago,*"
New York Herald, *September 25, 1875.*

⁂     ⁂     ⁂

Influenced by these interpretations, Jackson and Barber visited some of the most dramatic country and interesting ruins in the Southwest. Having already explored Hovenweep, the group now visited Casa del Eco (known today as Seventeen Room Ruin) on the San Juan River not far from Bluff; Poncho House Ruin in Chinle Wash; and a multitude of lesser-known remains. The previous summer, Jackson had visited Mesa Verde, studying those antiquities. Extensive field notes, accurate sketches, and well-positioned photographs provide some of the earliest detailed descriptions of what these two expeditions found. Just as Hayden's 1871 geological survey of Yellowstone proved influential in raising public awareness that resulted in its becoming a national park, so too did Jackson's work increase interest in the prehistoric cultures of the Southwest, a number of which have since become national or state parks.

Jackson's journey this time, however, required real effort. The expedition's route took them along the San Juan River to Chinle Wash; the group traveled to the end of the Wash before crossing the burning summer desert to the three Hopi mesas—First, Second, and Third. The group recorded temperatures at their camp at the junction of Chinle Wash and the San Juan River as 125 degrees in the noonday sun and 140 degrees in the sand at their feet, with the water at 88 degrees. After leaving the river, locating palatable water became a primary concern, encouraging Jackson to cache equipment for lighter loads on the animals, to send back to a base camp part of his crew, and to gauge travel

The Photographic Division of the Geological Survey, in photo taken between July 18 and 23, 1875. *Standing, left to right:* Harry Lee, guide; W. H. Jackson; and Bill Whan, packer. *Sitting:* Bob Mitchell, packer; E. A. Barber, naturalist; and William Shaw, cook. *Courtesy Scotts Bluff National Monument, SCBL 669.*

time and distance by the chance of water being available. The San Juan River also served as a general boundary line between Ute and Navajo territory. South of it, the party encountered Navajos who provided substantial information about the terrain and traded goods with the weary travelers. Barber picks up the story on August 10.

### E. A. Barber ❋ Rio de Chelly, northeastern Arizona, August 10

Leaving our fourth camp on the banks of the Rio San Juan, we took a southwesterly course up the Rio de Chelly, keeping a little to the west of its canyon on the mesa above.[5] Our next camp was pitched after a short march (for we were limited entirely by the watering places, which were very few along our route) beside a spring of tolerably good and cool, but alkaline water, which we so dug out and collected together as to secure sufficient for our own uses and the thirst of our mules. Near this, and in the canyon of the stream, a large colony of ruined buildings was found, among which some very perfect and valuable implements, ornaments, and ancient pottery were found.

It was noticeable that the general character of these relics in the bed of this channel from its very mouth differed in a considerable degree from any we had yet seen. The pottery showed an advancement in the intensity, durability and variety of its coloring. Here we found fragments of earthenware painted in three colors—red, orange, and black. We also picked up some entirely new to our experience. This was a highly glazed yellow variety with red ornamentations.

At the mouth of this river are numerous etchings on the smooth rocks, representing men and devils in many fantastic attitudes and with clasped hands, but among all the rock drawings we have yet seen there was not one representation of a horse, although goats [desert bighorn sheep—*Ovis canadensis nelsoni*] appear in nearly all of these ancient inscriptions. This would seem to indicate that the artists possessed goats but knew nothing of horses. We know that the Moquis, hundreds of years ago, raised goats and at the present day hunters report a few wild goats in some of the canyons of these streams. They are supposed to be the remnants of the ancient domestic goats, run wild, and are entirely distinct from the Rocky Mountain goat—capra Americanus, of Richardson. We find in all the paintings, etchings, and inscriptions of the Utes and Navajos of the present day, rude imitations of horses, which are more numerous than any other particular objects, and from this fact it may be reasoned that those drawings wherein goats are figured and horses are wanting are undoubtedly the productions of neither of these tribes, but were executed by a much older people. Indeed in many places they indicate a great antiquity, as the stone on which they are engraved has been worn gradually and slowly away until some of the designs are almost entirely effaced. Even where the rock overhangs, the sandstone has been worn by the fine dust and grains of sand blown against it by the wind.

At the mouth of the Rio de Chelly [Chinle Wash] we saw also some of the first attempts at painting on the rocks. One picture resembled a globe painted in red and yellow, two or three feet in diameter, and others were unlike anything with which they might be compared. It

Poncho House in Chinle Wash is the largest cliff dwelling ruin in Utah and one of the most dramatic sites visited by Jackson in 1875. His extensive description of the site (not included here) and excellent sketches and photos represent part of the first professional archaeological study of Anasazi culture in the Four Corners region. *W. H. Jackson, Courtesy Palace of the Governors Photo Archives* [NMHM/DCA], *plate L, Hayden,* Tenth Annual Report, *"Report on the Ancient Ruins Examined in 1875 and 1877."*

would be impossible to determine to which age they belonged, but it is very probable that they were of Navajo workmanship. Fifteen years ago this tribe roamed as far north as Utah and Colorado and for a while many of them availed themselves of these ruins as dwellings and places of security from their enemies, as many Indian tribes, among whom were the Utes, were supposed to stand in awe of this whole mysterious country. Today, however, we can distinguish between the original walls and those re-erected by the Navajos, as the latter have simply been piled up loosely from the debris of the fallen plastered walls. We see many buildings in which a portion of the stones are still cemented neatly, although indicating a great age, while a breach or an entire side, perhaps, is filled in with a carelessly thrown together pile of rocks. But these Indians were driven from these strongholds during the late war by the military, assisted by the Utes, and since then they have confined their operations to the southern limits of the ancient country.[6]

Our next camp on the same stream was a dry one, affording no water other than what we carried with us in a two gallon keg and our canteens save a small, thick muddy puddle in the bed of the stream. This sufficed for the mules but we were all limited in the use of our drinking water. From here we pushed on up the river for another twenty-five miles to within sight of the Navajo cornfields. Here we found flowing water in the stream, but so muddy that even the mules refused to touch it. From the fine red sand and clay of the marl sandstone country through which it flowed it had acquired the consistency and color of red lead paint. It was as thick as molasses and when anything, as the hand, was dipped into it, left a thick, pink coating. It was impossible to use it even for washing purposes for one might as well thrust anything into a tub of dyeing material. A water kettle, which was dipped into the stream, presented the appearance of a pink clay vessel the moment its surface was dry. We tried to filter the water, but found it impossible, as the sediment filled the pores of the paper before a drop of liquid could pass through, thus rendering it waterproof.

At length, however, we succeeded in finding water some distance from the banks of the stream below the sand, through which a hole was dug six feet deep. This had to be kept from caving in like quicksand by a cylinder of cottonwood bark, which was sunk in the hole, and from which we scooped the mud and sand. In the course of an hour we had cool water, which, although not clear, was infinitely preferable to that of the creek. From this well we watered all of our animals, dipping out the water in tin basins and serving to one at a time.

Presently two happy, pink Navajo papooses came down to our camp. They were perfectly naked and had been wallowing to their hearts' content in the stream, through the heavy pink deposit of [last line missing] . . . like the Utes, but silently accepted what was given them, or even refused a meal when invited to eat, which is a thing a Ute was never known to do, unless he might be sick or on his death bed. Only once in a while an old fellow might ask for a pipe-full of tobacco, but this was the extent of their alms asking. Their usual cordial greeting was "Wano-hay, John!" the first word being corrupted from the Spanish "bueno," and every white man they see they call "John."

Everyone was attracted by the leather on our saddles, canteens, and aparejos, and was perfectly ravenous for leather of any kind. Some of them brought down several of the most exquisitely colored blankets of their own make that we had ever seen to swap for leather. For one of the flaps on the stirrup strap of the saddle they wanted to trade a fine saddle blanket valued at $5, the lowest estimate. They had no eyes nor ears for anything but leather and they seemed determined to trade with us for the leathern flaps of the canteens, and insisted on our cutting off the leather from the inside of the aparejos. What they do with so much of this article it is difficult to say, but they probably use it for making whips, reins, and soles for moccasins.

These Indians differ materially from the Utes. They are more industrious and independent, raising quantities of corn or maize, pumpkins and watermelons, and keep large herds of goats, sheep, and horses. They weave blankets after the manner of the Moquis, from whom they undoubtedly obtained the art originally, and the blankets are heavy, perfectly water-proof, and woven in standing, brilliant colors, into geometrical figures and designs, entirely by hand. We witnessed the operation in several of the huts, the squaw working whenever she has nothing else to do, and frequently a blanket will occupy several months in its manufacture. They are made entirely of wool taken from the sheep. Some of these blankets command a fabulous price in the market, but they will wear for an indefinite time and are worth five of the best American-made. There is a certain kind of flat, circular bead ornament made from a species of marine shell, which the ancient Moquis used to manufacture and which are occasionally taken from the old graves and ruins for a string of which the Navajos will trade five or six of their best blankets or a good horse, so highly valued. We discovered only two or three single specimens of these wafer-like beads about the circumference of a pea, but we did not exhibit them to the Indians.

We soon discovered that their corn was ripe and in a few moments had a sack-full negotiated for, which we were eagerly husking. This, indeed, was a treat that we dreamed not of, but we determined to live high as long as we were in the country. For a few matches or a little tobacco or a quarter of a dollar (two bits, as it is called in the West), we purchased a quantity from one man, and in half an hour every squaw and papoose in the vicinity was carrying a blanket-load of fresh corn to our camp. We took all that was brought, showing no partiality in our selection and soon had piled up several bushels of the palatable vegetable. Much of this we used at supper and that man of the party fared badly who did not dispose of eighteen ears. This is no exaggeration, and for days after, so long as we could obtain it, the chief article of diet on our bill of fare was corn—boiled, roasted, cut down, and fried. By economical use a bushel lasted us two meals, but as long as there was plenty at low rates we did not limit ourselves to this quantity. The corn is what is known as Mexican corn, growing in small ears with red and blue grains, like our ordinary Eastern popcorn.

The Navajos were around us all evening until a late hour trying to trade for our leather. One old fellow stayed with us all night, making himself perfectly at home. These Indians dress in a manner peculiar to their tribe and differing considerably from any other, wearing almost invariably a red handkerchief or bandana twisted around the head, having their long hair tied up behind, in a loose roll or loop in an effeminate manner. The clothing consists of a calico shirt; loose, wide yellow linen breeches, reaching down only to the knee; with leggings of fancy patterns tied with red worsted garters, made by the squaws; and un-beaded moccasins with stiff soles. The females wear their hair usually parted in the middle and hanging in two plaits at their sides. Their nomadic mode of living interferes with the erection of any permanent structures of abode, and they usually sleep in small temporary dome-shaped tents made of cedar or cottonwood boughs. The winters, which are very mild in the country where they live, require no more substantial dwellings, so that when it is desirable to move from one place to another the lodge is deserted and another quickly built in a new spot. As we travel through the country we notice many of these old shells standing where they have not been visited for long years. Considering all things, the Navajos are a superior tribe of Indians to all the wandering bands which inhabit the western country. It is, in fact, a matter of doubt whether they originated in the same stock as other tribes, and it may be possible that they descended from a people of greater culture and a higher civilization.

"Ancient America: Races of Men Flourishing Here a Thousand Years Ago,"<br>New York Herald, September 25, 1875.

### William Henry Jackson ❉ Pioneer Photographer

We were now in the land of the Navajos. Many of these Indians were in the neighborhood and all one afternoon they crowded our camp eager to do some trading. We bought a lot of green corn and melons from them, paying in silver, but what they wanted more than anything else was leather. They looked with covetous eyes upon our equipment of saddles, cantinas, and aparejos. Since we had heard much of their thieving propensities, we took extra precautions to have everything made of leather as near to us as possible when we made our beds for the night.

After careful consideration I decided to divide our party here [August 10] and continue the trip with only Barber and Harry [Lee, guide] and two packs, sending the rest back to Canyon Bonito to await our return. The prospect for water and grass was altogether too precarious to warrant taking the whole train any farther. At Bonito there were both and the animals could recuperate in our absence. While we were getting ready for the separation, the Indians brought in quantities of green corn for sale, so we bought as much as we could carry.

With the boys off on the back track, we set out ourselves at a lively jog trot for "Moquitch." We soon came to an extensive farming region and for several miles passed through a succession of cornfields in the harvest season. Numerous small hogans (the Navajo name for their earth lodges) were scattered about and many of the Indians came out to the trail to meet us, always with the salutation "buena hay" or "adonde va!" Leaving the cornfields, we struck off southwesterly, skirting on our right the line of high cliffs of the Great White Mesa. Until noon we traveled rapidly; then we stopped for an hour under a group of peculiar red rocks, near which was a small pool of water. Our thirsty animals would not touch a drop of it, however, probably because of the sheep odor.

Just before sundown we came to a spring in a ravine, around which were camped several families of Navajos with a multitude of dogs. As we rode up, we were surrounded by a yelping pack of curs, which raised such a rumpus that it was difficult to get a word with the Indians. The dogs were eventually quieted and we made our camp in peace. Several of the Indians who had their summer hogans in the neighborhood were in our camp all the morning, importuning us to trade. They said there was to be a big corn dance next day and they wanted us to remain for it, but we could not accept their invitation as our time was too limited.

In the morning we struck out in an almost beeline over the broad, open valley, passing point after point of the great mesas. About noon, while still fifteen to twenty miles distant, we could make out with the glasses, the mesa upon which stood Tewa, the first of the Moquis towns. It was the last of the mesa promontories; otherwise we might have passed it without noticing the line of rock-built houses upon its summit, so like are they to their surroundings. Riding on rapidly, we were soon among Moqui cornfields, where we met a herder who directed us to a place where we could get water. Because of the many trails we had difficulty finding the tank or reservoir. It was a shallow well, walled with stone.

Passing through a small peach orchard, we met a man who pointed out the right trail for ascending the mesa with our animals. The trail was cut out along the face of the bluff, being walled up in places. Part of it was like a stairway. We made the four-hundred-foot climb, with ease and came out finally at the very door of the Captain's house.

*Jackson and Driggs,* Pioneer Photographer, *253–56.*

## E. A. Barber ❋ Moqui Towns, Arizona, August 15

From our camp near the Navajo cornfields we separated into two parties, three of us starting out with two pack mules, carrying our provisions and the photographic kit for the Moqui towns situated some eighty miles to the west. The rest of the party with the train was to return forty or fifty miles to our previous camp on the Rio de Chelly [Chinle Wash] near the diamond fields, there to wait for us.[7] It had been the intention to take the whole train over to the Moquis, but we learned from the Indians that the distance was much greater than we had supposed and water was very scarce, so that it would have been almost an impossibility to have taken fourteen animals through the dry country in safety. We proposed then to make a side trip, accomplishing the eighty miles in two days.

Taking with us, therefore, Mexico and Blinkey, the only two reliable and swift pack mules in the party, we set off at a good round trot and kept it up steadily all day, stopping only an hour or so at noon to rest and take a little lunch. After leaving the train we passed through the cornfields which extended up the valley for a number of miles.[8] Each farm was separated from the next by not so much as a mound of soil or a ditch, but we could tell pretty accurately where one ended and the next commenced by the position of the huts which stood in the midst of them. As we rode through the corn on the trail, we had to keep our animals at a rapid gait to prevent their snapping at the stalks which grew so close to the trail. Each hill contained several stalks which grew scarcely three feet high.

As we passed the wigwams the men came running out to see us and inquire where we were going. Everyone seemed to be busy about something, either herding their horses, moving their goods from one place to another, or engaged in some household occupation. We observed two or three of the men knitting stockings with steel needles; their work appeared as neat and creditable as that of any old lady who had knitted all her life. From some of these Indians we received directions regarding the trail we were to follow. Directly our course went straight for the end of a long gray mesa which we had noticed on our march for several days previous. We rode on until late in the afternoon before we reached it, but as there was no water here, we had to ride ten or fifteen miles beyond. At sunset we camped near another Navajo settlement, over forty miles from where we had left our train.

The next day we rode nearly forty miles through some of the most singular mesa country we had seen on our trip. Our trail took almost a straight line through a broad, perfectly level valley, where a railroad track might have been laid without grading, as the mesas on either side appeared one after another, seeming almost endless as we advanced. Their end pointed toward the valley and they ran back each way for several miles. This was on the 12th of August and a little past noon we approached the most eastern of the Moqui villages, three of which we could see for a distance of several miles, perched upon the level top and at the extreme point of a long mesa.[9]

Shipaulovi on Second Mesa, 1875. This two-story pueblo, with a central courtyard for dances and ceremonies, is surrounded by structures built with rock and covered with adobe. As with the other Hopi towns visited by Jackson, his group was welcomed with food and hospitality. *Courtesy Long Island Historical Society Collection, Box 1, 3086, American Heritage Center, University of Wyoming.*

As we neared its foot we were first made aware of the vicinity of human beings by observing several peach orchards growing in the sand in the valley below the plateau, and also by the presence of many flocks of sheep and goats with their respective Moqui shepherds in attendance. Then we passed through numerous corn patches and open gardens of beans, squashes, watermelons, and pumpkins. We were directed by one of the shepherds where to find water for our horses before ascending, which proved to be at the foot of the bluff in a deep depression that had been improved and walled up from time to time by the natives. The water of this spring or reservoir was cool, but unpleasant to the taste and alive with small insects and larvae, but it sufficed for our thirsty animals.

Taking the well-beaten track from here, we rode on until we approached a broad, steep, smooth road, which led to the summit of the mesa. This was some six feet broad and could almost be used as a wagon road. We could see scores of nude papooses standing on the cliffs overhead and running like goats along the edge or leaping across a chasm from one point to another. They were all attracted to the edge of the mesa by such an unusual spectacle as the approach of white strangers. From their positions they could command a view of the surrounding country for fifteen or twenty miles. We had undoubtedly been observed when far out upon the valley hours before.

As we climbed the last step at the top of the path and dismounted from our animals at the entrance of the town, two men advanced to greet us—one, the foremost, a bright, fine looking young fellow, dressed in a full American costume with a cocked hat and red feather. He took off his hat, shook hands, and in broken English, interspersed with Spanish, bade us welcome. The other, an older man, did likewise. These, we discovered afterward, were father and son—the elder, the "Capitan" [captain] or Governor of the town. By this time the tops of the houses and the open courts were covered with people. Old men dressed in tropical raiment; women of every age, eager to get a glimpse of us; and hundreds of papooses perched on the walls around and above us—all seemed to bid us welcome in their beaming faces which were turned upon us.

After we had shaken hands with several more of the prominent men, our mules were taken from us and lavishly fed with corn while our hosts invited us to enter the house. Following up a ladder to the roof of the second story and from thence to the third by a series of stone steps, we passed through a low aperture into a room on this floor. Here we were bidden to be seated on a raised platform at one side of the room, on which had been previously placed robes made of woven rabbit skins. Behind us a maiden was grinding corn in the primitive manner of the Moquis. Scarcely had we become seated when a beautiful girl approached and set before us a large mat heaped with piki bread. At the same time the chief's son placed for us some broiled meat to which we finally did ample justice, but our attention was directed to the peculiar bread, which was particularly palatable and which will be presently described.

The pretty Moqui Princess who had waited upon us sat down in another part of the room and resumed her occupation of cutting corn from the cob into a dish.[10] From where we sat we could gaze upon her unobserved with many an admiring glance sent in that direction. She was of short stature and plump, but not unbecomingly so. Her eyes were almond shaped, coal black, and possessed a voluptuous expression, which made them extremely fascinating. Her hair was arranged in that characteristic, Oriental manner peculiar to her tribe, which denoted her a maid. It was parted in the center from the front all the way down behind, and put up at the sides in two large puffs, which although odd to us, nevertheless seemed to enhance her beauty.[11] Her complexion was much lighter than that of her family and every movement of her head or exquisitely molded hands and arms or bare little feet, was one of faultless grace.

All the surroundings of the place, our reception, and the presence of this damsel, so unexpected and novel to us, overwhelmed us for a time with a mute surprise, and we could only silently eat and look about us, almost believing we were acting in a dream. We had entered abruptly and awkwardly . . . [last line missing] of the modest and beautiful Num-pa-yu—signifying in the Moqui tongue a snake that will not bite—every head was uncovered in a moment and each of us felt clumsy, dirty, and ashamed of our torn garments and unshaven faces. Harry, our guide, conversed with the son in Spanish and so we were enabled to make our errand understood.

On this first mesa, approaching from the east, stand three towns:— Tewa, pronounced locally Tay-wab, Se-chum-a-wee, and Moqui, pronounced Mo-kee. The second is sometimes given with the first, as it is but a small village separated by but a few hundred feet; nevertheless, it is one of the seven Moqui towns. As we strolled along the ancient courts and streets of these interesting places our attention was attracted on all sides by hundreds of curious sights. First were the buildings themselves, built perhaps five centuries ago, still standing, some in perfect preservation and others deserted and crumbling gradually away. Where one house ended and another commenced it was impossible to tell. Frequently the successive stories were occupied by different families with usually two rooms the extent of space. There was but one jumble of walls, one above the other, for four stories. Rooms had been dug into the solid rock beneath our feet and we were only aware of their existence by observing square holes in the ground as we passed along.

The successive stories of a house usually recede, something after the style of the Egyptian pyramids, until in some cases, four stories or even five, counting the subterranean, have been reached. The doors and windows were all small apertures in the walls through which one must stoop to enter. The underground rooms were usually workhouses where blankets were woven or the piki was mixed and baked. One thing was particularly noticeable in the style and architecture of all of these buildings, and that was a marked similarity to the ruins of those ancient buildings from which we had just come. The walls of the two were built and plastered out of the same materials and in the same manner. Many of these Moqui houses were plastered externally with a layer of adobe smeared on with the hand, just as we had seen in some of the ruins along the San Juan River. Here it may be said that we had the pleasure of observing the fair Num-pa-yu employed at this work.

The doors and windows of the two are similar, being wider at the bottom than the top; but the greatest point of resemblance between the two is in the roofs. For a long time we did not discover a ruin possessing any indications of ever having been roofed until one was seen in the canyon of the Rio de Chelly, which had been so thoroughly protected from decay by the overhanging rocks that the roof was almost as perfect as when laid. This was made exactly as the roofs of all the Moqui houses, being composed of parallel poles of cedar filled in with willow twigs and leaves. We noticed many of the depressions among the ruins which were evidently the subterranean workhouses of the modern Moqui towns.[12] In the extensive ruins, previously described on the Hovenweep, there were seven of these depressed rooms. To be sure, the ruins of the ancient people which still stand are more scattered and are built in different sorts of places from the mesas on which stand the seven towns, but this is accounted for by the necessities of those bloody times.

On the evening of our arrival, we strolled through the streets to pass away the time and learn as much of the manners and customs of the people as we might pick up. The hundreds of dogs which infested the place heralded our coming and followed us in packs, never, however, attempting to bite. Thus we were accompanied by a band of music wherever we went. Making ourselves at home, we entered without bidding wherever we liked. Climbing up one of the ladders we passed into a room where a robe was spread for us to sit upon and piki was set before us. In every house we visited we were treated in this hospitable manner. Passing along a court we would pause to look down some shaft at a family at supper below, reclining around a low table on which sat the mutual bowl of food into which each thrust his hand and brought forth what he wished. In all the houses we noticed immense quantities of corn, dried on the cob, which was stored around the walls or piled up along the sides of the rooms like cord wood. This was to provide for a possible failure of the crops so that a famine would be prevented. The corn was usually the red and blue grained variety which the Navajos raise.

At sunset the men came in from their day's labor in the fields in squads of four or five, almost naked with their hoes over their shoulders and their boomerangs or bows and arrows and whatever small game they might have killed during the day in their hands.[13] The hoes and weapons were laid in a pile in the center of the court and all hands repaired to their respective dwellings to sup. We noticed that the only weapons these people possessed, with the exception of half a dozen guns in the tribe which were only obtained recently, were weapons of the hunt, consisting of wooden boomerangs and small bows and arrows for killing rabbits, the arrows without points of any kind. This would designate them a peaceful nation as were their ancestors, and we find no trace of any ancient weapons among them.[14]

The first night of our stay we camped to the north of these towns, a quarter of a mile away, on the plain beyond one of the principal reservoirs. This was some ten feet in depth, surrounded by a circular wall fifteen feet in diameter and descended by stone steps. At daybreak we could see several figures, standing like sentinels on the parapets of the houses, watching for the sun to rise. As the sun appeared slowly above the eastern horizon, these figures dropped away slowly one by one and stole down from the mesa to the spring below, each with a huge jug wrapped in a shawl and supported from the back. All the women and many of the men repair regularly every morning to the springs of which there are three or four at the foot of the mesa, and carry up water to last during the day. The jugs are spherical with small necks which are flattened on one side to fit the back of the bearer. They will hold generally about four gallons being filled usually by means of a gourd with a hole at the end of the handle. This mesa stands about four hundred feet above the springs; the paths on either side are cut in the rock in a succession of steep, winding steps.

Ascending to the mesa early in order to photograph the towns, we rambled around once more in search of good specimens of modern pottery to bring away with us as mementoes. It was with no little curiosity that we stopped and passed the threshold of one of the houses to witness the interesting process of the manufacture of piki or Moqui bread, which we had so frequently eaten since our arrival. Under a large, flat, smooth, horizontal stone some two feet long, a foot and a half wide, and three or four inches thick, a hot fire was burning. Before this a woman sat on the floor baking. In a pot by her side was a thin, pasty mixture of a greenish flour (made from red and blue corn), cedar ash, and water. Into this the woman dipped her hand and smeared a thin coating over the stone or oven which had been previously greased to prevent adhesion. In a few seconds the sheet of piki was removed and another baked. Twenty or thirty layers of this folded twice formed a loaf, and when dry it was extremely brittle and palatable.

The process of grinding the corn into flour and converting it into this bread is an almost endless job for the women, but they take it as a matter of course and are always laughing and apparently happy. The flour made by them is of two kinds, the greenish blue and the white. The latter, made from the white corn, when finished, is as fine and good as any of our manufactured brands. This passes through three mills: the first breaks up the corn, the second grinds it coarsely, and the third pulverizes it. These mills consist of stone boxes placed in a row, which may be seen in every house, in each of which is an inclined, square, smooth rock on which the corn is placed and rubbed with a long stone or roller, some fourteen inches in length and four wide. The grinding is invariably done by the women, who labor at it from morning until evening, and frequently during the whole night.

The mesa, on which are built the three towns mentioned above, is a long, narrow plateau, extending from northeast to southwest. The end on which the towns stand is not over two hundred feet in width, and that portion of it between Sichomovi and Moqui, in one place, is not over twenty feet. In crossing along the trail one can see down for four hundred feet perpendicularly on either side. The trails between these towns are worn deeply into the rock, in one place twenty inches and two feet in width. Considering that this has been done entirely by the feet of the Moquis from generation to generation and for the most part by their bare feet, we may gain some faint idea of the length of time they . . . [text missing from document] corrals formed by long, narrow, horizontal shelves, which are walked around the outer edge. Up the rocky terrain into these the flocks of sheep and goats are driven every night, where they remain till morning. In one of the ruins near the Rio de Chelly we noticed one of the same sheep corrals, which adjoined a large ruined building perched on a cliff in a large cave.[15] In every house may be seen several fantastic toys or gods carved out of rotten wood, brilliantly painted in many colors, and decorated with feathers.[16] These are the gods used in the great dances of the tribe, and, although they are very highly prized among the Moquis, we were fortunate enough to obtain a couple.

"Ancient America: Races of Men Flourishing Here a Thousand Years Ago,"
New York Herald, September 25, 1875.

❊          ❊          ❊

Jackson, in his book *The Pioneer Photographer* (1929), adds detail from his perspective of the work that he pursued while at the Hopi mesas. They are less detailed and without the polish that Barber, as a newspaper correspondent, gave to his prose for his reading public.

### *William Henry Jackson* ❊ Pioneer Photographer

Our introductory visit over, we were directed to a place on the west side of the mesa where we could camp. Two boys were sent along to show us the way. Our photographic apparatus was left in the Capitan's house for future use. Since there was no grass in the neighborhood, we laid in an additional supply of corn for the animals.

Breakfast was late next morning, owing to the scarcity of fuel, but with that disposed of and the animals securely picketed, we went up into Tewa and began operations by taking a picture of Captain Tom and his attractive sister on the terrace of their house. Then we carried

VESTIGES OF BYGONE AGES 147

our boxes to the other end of the mesa and made several views around Walpi. Crowds of naked youngsters followed us around and perched upon the rocks, watching with eager interest all we were doing.

In the afternoon we started off for the other pueblos. Oraibi, which was too far away for the time at our disposal, was the only one omitted. Views were obtained at Shungopavi, Mishongnovi, and Shipaulavi, and at each pueblo the capitans entertained us with the usual layout of wafer bread and stewed peaches. Wherever we went, we were surrounded by curious throngs, pressing upon us so closely that we had but little room for getting our meals. For the two nights we were away from First Mesa, we had to make camp on the bare rock, where there wasn't a spear of grass for mules and horses. Corn on the cob without roughage was hard on them.

On our return we took our whole outfit up into Tewa and made our camp in its little court or plaza, where again we had nothing but corn for the animals. During the afternoon two other white men came in, W. B. Truax, the new agent on his first visit to the pueblos, and Billy Keams, the agency trader.[17]

Buying modern pottery and baskets as well as fetishes and small idols from Tom and his family, we spent all our cash and also bartered away nearly everything else we had to trade. When we finally gathered up all our purchases, we wondered how we were going to carry them. My photographic work was concluded by making another negative of Num-pa-yu. Later in the evening we had a farewell party in the house of the Capitan of Walpi. Here the three of us, with Truax, Keams, and five or six of the Moquis, gathered in a porch or vestibule, and by the light of the moon only, joined in a feast of wafer bread and stewed pumpkin. Our fingers were the only utensils available as everyone dipped into the same bowl.

*Jackson and Driggs*, Pioneer Photographer, *259–61.*

## E. A. Barber ✳

At noon of the day after our arrival we packed up and started across the valley in a westward direction from the other towns, situated on mesas from eight to fifteen miles distant. By some misunderstanding of our direction we passed within three miles of Oraibi, the largest

"Numpayu, A Moqui Maiden" was taken on August 14 in the Tewa village. Jackson and associates were smitten by the beauty of this woman, whose hair whorls indicate that she was not married. Nampeyo, who became a celebrated potter, also provided an interesting contrast to how other Native American women were viewed by this group. *W. H. Jackson, Courtesy Palace of the Governors Photo Archives* [NMHM/DCA], *#49806.*

town, which we afterward saw from a high point. Since our time was short we did not retrace our steps to it. At sunset, however, we entered the plaza of Shung-a-pah-wee [Shungopavi]. We camped just at the entrance of the town, picketing our animals to one small bush which was the only sign of vegetation on the rocky top of the mesa. We obtained three or four small pieces of wood from one of the inhabitants and had to walk a mile after sufficient water to boil our coffee. Wood is so scarce in the vicinity of all the Moqui towns that it is packed on the backs of men a distance of eight or ten miles from the valley below. We cannot wonder at this when we consider how many centuries these people have occupied this spot, especially as the country, being so sandy and barren, never was well-wooded.

Obtaining some negatives of the principal buildings of Shung-a-pah-wee, we rode over to the next town on our return route, known as She-pau-lah-wee [Shipaulavi], and were welcomed as we had been at Tewa, by the head man of the place, Na-kwap-she-o-ma. After partaking of some piki, dried peaches, etc., and indulging in a social smoke sitting on a circle of robes spread on the floor, we passed out to the hollow square, around which the town was built and obtained negatives of the principal views of the place and also of Moo-sha-neh [Mishongnovi], the seventh town, built on a high point of a few hundred yards beyond a deep valley. In returning to Tewa we passed close to the base of Moo-sha-neh, but did not stop on our way down the mesa since we had already tarried longer than we had intended. We caught a glimpse, however, of some albinos who live here and belong to the tribe.

At the base of this mesa we stopped to water our mules at a fine, large spring where we observed some decorations on the walls placed there by papooses, probably in the shape of painted sticks and colored feathers which fluttered from them.[18] Near this spring lay several flourishing gardens, fenced in by high stone walls in which were growing luxuriantly onions, beans, castor oil beans, cauliflowers, and some ornamental blossoms. Returning hastily to Tewa in order to take a few more desirable views before evening, we met the agent and trader for the Moquis, who were the only white men we had seen since leaving the La Plata River.

About dusk the whole party repaired to Moqui to take supper with the governor of that town, a sociable man and one who could speak

Jackson's skill as a photographer was matched by his talent at drawing. He sketched the "interior of a Hopi home" at Tewa and included a lot of ethnographic detail: hair styles, corn-grinding bins, two rabbit clubs hung on the wall, different types of pottery, sleeping arrangements, and the ever-present naked children. *W. H. Jackson, Courtesy Palace of the Governors Photo Archives* [NMHM/DCA], *#122774.*

a little English. Arriving at his house we were bidden to be seated on blankets and robes in a circle around a large basket of piki and an immense bowl of prepared pumpkin. In the party there were five white men, four or five Moqui men, and three Moqui women. Dipping into the dish of dried pumpkin with the first two fingers of the right hand, we alternately scooped out pieces of the pumpkin or broke off bits of piki and in this primitive manner we enjoyed the meal heartily.

We camped that night on the plaza of Tewa and, but for the wanderings of our hungry mules and the fleas which infested the place, we might have passed a comfortable night. The full moon poured her light around on all objects, making it light as day as we spread our blankets out in the level, rocky street. Our animals were fastened by long ropes to large flat slabs of stone, save one, which was tied to a ladder leading down into an underground room. All night we were kept awake by the mules dragging the stones all over the place, and did we ever sink into a doze for a moment one of them would approach and we would be wakened just in time to escape being crushed by one of these rocks. Through the whole night the sound of the flour mill floated out on the drowsy air from some dwelling and sleep seemed to be a thing which never visited the place.

Long before the sun sent his rays up from behind the eastern horizon, scores of females were out on the housetops with their jugs on their backs, waiting for the first ray to light them on their way to the spring. All over the roofs reclining figures who had not yet waked, might be seen rolled up in their blankets. As the sun appeared above the long line of mesas extending eastward, all was bustle and noise; the routine of another Moqui day had commenced. It was the Sabbath, but all days were alike here and the day's work proceeded as usual. At daybreak we were startled by a crash and discovered that the mule which had been tied to the ladder had pulled off the whole roof of the house which was precipitated to the bottom.

The men of the Moqui tribe wear their hair in a fringe cut off square just above the eyes from ear to ear and hanging down behind to the shoulders, or else gathered up in a knot after the fashion of the Navajos. Many also adopt the style of the latter in the head bandage. The married females usually part their hair in the center and wear it in two long side plaits. The dress of both sexes is very similar to the Navajo costume. All the children, until ten years of age, run perfectly naked. The Moquis possess nothing in the shape of horses except a very few burros or jackasses, and these they use for packing wood from the plains or riding occasionally from one town to another. At Shung-a-pah-wee we passed a graveyard just on the suburbs of the town. It was composed of graves marked out in squares, around which flat stones were set on edge, and over the whole much sacrificial pottery was strewn and broken, precisely as we had observed in so many of the ancient burial places connected with the ruins. We were also informed by the chief of Tewa that their dead were buried below the bluff in the valley.

Unlike many other tribes of Indians, the Moquis possess a great affection for their offspring. One old woman whom we visited presented her three little children to us, and with tears in her eyes, told us she had had two others, which (with a wave of the hand upward) had gone to a better land.

There can be no doubt that the Moqui tribe is a branch of the American race of men, but just as in the Caspian some nations are further advanced and more refined than others, occupying a higher place in the scale of human advancement. These Moquis are a more civilized, intelligent, and industrious race than any of the pastoral American tribes. The high foreheads and full, intellectual heads of the majority of them would alone place them in advance of all other Indians.[19] Their towns, lying as they have done for centuries on the mesas of Arizona in longitude 110 deg. to 111 deg. West, and latitude 35 deg. to 36 deg. North (not on the Little Colorado and San Juan Rivers, as some authors report, but a good two days' journey from any large stream), will probably remain where they are for future centuries; for, although of late they have been importuned to leave their present abodes and relocate in a more fertile country, they have refused to be removed from these pre-historic spots made sacred by a long line of ancestors who have passed away forever, leaving but the results of their labors to be carefully preserved and guarded by their posterity. The Moquis are growing fewer every year and now they have dwindled down to perhaps 1,500. The line of empty houses to be seen in each town tells a tale of its own which must sink sadly into the hearts of all who pause to think of the approaching fate of the Moqui race.

*"The Hayden Survey: Interesting Picture of the Moqui Towns in Arizona,"*
New York Herald, *October 1, 1875.*

### *William Henry Jackson* # Pioneer Photographer

Next morning [August 15] we started off on a jog trot for the return trip. We made the camp on Bonito Chiquito by sunset of the third day and found everything all right. The boys were glad to have us back. The next day while we lay over to let our animals recuperate, Barber and I went down the canyon afoot over the bed rock about two miles to a two-story cave house. Here we made careful measurements with sketches for a future model. Another day took us back to the Cave Town on the Chinle. Then sending the train on to the San Juan, I went over to the big cliff ruin again and made several more negatives of it. It grew oppressively hot before we were through, but I stayed with the work until I had photographs enough to give all the data required for making a reproduction.

We arrived at our former camping place soon after the train. The caches we had made in the sand were found undisturbed. A refreshing bath in the river, even though the water was quite turbid from heavy rains farther east, prepared us for an invigorating sleep. Our next objective was the Blue Mountains—the local name for the Abajo and La Sal peaks in eastern Utah.[20] It was a mysterious region, reputed to be the haunt of a band of outlawed, renegade Indians recruited from the surrounding Utes, Navajos, and Apaches. We approached this region, therefore, with some apprehension, but had confidence in Harry Lee's familiarity with the country and in the probability that he would know some of the Indians we might meet. . . .

*Jackson and Driggs,* Pioneer Photographer, *261–62.*

# CHAPTER 6

# "Something Serious Had Occurred"

## La Sal Mountains to Parrott City

### AUGUST 15–19

JACKSON'S LITTLE TIFFS WITH THE UTES AROUND COMB Ridge and Whiskers Draw, and in Montezuma Canyon, proved to be slight inconveniences. Little did the photographer know that the day he left the Hopi mesas, having spent the previous evening feasting on pumpkin and piki bread in the moonlight, the Gardner and Gannett party were embroiled in a firefight that made them equally thankful for the illumination. Nor did Jackson realize that, less than two weeks later, he would be riding around the battlefield, that the horse and mule tracks he encountered belonged to his friends, and that the Utes he met undoubtedly knew what had transpired.

The unified Gardner and Gannett parties were last seen camped on the southern grassy slopes of the La Sal range below the twin peaks of Mount Tukuhnikivatz and Mount Peale. Bad weather reduced visibility, forcing the group to wait days for the rain to stop, the cloud cover to lift, and triangulation to commence. Since the camp was somewhat concealed by pines and aspens, the surveyors remained undetected by the Indian encampment below and to their east. There was no reason for alarm, so Peale, who had a peak named after him at this point, whiled away his time by plowing through his stash of novels. Others performed camp duties, hunted, and monitored the growing number of tepees, which had recently expanded from nine to fifteen. August 14 saw the completion of the parties' surveying tasks, and so the following day, the men moved toward Blue Mountain and their next station. The encampment of Utes below did not seem to present any real threat, especially since the expected route of the party angled away from it. But on August 15, after the Hayden men broke camp and headed down through the valley, the Indians attacked.

The running battle that ensued was described by the two correspondents accompanying the Gardner/Gannett party, Cuthbert Mills and Robert Adams; in James Gardner's report to Hayden; and in A. C. Peale's diary. Since all of these sources cover the same sequence of events, we have arranged excerpts to provide a chronological narrative with as little redundancy as possible. All of the documents were written retrospectively, even Peale's diary, so that the dates included here represent our understanding of when events took place, not the date of writing, filing, or publication.

## HOSTILITIES COMMENCE

### James Gardner to F. V. Hayden ✢ Parrott City, Colorado, August 22

About sixty miles travel southward of our station lies the Sierra Abajo. The country is desert, interspersed with barren ridges and impassable canyons. Only one spring is known in the whole distance. Seeing from our mountain that the abrupt escarpment which terminates this table on the north was only broken in one place and this was in the exact direction in which the spring was laid down on Macomb's map, we directed our march toward this point on the morning of the 15th, hastening to get away from the dangerous region.[1]

"*Professor Gardner's Report,*" Chicago Daily Inter-Ocean, *September 8, 1875.*

### Cuthbert Mills ✢ August 15

All the triangulation and topographical work being finished, camp was struck early on the morning of Sunday, the 15th inst. and the march commenced for the Sierra Abajo, forty miles or so to the south. About 10 o'clock the two trains had reached the foot of the mountain slopes and began to cross the sagebrush plain which finally ran down into the desert and canyon country. Fresh Indian signs were observed some distance along the trail, apparently of two horsemen, and an hour or two later the head of the first train came suddenly upon a couple of Indians—an old man and a youth—who were in a little watered patch rudely planted with corn. When we, who were behind, came up, the two were flying through the sagebrush to the left of us, as if legions of fiends were after them. Ben Northington had called out to them in Spanish, but their only reply was to spur their horses the faster. He declared that five others had run into the brush, indicating some rocky knolls covered with scrub pine a little way off, but I think most of the party put this story down to the effects of imagination and were inclined to be merry over our first Indian encounter.

The corn patch of these Indians was irrigated from a small rill. This was the last running water we saw from that time till the Mancos was reached on the following Thursday evening, a distance of nearly two hundred miles. By noon the trains were completely in the desert, winding through a fearful region of broken sandstone ridges, dry, sandy water-courses with straight sides called arroyos, piñon pine knolls, and wide stretches of glaring white rock. The heat was so intense that the sand and rock seemed to burn the feet. The water in the canteens had long been exhausted; not the slightest indication could be observed where more might be found or a mouthful of grass for the stock. A "dry camp" that night seemed certain.

Late in the afternoon some water, red with mud and gravel, was discovered in holes in the rocks beside the trail. Of this the mules drank eagerly as did many of the riders. A proposition to camp was advanced, but it was hoped that a better place might be found further on so the trains continued the march. The trail soon descended into a wide, dry basin, so arid, so lonely, so scorched up and wild, it seemed to realize the ideal of the valley of the shadow of death. The only way into it was over the sandstone; the only way out of it was through the close canyon into which it narrowed at its southern end. To get out at any other point was to climb stone walls varying from five hundred to a thousand feet high. The ground plan of the valley was irregularly cruciform, having a transept, to speak architecturally, as wide and as long as the nave. A broad river had once drained it, but all that remained of this was a dry sandy bed, overgrown with sagebrush.

It was between five and six [o'clock] when the trains descended the last slope into this basin, having been marching without intermission since daylight. The Gannett train was somewhat ahead, Mr. Gardner being in front of both, and the two packers, Shep Madera and Kelsey, bringing up the rear of ours, while Charpiot rode the bell mare, as usual. Mr. Adams, who rode beside him, looked back over his shoulder, and turning to me said very quietly: "The Indians are on our trail."

A "green" man is ever the object of all sorts of attempts to scare and this seemed one of them. "You don't believe me," he continued in the same tone. "Look again." True enough, a party of them were tearing down the slope behind us in such a cloud of dust that it was impossible to tell their numbers till they pulled up to speak to the packers. We barely had time to see there were only five of them, when another cloud of dust came whirling up from which four more emerged. They made no hostile demonstration, but it was evident they had not overtaken the trains by accident and this looked ugly.

At this time some water, or rather mud holes, were discovered in front which, of course, caused a general halt. In a few minutes all the party were gathered together and the Indians were engaged with an earnestness which was too lively to be entirely disinterested, in assuring the "big chief," (Mr. Gardner,) and everyone else, that there was no more water for miles. "No more wa'er," said one old villain, throwing wide his arms, "no more wa'er, heap way up." They wanted us to camp there and spent ten minutes trying to persuade everybody that we must do it or perish from thirst. While the talk was going on, the rascals were skirmishing around the party, counting our guns and noting their make, and generally taking stock of us.

These suspicious movements were too obvious to be overlooked and Mr. Gardner decided that at all hazards he would not camp there. About a hundred yards from the water holes there was a ridge of broken rocks by which they were completely commanded. "A ——— bad place to fight in," said Ben Northington, taking a survey of the situation which Mr. Gardner had already done before him and arrived at the same conclusion. Still no one seriously thought of a fight, the Indians being comparatively small in number, but there was one man in the party who very decidedly made up his mind that he might look for a lively time on guard that night.

*"The Hayden Survey: What the Sierra La Sal Indians Did for It,"*
New York Times, *September 9, 1875.*[2]

## *James T. Gardner ✳ August 15*

About half-past four, when I was ahead searching for water-pools in a ravine and Mr. Gannett was half a mile in the rear of the train taking topography, nine Indians came riding after him, making signs of friendship and then shaking hands. He rode on with them to the main party, when they desired to shake hands with everybody. Messrs. Gannett, Peale, McCreary, and Northington recognized three of them as being with a band of women and children that they had met on the reservation twenty miles east of the Dolores where the band was engaged in hunting. The Indians recognized Mr. Gannett's party and recalled some incidents of their former meeting. McCreary also said quite confidently that he had seen the spokesman of the party at the Los Pinos Agency at the ration issue on July 1st. This, with the fact that they called themselves Yampa Utes and showing a mutilated paper from the White River Agency, quite disarmed suspicion. They were very anxious for us to camp at some mud holes close by, but we found that neither men nor animals could drink the nasty fluid. They then tried to trade for tobacco and powder. As we had neither to spare, we shook hands, and bidding them "adios," started forward over the hill.

*"Professor Gardner's Report,"* Chicago Daily Inter-Ocean, *September 8, 1875.*

## *Cuthbert Mills ✳ August 15*

The order to advance was given, the trains moved away and passed up over the ridge. Those who were behind, remarked that the Indians were following. "They wanted to camp with us and get supper on the cheap," replied Shep Madera. At that moment a shot was fired and Kelsey saw the fellow who did it—a villainous-looking scoundrel, with a couple of feathers stuck crosswise through the crown of his felt hat—jump away into the brush. The shot had the effect of bringing several to the rear of the trains, but as no other followed, Mr. Gardner thought they had fired at a rabbit or were trying a small scare, and was riding to the front again when another shot was fired. The bullet struck up the dust in the midst of the little rear group. There was no mistake about this—it meant fight and a nice condition we were in to make it—in a complete trap, at the close of a long and intensely-tiring march under the burning sun, with utterly fatigued animals, no feed for them, and, beyond all, no water, except at the holes behind where the Indians could kill any man or animal attempting to drink. The scoundrels knew well what they were about when they waited till we got into that desert valley. They appreciated the value of water in their country.

*"The Hayden Survey: What the Sierra La Sal Indians Did for It,"*
New York Times, *September 9, 1875.*

## James Gardner ✳ August 15

No sooner had the rearguard passed the brow than the Indians commenced firing from behind it. Kelsey and Adams came very near being killed, bullets striking the ground close to them. Being in the advance, I rode at once to the rear. The boys begged to be allowed to charge the Indians, but I considered it unadvisable, considering that they were protected by a hill and mounted on swift horses, and we on tired, slow mules. I, therefore, ordered the train forward in a trot to get out of range of the hill behind; then, taking Madera and McCreary with me, galloped toward a hill on the right and in advance under which the train must pass to reach more open ground. The redskins were already upon the opposite slopes but we drove them from it and held the point till the train was out of shot [range].

*"Professor Gardner's Report,"* Chicago Daily Inter-Ocean, *September 8, 1875.*

## Cuthbert Mills ✳ August 15

The second packer in Gannett's division was Charles McCreary. He had served in almost every army since he could hold a musket, fighting apparently for pure love of the excitement. He had one idea about fighting—charge the enemy the moment you see him, and the instant that opening shot came among us his revolver was out, and rushing to Mr. Gardner and all through the party, he begged and implored that a charge might be made on the spot. "We can kill every —— now," he urged. But a charge on tired mules against men posted among rocks with good horses at command would certainly have resulted fatally

Ute warriors were well known to American Indian and white opponents as skilled trackers and implacable foes when operating in their homeland. The Winchester rifles these men are carrying were a favorite because of their magazine capacity of fifteen rounds, their rapid-fire capability, and their maneuverability on horseback. Their maximum effective range, however, was only about two hundred yards. *Courtesy Denver Public Library, Western History Collection, H. S. Poley Collection, H. S. Poley, P-54.*

to those who made it. Mr. Gardner declined to order it but hurried the trains to an open space in the valley, the enemy dropping in a few shots to help keep the pace up.

The place we stopped at was nearly at the intersection of the cross valley, and to the right of us was a long, sparsely-timbered ridge, affording an excellent place from which the Indians could fire. Mr. Gardner called Madera and McCreary, and the three of them rode hard to get to the point first. They were just in time for the whole band was coming along its sheltered side full tilt. Three shots scattered the entire crew—in fact, they scarcely waited till the little party could dismount to fire. Having cleared the ridge, the three returned to the trains where there had been some brief confusion. A circular barricade was formed of the aparejos and cargo, the mules were picketed around outside, and, in western phraseology, the party was "corralled."

While this was being done the Indians again reached the ridge and kept up a fusillade on us, but most of their shots fell short, others flew overhead, and one came nearer than twenty or thirty feet. They could not get the correct range. One or two shots were fired in return by our party, just to show them the range of the guns, which it became quite clear next day that the enemy remembered and respected. In a little while they commenced firing at us from the other side of the camp, those who were doing it taking elaborate care to keep themselves well hidden in the sagebrush. Even at seven or eight hundred yards, not one of these valiant Indians would come out and shoot openly. Pickets were placed at points about fifty to seventy-five yards distant from the barricade, and the reliefs arranged for the night.

*"The Hayden Survey: What the Sierra La Sal Indians Did for It,"*
New York Times, *September 9, 1875.*

## A. C. Peale ✳ August 15

Charlie McCreary, Gardner, and Kelsey then went to the edge of the bluffs while we camped in the center of the top of the bluff. We made a barricade of our cargo and aparejos with the mules on both sides. We then put out three pickets, Gardner, Adams, and Kelsey. I kept guard in camp. We had a lunch of bread and cold ham. The Indians kept firing until midnight. Several times the mules got tangled up, being in want of both feed and water. Atkinson and I held them. Once while we were out with Ben and Gannett, a shot struck Polly, the bell mare, above our heads and we tumbled into the barricade promiscuously. My foot caught in a rope and I went in head first. None of the balls struck in the barricade, but went whizzing over our heads. Shep Madera, Ben Northington and Charlie went on guard and I lay down and slept.

*Peale Diary, August 20, 1875, Howell Papers.*[3]

## James Gardner ✳ August 15

Taking the advice of my most experienced men, we camped in a sagebrush plain, as far as possible from the hills. The position was, however, exposed to fire at three hundred yards from a ravine that would shelter the enemy, and from a ridge five hundred yards distant. I formed a skirmish line of Adams, McCreary, and myself three hundred yards from camp and so placed as to command these positions and protect the rest of the men, who were unpacking and building a circular barricade of the aparejos and baggage. The Indians were thus forced to fight at very long range for we were hidden in the sagebrush and fought to excellent advantage. They took position on a hill from which most of their bullets just fell short of camp.

"*Professor Gardner's Report,*" Chicago Daily Inter-Ocean, *September 8, 1875.*

### Cuthbert Mills ❋ August 15

It was certainly not a pleasant night we spent. The unanimous opinion of those who knew most about Indian methods of fighting was that the band was an advanced guard thrown out to delay us till reinforcements should come up, and that at daylight the worst attack might be looked for—that and dusk being their favorite hours for surprises. They would probably be quiet during the night, preparing for the morning.

Our arms and ammunition were carefully inspected. There were seven breech-loading rifles, more or less good, and four large revolvers, which it was quite obvious, were of no use against those long range loving cowards. The ammunition was neither very abundant nor very good. Meantime, for thirteen persons, about two quarts of muddy water were left in the canteens. This was much worse than the Indians, who, by the way, exhibited no desire to wait for morning before recommencing active operations.

Firing went on till 12 o'clock. The enemy would crawl through the sagebrush and shoot; if one of the pickets caught the flash he let fly at it, and it was safe to reckon that no more shots would come from that spot. Sometimes the pickets got a third shot in return from another quarter and Adams, who had taken rather an exposed position, had it made so warm for him that he had to fall back. Between eleven and twelve [o'clock] one of the mules commenced a violent kicking, threw the whole herd into confusion, and Gannett, Dr. Peale, and some others attempting to straighten them out, brought in half a dozen shots in a trice. One struck the barricade, another flew just over it, a third whistled by Gannett's head and hit the old bell mare he was tying on the hip. She lashed out hard and our fellows came tumbling over the barricade pretty quick. All was quiet for some time after this, then some more shots were fired from a particular point of brush to which Kelsey's attention had been directed. He sent a couple in return from his flanking position and that was the last firing, I believe, done that night.

*"The Hayden Survey: What the Sierra La Sal Indians Did for It,"*
New York Times, *September 9, 1875.*

## Day Two of the Fight

### *James Gardner ✻ August 15–16*

At sunset I formed a new picket line of Adams, Kelsey, and myself two hundred yards from the barricade with orders to keep back the Indians whom we now expected would crawl through the sagebrush and attack us by the light of the just risen full moon. They came as anticipated and for five hours we fought them in their own fashion, creeping through the sagebrush and firing at the flash of their guns. One of our animals was wounded. We were beginning to suffer much from want of water and food. At midnight they drew off, and we were relieved from duty by Madera, McCreary, and Northington.

While the rest slept for two hours, I lay and tried to plan for the next day. We had reached the edge of the great plateau and were in an irregular valley running up into it, the surrounding cliffs a thousand feet high. Southward the valley narrowed gradually to a canyon, up which the trail went to the spring. The Indians would undoubtedly be re-enforced in the night by the remainder of the band, and while a part would take up the best positions for ambush in the canyon, the remainder, mounted on their swift ponies, would fight us from every knoll as the slow moving train pressed on. We had eighteen pack animals. Could they but keep us in this valley a day longer, we would become frantic with thirst and rush to certain death up the canyon. It was a well laid trap.

I saw but one hope and that was to reach the summit of the plateau where we could fight them on more equal terms and move forward hoping to find water. Near our camp the cliff was solid sandstone from top to bottom, but in the distance the slopes were covered with piñon, among which rocky debris was visible. Everywhere the crest was formed of an unbroken vertical wall of rock, the projection of the hard capping bed.

At 2 A.M. I ordered the mules saddled and packed. As day dawned I thought there was a point to the southwest where we could reasonably hope to climb the cliff. Gannett and Adams had been sent out before day to hold the ravine from which an attack was feared with the first light. They kept the Indians from occupying it and we packed undisturbed. I took Gannett, Adams, and Madera with me to skirmish in advance of the train, to the right and left, while Mills, Kelsey, and Northington were to fight in the rear and keep the enemy from occupying the hills over which we had passed before the train was out of shot. In this order we started at dawn and the battle signal came quickly in short, wild yells from an Indian posted on a rocky pinnacle above us.

"Professor Gardner's Report," Chicago Daily Inter-Ocean, September 8, 1875.

### Cuthbert Mills ❊ August 16

At 3 o'clock the first streak of day appeared, and preparations were made to pack and move. Momentarily the attack was expected from a much larger number of Indians than we had first seen, but not a shot was fired during the hour the packing went on. The day was bright when Mr. Gardner, who had been on duty nearly the whole night, rode to the head of the train and led the way up the valley. Where are they? was the question everybody was asking. "Hi! Hi! yah hi-i-i!" seemed to come to us in answer, and from the shelter of a rock abutment to our left, out dashed half a dozen of the Indians, making in a direction as if to cut off our advance, but taking good care to keep at very long range. "Hi! yah i-i," echoed another party of them, riding into view on the right, and from far in the front the yelp was taken up by a couple more. They seemed to be everywhere, all riding round and about at the hottest speed so as to present no mark, a practice they kept up all the time they were in the open.

"The Hayden Survey: What the Sierrra La Sal Indians Did for It," New York Times, September 9, 1875.

### James Gardner ✳ August 16

Down they came from their hiding places on those flying ponies. They immediately occupied the eminences within shot of which they supposed we would pass. We were successful in driving them from every one for the first hour, but soon our hungry and thirsty mules utterly gave out and refused to be spurred from a walk. Several times Madera and I would attempt to reach hills which the Indians were also aiming for. They would gain the summit first and then our retreat across the open was attended with great danger. Here the rearguard came to our assistance and Mills and Kelsey did some splendid shooting at one thousand yards. In spite of all we could do, the bullets kept dropping near the train.

*"Professor Gardner's Report,"* Chicago Daily Inter-Ocean, *September 8, 1875.*

### Cuthbert Mills ✳ August 16

The way was taken up the western transept of the valley where a break in the high wall at the end seemed to afford a place where the train could get to the plateau above. Now commenced a game of long shots, which if we had not been so anxious about getting out of this natural trap, would have been quite amusing. Some of the Indians rode to our rear, a fellow on a powerful gray horse kept to our right, and Kelsey, Ben Northington, and I fell back as a rearguard. The enemy commenced banging away at us and the gray horseman was especially active in wasting his ammunition. This was endured for some time and then Ben, losing patience, exclaimed: "Dash me but I'll try a shot at that fellow, though I am short of ammunition," and dismounting he did so; then shook his head. The shot was a wide one.

In a few minutes he tried another, when I suggested that my ammunition being plentiful, I had better do the wasting. At this time they were paying attention to us from the left. There were three there—two close together, the third a little way behind. I aimed at him and as the gun cracked, our fellows gave a shout of derisive laughter. The bullet struck up the dust just at the horse's heels and the rider gave the animal such a sudden stroke with his whip that it jumped and fell headlong over the sagebrush. When it scrambled up the Indian was still in his seat. He had never lost it. Little duels of this kind went on all the way up the valley, but without hurting anyone. The gray horseman's bullets flew over, in front, behind, short, and about us. Only one came any nearer than six feet, and that made close music in Kelsey's ear. The Indians were too cowardly to come any nearer than six hundred yards, while an old fellow trotted up on a distant high rock, directing their movements with a ragged red flag. Any little ambush the rearguard made to await the approach of the attackers they were warned of and kept far away from.

*"The Hayden Survey: What the Sierra La Sal Indians Did for It,"*
*New York Times, September 9, 1875.*

### *A. C. Peale* ❈ *August 16*

The Indians, seeing that we were making for the gap to the west, got on the mesa and galloped to the bluff. We then turned and went back to the trail and had almost reached it when the Indians came back and headed us, for when we got in the canyon they opened fire on us from the right side. We were quick enough to prevent them getting on the left to which we ran for shelter. Atkinson's mule was wounded here as the balls whizzed about us in a lively manner. In going up the bluffs on the left side, Judge changed his saddle from Jimmy, a white mule, to Polly, but not having time to cinch, jumped into the saddle and rode up the hill.

*Peale Diary, August 20, 1875, Howell Papers.*

### *Cuthbert Mills* ❈ *August 16*

There was nothing serious in this style of fighting, but the Indians, apparently divining our intentions, made directly for the place where it was intended to take the train up out of the valley. We saw them riding up the slope for the rocks above like madmen. A few shots dropped that way hastened their ascent. That way of escape was cut off. "We must go back and fight our way up the trail," said Mr. Gardner.

The trains were turned, the enemy soon saw it and came tearing after, the long shot game with the rear guard recommenced, and about the time the train got near the central part of the valley, they disappeared, much hastened by a close shot from Kelsey's rifle. While the train was delayed here in re-fixing some loosened packs, Mr. Gardner and Adams rode ahead to occupy a ridge we should have to skirt in following the trail. They expected to have a fight to get it, but the enemy was not there, and all being ready, we came on and turned a point of rocks which presented a flat face to the ridge occupied by Mr. Gardner. Between that and the wall of rock was about four hundred yards of open.

Just as the train got well into this space and clearly exposed, the whole of rocks on our right flank seemed charged with exploding rifles. It was nothing but whiz-bang, whiz-bang, whiz-bang; the worst of it was that not so much of the enemy could be seen as even the smoke from their guns. The bullets buzzed around us like a swarm of bees. In fact the Indians seemed so intent on rapid firing that they did not stop to take aim, and strange as it may appear, the only damage done was to Mr. Atkinson's mule which was shot under him. He fell off and McCreary ran to pick him up, thinking he had been hit, but he rose, said he was all right, and led his mule which was only wounded over the ridge to the left.

Of course there was some confusion while we were in this warm corner. The colored cook [Judge Porter] who rode the bell mare of the Gannett train became wildly demoralized, but sturdy old Charpiot, though he had never a weapon in the world, rode his mare steadily over the ridge without a boggle. "I did what I could," he said, afterward. "I rode on and let them shoot at me." The packers tried to hurry the mules over the ridge and Shep Madera stopped to take a shot over his saddle, when two bullets came so close to either side of his head as to fairly make his hair curl. Every mule was finally gotten over the ridge and on the protected side of it the trains were again gathered together. Some of us lay down on the edge and watched for a puff of smoke to shoot at. It is a fact which seems almost incredible that though the Indians kept firing all this time, so close was their concealment that not one could be seen.

*"The Hayden Survey: What the La Sal Indians Did for It,"*
New York Times, *September 9, 1875.*

### *James Gardner* ✳ *August 16*

We thus marched around the whole of the open valley unable to find a place to get up the bluffs. Five hours passed in this fruitless search. The fierce sun was beating down and our thirst became intolerable. I then determined to fight our way up the canyon to water, at all hazards. Better that half of us should fall than all perish. On the east side of the canyon's mouth there were piñon-covered hills, on the west low sandstone walls capped with woods. As the Indians had always headed us off as soon as our intentions were seen, Mr. Adams and I rode far ahead of the train and took up our positions among the pines on the east side of the canyon, thus compelling the Indians to take their position in the west side. It was about four hundred yards across.

The train then moved forward, but in order to cross a deep gully, was obliged to go within three hundred yards of the rocky promontory. Here the Indians poured a terrible fire on the men. Atkinson's mule was shot under him. Charpiot, mounted on the bell-horse, moved steadily forward toward the only cover, the hill which Adams and I were holding, and at last got the train behind it. His perfect steadiness in this emergency was admirable. Madera bombarded the position of the Indians, though none were visible. Only the poorness of the Indian aim saved our men.

*"Professor Gardner's Report,"* Chicago Daily Inter-Ocean, *September 8, 1875.*

### *Robert Adams* ✳ *August 16*

How many Indians opposed us we cannot certainly tell, ten only were counted at any one time. These were principally armed with muzzle-loading rifles, but several had Henry breech-loading guns which enabled them to shoot at very long range. It was their swift ponies that gave them such great advantage over our worn out mules and enabled them to choose commanding positions and occupy them ahead of us. It was in this way they secured the two positions from which they poured such terrible volleys upon us in spite of all the haste we could make. There were but seven armed men on our side to protect six others, utterly defenseless, and a pack train of eighteen animals, which when strung out in single file the way in which we were obliged to march, left none for aggressive fighting.

*"Hayden's Survey: The Late Fight with Indians,"*
Philadelphia Inquirer, *September 23, 1875.*

## *Cuthbert Mills* ✱ *August 16*

It was evident now that every point to which we could make would be occupied, for the fleet horses of the enemy enabled them to ride round us at their pleasure. To go forward was to fight, to go back was to fight, and always with an unseen enemy. The sun was beginning to burn us up again; we had had no water since the noon previous and knew of no place where it was to be found. Some signs of faltering began to show themselves in the party. Mr. Gardner thought it necessary to get some expression of opinion. He called us together, showed the desperate straits we were in, and asked each to give his vote, whether it should be go on or go back. His own desire was to go forward, but he would defer to the majority. As usual, most of the suffragists declined to give a vote either way; two were decidedly in favor of going back, three as decidedly in favor of going forward. "Forward it shall be, then," said the chief and the advance immediately commenced.

*"The Hayden Survey: What the Sierra La Sal Indians Did for It,"*
New York Times, *September 9, 1875.*

## *James Gardner* ✱ *August 16*

Here I held a council of war, to see who has ready to go forward, come what might and found that those who had borne the brunt of the battle from the first were still ready to go on. Mr. Adams, especially, was vehement in his expression of opinion. We, therefore, moved along the foot hills on the east side of the canyon keeping among the trees, thus escaping the enemy's fire from the opposite bluff.

The Indians, judging from our movements that we had determined to go to the spring, took position up the canyon about three-quarters of a mile where the walls shut in so steeply that we must go down into the narrow bottom. On seeing this we turned abruptly up the tree-covered slope on our left, Mr. Gannett piloting the train with great skill while Madera and I pushed ahead to reach the foot of the sandstone wall in the direction where both Mr. Gannett and I thought there was a break. In the rocks we were fortunate enough to find a hole with a little muddy water with which, though very alkaline, we wet our parched mouths.

"Professor Gardner's Report," Chicago Daily Inter-Ocean, September 8, 1875.

### Cuthbert Mills ✳ August 16

The route taken from this point was one which would have saved the train if anything could possibly have done it. Mr. Gardner calculated that after driving us over the ridge the Indians had gone up the valley and occupied the entrance of the narrow canyon through which the trail ran. He therefore led the way along the slope of the bluffs opposite to the side we had been fired on from, kept the train well concealed in the timber, and then making a zigzag turned back and up the face of the wall, making for an indentation up which it was probable a trail might be found. On the way up (the bluff was at least five hundred feet high) a little puddle was found. It was a joyful find and every man drank deeply of the alkaline mud. There was enough for the animals, but word was brought that the Indians had been seen to cross the valley far up and to climb the rocks with the evident intention of getting above us.

The train was hurried on, but five packs came off and had to be repacked, and much time was occupied in making the ascent of 250 of the 500 feet. Let it be understood that the top of the bluff was a perpendicular cliff like a parapet, fifty to sixty feet high. Below it was a slope of huge rocks and earth, overgrown with piñon pine. This was the character of the bounding walls of the valley for ten miles round. The point we were making for was where this parapet had fallen down.

I think we had certainly been half an hour trying to climb up and over that mass of rock and had reached a comparatively level spot running on the same line with the wall, therefore placing the flank of the train toward it, when a volley was shot into us from what seemed a few yards off. Once more those cowardly but active wretches had headed us. They were up just under the parapet, as thoroughly concealed as they had been on the point of rocks. A second volley came a minute after and a pretty little white mule of Gannett's doubled its legs and fell dead without a kick, shot squarely through the heart. Another mule was killed and another wounded at the third fire.

Then it was every man to shelter, but not to fight. Off our mules we came, down behind trees and stones, rifles cocked and ready, waiting for the faintest show of the enemy. But it was not to be. Just as before there was nothing but the crack of their rifles.

*"The Hayden Survey: What the Sierra La Sal Indians Did for It,"*
New York Times, *September 9, 1875.*

## James Gardner ✱ August 16

When Mr. Gannett with the train got within three hundred feet from the top, the Indians succeeded in getting above them and commenced firing from behind rocks and trees at sixty yards range. Three mules were killed, but the men found shelter behind rocks and trees.

*"Professor Gardner's Report,"* Chicago Daily Inter-Ocean, *September 8, 1875.*

## Cuthbert Mills ✱ August 16

Adams was kneeling a short distance from me, watching. Despairingly I asked him if he saw any possible sign we could shoot at. "Not even a puff of smoke," was his reply. Neither could I, yet one of the fellows could evidently see me for first he cut off a twig just over my head to the right and when I shifted a little to the left sent a bullet to that side. Though watching with all possible intensity, the scoundrel had so thoroughly concealed himself that the smoke of his gun, which I was waiting to shoot at, was not visible.

Charpiot lay under a tree nearby. He could only lie there and helplessly wait, though the bullets were whistling through the branches a few feet over him, but he never betrayed a sign of fear, only looked serious. He had fought Indians on the Plains when he was a wealthy man and had his bull teams crossing them all summer, but he had never been in so tight a place as this before. The circumstances most in our favor here was that each Indian was so intent on making his own concealment perfect that he necessarily commanded a very small range. The pause in this situation was certainly the most trying moment of the six hours' fighting we had done that morning. It

This steep talus slope of loose sandstone and boulders, covered with trees and capped with a tall rimrock, made the ascent for Gardner's party difficult, even after finding the hidden deer trail. *Courtesy J. V. Howell Collection, Hayden Party Photo File 3, American Heritage Center, University of Wyoming.*

seemed as if nothing was being done and that nothing could be done. But something was.

Mr. Gardner, Adams, and Shep Madera got forward and round an angle of the bluff where they discovered that there really was a sort of trail running up the indentation in the wall which we had observed from the valley below. Up this they climbed, leading their saddle mules, and reached the top. The first thought was to get a shot at the Indians below, but as if everything was to be against us, they found that the parapet had a second bench which made approach to the edge impossible. On the way down Madera heard one of the Indians shoot and saw the smoke from his gun about fifty yards to the left and right above where we were. He waited till it cleared away and was delighted to see the Indian cautiously raise his head and shoulders over the rock to see the effect of his shot. Shep let him have it on the instant and down went Mr. Indian, either killed or wounded. Down below we heard the old breech-loader speak. Nothing could be seen but we knew someone of our side had at last got a sight of the enemy and the shot was echoed with a cheer. It was the first ray of hope in that trying half hour.

*"The Hayden Survey: What the Sierrra La Sal Indians Did for It,"*
New York Times, *September 9, 1875.*

## *James Gardner* ✳ *August 16*

Adams came up from the party below and joined us behind a large rock. Here we three held a counsel. To their encouragement and gallant enthusiasm, I am forever indebted. Finding that our large rock was looked upon by the Indians as a place to be dreaded, we quietly left it to keep silent guard and slipping along the foot of the vertical sandstone wall, here one hundred feet high. At last I found a deer trail which threaded its way through a break in the wall, brought us at last to the top of the plateau. From here we crawled along till directly over the Indians, but found them so sheltered that we could not see them. We examined the deer trail carefully and found it impossible for pack animals, but the saddle mules might be led up. With this discovery we returned to the main party.

*"Professor Gardner's Report,"* Chicago Daily Inter-Ocean, *September 8, 1875.*

## Cuthbert Mills ❉ August 16

In a few minutes Mr. Gardner and the others joined us and after a short consultation, he determined to abandon the packs as the only possible way of saving the lives of the party. It was clear that no mule carrying a pack could ever get up that trail.

*"The Hayden Survey: What the Sierra La Sal Indians Did for It,"*
New York Times, *September 9, 1875.*

## James Gardner ❉ August 16

All now joined in requesting me to cut the packs and attempt to save their lives and mules. Reluctantly I gave the order to cut off the packs, save four day's flour, bacon and coffee, take notebooks and overcoats and saddles, and prepare to fight our way up the deer trail, and force the passage at any cost.

*"Professor Gardner's Report,"* Chicago Daily Inter-Ocean, *September 8, 1875.*

## A. C. Peale ❉ August 16

Enough grub to last four days was arranged in two light packs with one kettle and frying pan. I put three of my blankets under my saddle and some small things in my saddle bags. The instruments were all abandoned. Total loss between $2500 and $3000. We opened and drank our canned tomatoes, packed our gear—about fifty pounds to the mule, and readied to fight our way to the top. All this was done under fire though partly sheltered by the rocks and trees. Our thirst and hunger were relieved by cutting open some cans of tomatoes, which we drank raw, and by a bottle of French olives, then started up the trail, the rifles ahead. The Indians kept quiet and we gained the top and found ourselves on a plateau in open country. We started across at the gallop and trot. This was about one o'clock.

*Peale Diary, August 20, 1875, Howell Papers.*

## Robert Adams ❉ August 16

How such a delicacy [French olives] came among the supplies we know not, but it was discovered one hot day, when it was proposed to eat them.

Mr. Gardner advised delaying that enjoyment for the desert of New Mexico, toward which we were wending our way. Adams, who was putting up the supplies [in preparation for escaping up the deer trail], came across it, and knocking off the top against a rock, offered it to Mr. Gardner, with the remark, "We had better eat these, for I think we won't find a better place than this." All agreeing, they soon disappeared.

*"Hayden's Survey: The Late Fight with Indians,"*
Philadelphia Inquirer, *September 23, 1875.*

### Cuthbert Mills ✷ August 16

The packers received the order to "cut loose" with feelings which actually brought out tears. Had there been time everything would have been piled up and burned; as it was they went to work with knives and cut everything from the backs of the mules in such a way that scarcely a whole rope, an unbroken package, an un-smashed can or box, or anything cutable or breakable was left. Four days' provisions were packed on the mules, all the scientific notes and memoranda were taken, and all the ammunition, and then we started up the trail, every man's immediate worldly possessions being on his back and in his saddle pockets. Each man led his mule and held his weapon, pistol, or rifle ready. That we should all get safely to the top very few expected. The loose animals were driven on, and of course, being unencumbered, climbed the bluff without difficulty.

*"The Hayden Survey: What the Sierrra La Sal Indians Did for It,"*
New York Times, *September 9, 1875.*

### James Gardner ✷ August 16

I supposed that as soon as we started the Indians would run along the slope above us and occupy every rock that commanded the trail. My physical strength was almost exhausted for want of food and water when Mr. Gannett happily thought of canned tomatoes. These he poured down me for I had sunk on the ground. When all was ready I rallied again and led the way up the trail closely followed by Adams. It was the critical moment when the Indians might have killed half of us, but the cowards had been taught such a lesson by Madera and I getting above them that they dared not charge and we reached the summit in safety, leaving behind us three dead mules and one lost in the woods.

*"Professor Gardner's Report,"* Chicago Daily Inter-Ocean, *September 8, 1875.*

## ESCAPE

### *Robert Adams* ❋ *August 16*

Strange to say the Indians let us ascend in safety to the top, a fact only to be accounted for by the shot of Madera a short time before at an Indian who tumbled over and whom he believed he killed. This was the only shot within range we had during the fight as they were always concealed. On landing, a trot was taken up and continued until seven o'clock, six hours. We headed for the Dolores River, the only water we knew of, and that about thirty miles distant. The Indians, perceiving our intention, hovered about a mile to our left, evidently intending to head us off, not satisfied with our provisions, but hankering after our scalps and rifles as well.

*"Hayden's Survey: The Late Fight with Indians,"*
Philadelphia Inquirer, *September 23, 1875.*

### *Cuthbert Mills* ❋ *August 16*

At 1:30 the last man and last animal reached the top and passing through the narrow fringe of piñon pine emerged on an apparently boundless plateau covered with sagebrush and dotted at intervals with clumps of pine timber. One long breath of relief we drew. Here, at any rate, we could see our enemies if they attempted to follow us. It was strange that during the whole time the cutting of the packs went on and while we climbed the bluff after it, not a single shot was fired by the Indians except one just as we reached the top. That was far in the valley below and evidently a signal shot. The only explanation is that the Indians must have vacated their position when they found that men were above them, and the flank shot probably completed the business, for a greater set of cowards it would be impossible to conceive. It brought tears to the eyes of some of us that such a horde of sneaking coyotes could do as much as they did while we lumbered up with heavy pack trains could do so little. They had worked hard for their plunder, however, and a rich booty fell to them. In their famished eyes it must have seemed like the wealth of worlds.

*"The Hayden Survey: What the Sierra La Sal Indians Did for It,"*
New York Times, *September 9, 1875.*

### James Gardner ✳ August 16

We then pushed our jaded mules to their fastest trot, bearing southwest across the table land for I determined to strike for our supply camp on the Mancos River. The Indians being afraid of ambush went a long way round to get on to the plateau. We thus were far ahead when their pursuit commenced, and being unencumbered with packs, were able to elude them under cover of the woods, which in some places cover the plateau. They cut us off from one place toward which we were making for water, but at sunset we fortunately discovered a small spring and the lives of men and animals were saved.

*"Professor Gardner's Report,"* Chicago Daily Inter-Ocean, *September 8, 1875.*

### Cuthbert Mills ✳ August 16

The point we struck for was the Mancos River, more than a hundred miles distant on an air line, and by the only route open to us, perhaps double that distance. Our main thought was for water on the way there. From 1:30 o'clock when the party got on the plateau, they rode till 7:30 o'clock when a little oozing spring was found and a stop of an hour made for rest. We had seen the Indians following, but they evidently mistook the direction we were going in and struck off to the left for some heavy timber. It is probable that water could be found there so they thought we were making for it and went to wait our approach. After resting an hour, we started again and rode till 10:45 that night. On the way we ran into another Indian encampment. They came after us full tilt, yelling and shouting, but to our intense surprise, they proved to be friendly, being some of Ouray's Utes.

*"The Hayden Survey: What the Sierra La Sal Indians Did for It,"*
New York Times, *September 9, 1875.*

## Robert Adams ✴ August 16

About five o'clock we struck a trail running at right angles to the direction we were pursuing, when Mr. Gardner [divining] the intentions of the Indians and feeling sure it would lead to water, turned abruptly to the right, thus leaving our enemies so far behind that we did not see them again. Two hours' ride brought us to water, such as it was, when we halted an hour to let the animals, browse and eat ourselves.

*"Hayden's Survey: The Late Fight with Indians,"*
Philadelphia Inquirer, *September 23, 1875.*

## A. C. Peale ✴ August 16

A couple of hours after we saw the Indians behind us, striking to the left. They evidently thought we would go to the Dolores for water. We struck a trail heading to the southeast and followed it. At six o'clock we came to a spring and stopped to water the mules and take lunch. The mules would drink up all the water and we had to keep them away until it refilled. We had some tea, bread, and ham. Atkinson was on guard and when I had my lunch I relieved him.

At seven we were on the road again, travelling on the trot all the time. About nine o'clock we heard a dog bark and saw the light of an Indian camp ahead of us. We left the trail and went to the left of it. Soon we heard the Indians yelling behind us then getting on both sides of us, wanting to know who we were, where we were going, and crying "amigo" (friend). We paid no attention until we got on a hill, when we stopped and the Indians (five) came up. They were Utes. After a short talk we resumed our march. At 11 o'clock we stopped and with Mills going on guard, the rest of us rolled ourselves in our blankets to sleep. Atkinson and I doubled up.

*Peale Diary, August 20, 1875, Howell Papers.*

## Robert Adams ✴ August 16

Resuming the march, we rode until eleven that night, when we camped beside an alkaline pool. Up to this time, out of sixty hours,

we had been forty eight in the saddle, under fire twenty-four, and
had less than five hours' sleep.

*"Hayden's Survey: The Late Fight with Indians,"*
Philadelphia Inquirer, *September 23, 1875.*

## A. C. Peale ❋ August 17

Mills woke me at 1 o'clock and I went on guard, waking Judge at 3.
After a breakfast of slap jacks, tea, and canned corn beef, we started
at daylight on the trail. It gradually turned to the south and about
noon we met an Indian on it. He would not come near us so we did
not learn anything about the country or the trails to the Mancos,
where our supplies were, for which we were heading. We then struck
across the country, crossing deep canyons and at dark camped at the
bottom of one where there were several pools of slightly alkaline water.

*Peale Diary, August 20, 1875, Howell Papers.*

## Robert Adams ❋ August 17

We camped in the bottom of a canyon two thousand feet deep, where
we found water, but so alkaline that tea would not destroy its taste;
the boys' health began to be affected by it. The country over which
we were traveling was an unknown desert plateau, cut up by canyons
running in all directions. At first we tried to head these by riding
round them, but after traveling in all directions we were compelled
to abandon this plan, and, taking our direction, we held our course,
crossing one canyon after another. This made the third weary day,
especially as we struck no water until late in the afternoon, when one
of the boys found some rain pools. Here an exciting scene took place.
The loose animals made a rush to the pool and two men, clubbing
them with muskets, could scarcely keep them off until the boys drank.
Upon being permitted to drink, they rushed in biting, kicking, and
fighting each other, endeavoring to obtain what little was left.

*"Hayden's Survey: The Late Fight with Indians,"*
Philadelphia Inquirer, *September 23, 1875.*

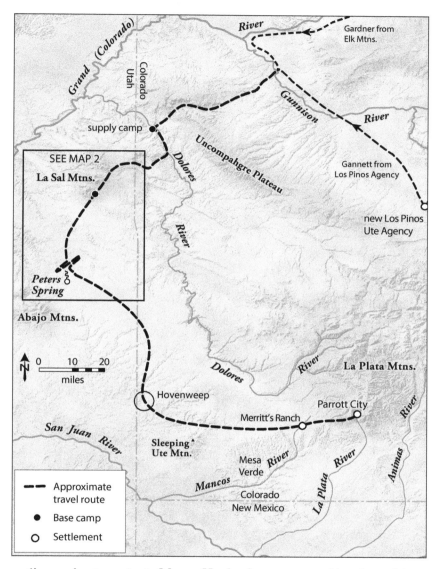

*Above and on pages 182–83,* MAP 3. Hayden Survey route and locations of the skirmish in southeastern Utah. *Maps by Ben Pease, based on maps by Winston Hurst. Copyright © 2016, University of Oklahoma Press.*

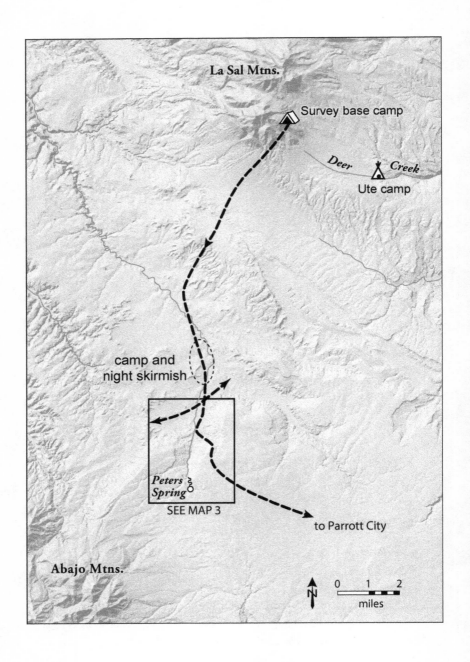

La Sal Mtns.

Survey base camp

*Deer* ⚑ *Creek*
Ute camp

camp and
night skirmish

Peters
Spring

SEE MAP 3

to Parrott City

Abajo Mtns.

N

0    1    2
miles

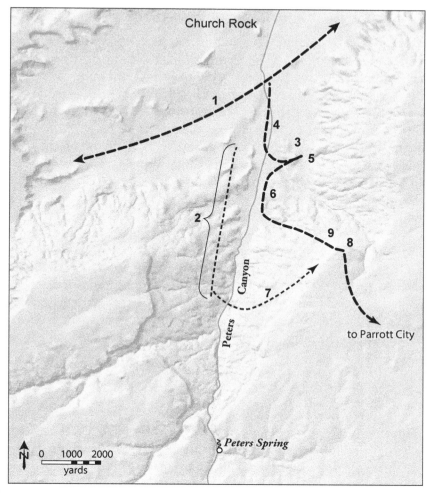

Church Rock

Canyon

Peters

Peters Spring

to Parrott City

0   1000   2000
yards

N

1. Five-hour skirmish in failed search for alternate route onto mesa
2. Ute ambush position on high ground west side of wash
3. Gardner and Adams ahead of main pack train find cover on wooded hill
4. Main pack train forced to within three hundred yards of Ute rifles to get across arroyo
5. Main pack train finds cover behind Gardner's hill
6. Party makes run for spring, using trees for cover, abandons run for spring; avoids ambush by heading upslope toward break in caprock
7. Utes reposition via bench to intercept surveyors, firing from caprock talus
8. Gardner, Adams, and Madera find trail, kill or wound one Ute in talus
9. Surveyors dump gear, escape up trail onto mesa

### A. C. Peale ✳ August 17

We had a jar of Libby's beef and made soup after which we made coffee and baked bread in the frying pan. The boys made coffee in the can which had the corned beef. After roasting it they had to grind it by smashing the beans with stones. Guard duty was given up and the boys all turned in for the first real rest since the fight. The only stop during the day was an hour at noon to rest the mules.

On Wednesday, August 8, we were up by daylight and on the road across the country. About two o'clock we camped on the Hovenweep in the canyon. On the bluffs above us were a lot of ruins which we examined in the afternoon. We started at daylight and struck a trail which led us toward the peak and to the McElmo from which we came out into a dry valley north of the Mesa Verde, where we struck a wagon trail leading in the direction we wanted to go. We overtook an Indian and his squaw but could get no information from them. At one o'clock we stopped to rest the mules. I lunched on dried apples. When we started we had a shower for which we were extremely grateful as we had no water from morning until we struck the Mancos about four in the afternoon.

*Peale Diary, August 20, 1875, Howell Papers.*

### Robert Adams ✳ August 18

At noon on the fourth day we struck Macomb's wagon tracks, which we knew led to the Mancos River, our destination. The boys gave a shout at this sign of an inhabited region, heartily joined in by those whose courage had not been up to the average point. Their joy was somewhat lessened by the lugubrious remark of Judge Porter, the colored cook—"I've seen dead men on fresher tracks than them 'ere." At five o'clock we reached the Mancos River, the first running water we had met in five days. Never did brighter sight greet the eye of man than that green valley with its mountain stream was to us. Early next day we reached Parrott City, where our supplies were, and had the good luck to find Mr. Holmes' party there, who had also come in to replenish their exhausted larder.

*"Hayden's Survey: The Late Fight with Indians,"*
Philadelphia Inquirer, *September 23, 1875.*

⁂   ⁂   ⁂

Late in the day on Thursday, August 18, the combined Gardner and Gannett parties, along with the surviving weary mules, arrived at the Merritt Ranch, just west of the Hayden supply depot. Cuthbert Mills summarized the past ordeal by writing, "During those days we had quenched a constantly burning thirst in little stagnant pools of alkaline mud and ate little beyond dough-cakes cooked in a frying-pan. The distance traveled in the retreat was 175 miles over a desert plateau dissected by innumerable broad canyons, most of them nearly one thousand feet deep. All these had to be headed or crossed."[4] A sense of exuberance, as well as the somber recognition of their narrow escape, blended into the returning party's mood.

## A. C. Peale ⁑ August 18

The first cabin was greeted with shouts although it had no occupants. We reached Merritt's ranch before dark and camped. There was no one at the ranch, but soon after camping, the owner and two other men came from the mining camp where they said Mr. Aldrich and our supplies were. They also told us that Holmes's party was five miles ahead of us on their way in for supplies. We got turnips and green peas from the garden at the ranch and had pea soup for supper.

*Peale Diary, August 20, 1875, Howell Papers.*

## James Gardner ⁑ August 19

In four days from the time we scaled the bluff I brought the party in here safe and well, having ridden two hundred miles from the scene of the battle. Out of sixty hours from the morning of the 15th we were in the saddle forty-eight. The fight was incessant from 5 o'clock P.M., on the 15th, till the afternoon of the 16th, except three hours in the night. Out of thirty-two animals we brought off twenty-eight. Three of these are wounded but not badly. Not a man was wounded and none are sick. The work is not much interfered with for the western part of the topography in the dangerous country was about completed.

*"The Hayden Survey: Gardner and Gannett Unite Their Parties and Are Attacked by Renegade Indians," Chicago Daily Inter-Ocean, September 8, 1875.*

## Cuthbert Mills ✳ August 19

The loss sustained by the party in the fight was three mules killed and one lost, three others and a horse wounded, all the instruments, baggage, and personal property of the party abandoned. What we saved were the scientific records of the work done on the trip, all the mules except four, and our lives.

*"The Hayden Survey: What the Sierra La Sal Indians Did for It,"*
New York Times, *September 9, 1875.*

## Charles Aldrich ✳ Parrott City, Colorado, August 23

This inchoate municipality had been exceedingly dull for many days; a score or more of the miners had gone quietly away to other parts; the Indians only came in pairs and about once a week at that; Captain John Moss, the great cogwheel furnishing all the motive power for the entire valley, was still absent in California and had not been heard from; Father Boren, the veteran prospector, was not finding, on an average, more than four or five silver-bearing lodes per week; and look whichever way you would, everything was quiet—almost lonesome. . . .

On Friday last, after breakfast, I went leisurely down the creek and brought up my little horse with a view to climbing the mountain north of "town" and hunting grouse up near the timber line, but on starting back to my quarters I saw half a dozen men on mules coming trotting from the west. Of course I was on the *qui vive* to greet any of "our folks" of the Hayden survey and at once recognized Holmes and Chittenden, whom, by the way, I was now looking for for a week. Presently one of the party rode down to greet me, and him I recognized as Mr. Gannett whose work lay far to the north and whom I did not expect to see before we all returned to Denver or Washington. Evidently there had been some change in the program and something serious had occurred to bring him here so far from his proper field of labor.

*"The Hayden Survey: Gardner and Gannett Unite Their Parties and Are Attacked by Renegade Indians,"* Chicago Daily Inter-Ocean, *September 8, 1875.*

# CHAPTER 7

# Getting Everyone In

## Parrott City and Southeastern Utah

### AUGUST 21–SEPTEMBER 5

UPON THEIR SAFE ARRIVAL AT PARROTT CITY, THE TIRED and hungry men of the Gardner and Gannett Divisions spilled out the harrowing story of their encounter with the Indians to Charles Aldrich and their colleagues in the Holmes Division, who had arrived at the supply camp the day before. They had traveled more than two hundred miles by mule in just over four days. The newspaper reporters accompanying the Hayden Survey knew that the events of the past few days were exactly the stuff eastern readers wanted to hear about the far West and rushed to post their stories. The first published reports hit the eastern newspapers on September 5.

Rest and recuperation did not last long. Several important and urgent tasks confronted James Gardner upon his return to Parrott City. No one had heard from William Henry Jackson since he had parted from the Holmes Division in early August. Was he safe? And then there were the two men that Gannett had left behind at a supply camp on the Dolores River. What had happened to them? Gardner immediately sent out two groups to find the answers. He needed to know that all members of the Hayden Survey were safe.

### STORYTELLING AT PARROTT CITY

The stories the men told around the campfire in the days after their return reflected a normal need to quell raw nerves by transforming events into tales of death-defying adventure, humorous yarns, and sentimental songs. And the newspaper reports, in part, echoed this. The crew members praised Gardner for his leadership, and he, in turn, complimented them on their fidelity and bravery. For their opponents, the Hayden men expressed nothing but contempt. The campfire stories and newspaper reports exposed the racial assumptions that the Hayden men took with them into the field as well as a profound ignorance of the specific Native cultures in whose homelands the Survey was working and of the larger political context for the Survey's scientific endeavors. The Utes understood that context full well—their lands and lives were under threat by the very expansion of the Anglo enterprise that Hayden intended his science to serve.

*Charles Aldrich* ❋

The next night after the "boys" arrived here they had a happy reunion. Their season of toil and danger was over and they enjoyed themselves to the top of their bent. Ten of the scientists got themselves, somehow, under the shelter of one little dog-tent. This little "dog tent," by the way, was elevated a couple of feet on a log foundation and was almost as roomy as an omnibus. In fact, there was still "room for one more" as long as our fellows kept dropping in. One individual, I know, regretted that a cramped seat and the current supply of smoking tobacco were about all he could offer in the way of hospitality. But this is a far-away region where luxuries are neither indigenous nor to be had for pay. The will was doubtless taken for the deed.

A couple of pleasant hours were passed in recounting the history of the fight with the Indians and smoking Mexican cigarettes. The evening closed with singing several humorous and sentimental songs. I have never heard better singing anywhere and I think they sang those good old songs with all the more spirit in consequence of the dangers through which they have passed. The singer par excellence was Frank Pearson of Philadelphia, one of the skilled and efficient topographers, but always a genial and pleasant fellow off duty. While he was rendering some choice piece in his own inimitable way, the burden of which was the old home, its surroundings, and "the old folks," I saw a tear on more than one cheek that was bronzed by this long summer's exposure.

"The Hayden Survey: Completion of the Season's Work in the Mountains of Southwestern Colorado," Chicago Daily Inter-Ocean, September 25, 1875.

## Robert Adams ⁂

Crossing through camp last night, I heard one of the boys singing:
'Twas here I dropped a parting tear,
To cross the sage plain bare;
And, oh! It fills my heart with joy,
That I did not lose my hair.

"Chain and Level: The Hayden Geological Survey,"
Philadelphia Press, September 9, 1875.[1]

## Charles Aldrich ⁂

With the Gannett party came out as a cook a big, burly, but sharp, shrewd, quick-witted colored man, who calls himself "Judge" Porter. He cooked for Clarence King years ago when he was geologizing in the Sierra Nevada Mountains and has spent much time in the Far West. His "perfeshun" is presiding over the cuisine of the camp and this he does right well. He makes no pretension as a warrior, and freely says: "I don't want no mo' Injun in mine." Some of us were talking of the trip through the canyon of the Rio Mancos to look up the ruins, but the "Judge" said[,] "it wouldn't do for him to go, case you kno' dar's $1,100 worth o' mules heah, and day might stray off, you know!" He says also: "Dis young man is just as fah west as he cahs to go!"

He had ridden a white mule up to the time of the fight, but on one occasion when the bullets fell thickest, he saw that his animal was drawing all the fire of the Indians, so in the midst of the melee dismounted and "swapped" for one of the usual brown or bay color. The "Judge" said: "It pear'd somehow that day was all fi'ing at me!" This incident was the source of much merriment and many jokes after the parties were all one hundred miles away from the scene of action, but the result proved that in changing his base in the heat of action the "Judge" "knew his gait," as these rough fellows sometimes remark, for "Jim," the white mule, was soon after shot through the heart. The poor animal deserved a better fate. He had been with the survey two or three years, faithfully carrying his burdens up and down the mountains. Instead of being shot down by these cowardly redskins, he deserved to be pensioned and taken to some region of perpetual summer, where he might spend a long and quiet old age "in clover up to his eyes."

*"The Hayden Survey: Completion of the Season's Work in the Mountains of Southwestern Colorado,"* Chicago Daily Inter-Ocean, *September 25, 1875.*

❊    ❊    ❊

Not all the reminiscences were humorous. A sense of how close they had come to losing their lives lay just below the sweet songs. The crew members sought to understand why they had survived.

## *Charles Aldrich* ❊

The fact that three animals were killed and three wounded show how hotly they were fired upon. That the men escaped with their lives seems almost miraculous, but this was due to several causes. First, our men were armed with long-range needle guns of which the Indians have a wholesome fear and so kept themselves most of the time too far away to permit of any execution from [their] muzzle-loading rifles.[2] Aside from this they seemed too much excited to aim with any sort of steadiness or precision. Second was the courage, coolness, and steadiness with which Professor Gardner had led his men, combined with his general topographical knowledge of the route necessary to be traveled. Third was the bravery and skill of Gannett, Madera, Mills, Holmes, and Kelsey, who fought with all the pluck and boldness of veterans, and made things lively for the Indians whenever they came within sight and range.

*"The Hayden Survey: Gardner and Gannett Unite Their Parties and Are Attacked by Renegade Indians,"* Chicago Daily Inter-Ocean, *September 8, 1875.*

W. H. Holmes penned the following caption to this picture: "My own party with parts of the Gardner party which had just reached my camp [Parrott City] after having been attacked by the Paiutes and had lost everything but their riding animals. They arrived a sad and hungry lot, 1875." *Left to right*, Frank Pearson, E. A. Barber, G. B. Chittenden, A. C. Peale, William H. Holmes, Henry Gannett, Charles Aldrich, W. R. Atkinson, T. S. Brandegee, and Harry Lee. Pearson, Peale, Gannett, and Atkinson were involved in the fight. *Courtesy J. V. Howell Collection, Hayden Party Photo File 3, American Heritage Center, University of Wyoming.*

## *Charles Aldrich* ❈

When I wrote my letter about the battle of the two Hayden parties with the Indians I was too much hurried to do my work as I desired. But since our messenger left with our letters and telegrams I have had more leisure to talk with some of the parties who were in the fight. All bear testimony to the great coolness and good judgment with which Professor Gardner led them through that merge of difficulty and danger. He not only anticipated emergencies as if by intuition— calculating in advance just what the insolent devils would resort to next—but took upon himself more of real exposure, labor, and hardship than fell to the lot of any other man. He never sent a man out to any post of danger where he would not go himself and where the danger was most imminent and the utmost vigilance required, to that position he invariably repaired. He might have "commanded" others to do this work and had the duty well-performed, but he bore his full share of privation, danger, and more. . . . If his record of scientific work performed is abridged temporarily, he has shown the highest qualities as a man of true courage and generous sympathies. . . .

Before this letter sees the light of the outside world the affair of the Indian attack on the Hayden surveyors will have been commented upon fully and the judgment of most people made up. What the circumlocution office will do in the premises I will not attempt even to surmise; but it seems to me that the surrounding tribes should be in a measure held responsible for those outrages. A demand should be made upon them for the desperados, with the distinct understanding that no annuities will be paid until they are delivered up to the civil authorities to stand their trial precisely like a white brigand. The value of the property destroyed or captured should be deducted from the annuities of the tribes to which the criminals belong.

When tried and found guilty let them be sent to a penitentiary, just as you would send a white man for a like offense, and if they cannot be learned some useful trade they can at least saw stone. A few applications of this sort of discipline, firmly and unflinchingly administered, would lessen the offenses of this kind. Here was a scientific party, laborers and all numbering but thirteen men, of who but six were armed, who while peacefully traveling through the country were villainously attacked and fought for two days by a set of Indians who presented certificates of good character from an Indian agent and whose actions must be well known to their respective tribes, for they cannot conceal the property which they carried into their camps. An example should be made of such "good Indians" that their fellow scalpers will never forget.

*"The Hayden Survey: Completion of the Season's Work in the Mountains of Southwestern Colorado,"* Chicago Daily Inter-Ocean, *September 25, 1875.*

## A Rescue Mission

Gardner had little time for compliments. He wrote quickly to Hayden, explaining what had happened, then turned to those men still in the field. Gardner sent two men to find Jackson, while concentrating his personal efforts on Dallas and Holman, whom Gannett had left behind at the supply depot on the Dolores River. What had happened to them? Gardner decided to lead a rescue party—imagining the worst, hoping for the best—to bring these packers to safety. With him went six of the stalwarts who had made the escape from the La Sals. On August 22, the group started toward the same general area they had fled days before.

### *James Gardner* ❋

The party was very much worn, but I could not rest. Messrs. Holman and Dallas were still at Mr. Gannett's supply camp in the country roamed by the Sierra La Sal bands. I knew their lives would depend upon reaching them quickly. A day's delay might be fatal. I let it be known that volunteers were wanted to go with me and bring them out. The following offered their services: Robert Adams, Jr., Shepard Madera, Cuthbert Mills, Chas. McCreary, Clarence Kelsey, Jacque Charpiot, W. R. Atkinson, and Chas. Aldrich. I chose the first six. They had proved very energetic and courageous fighters on the 15th and 16th, and I felt that we seven, unencumbered with pack train and defenseless men, were a match for the Indians.

*"The Sierra La Sal Utes,"* Rocky Mountain News, *September 17, 1875.*[3]

### *Cuthbert Mills* ❋ *Between the Gunnison and Dolores, Wednesday, September 1*

After the little affair between the Hayden surveying parties and the Sierra La Sal Indians on the 15th and the 16th ult., the first thought of the former was for the safety of the two boys left in the supply camp on the Dolores. From the scene of the disturbance the camp was about thirty-five or forty miles, and therefore not more than a day's ride to the well-mounted nomads who infest this region. What was worse, it was established beside one of the main trails to the southern country where all these Indians go to trade with the Navajos. It was remembered that the Indian camp we had looked down on from the Sierra had been increased by five [*sic*, six] additional tepees the day before the party left the mountain slopes. If that band had come along the Dolores trail, then, without doubt, the survey was short two members. Supposing they had not, and that the boys were still safe, it was important that they be brought out with the least possible delay.

Kelsey and McCreary offered to go in alone and do it, but Mr. Gardner declined to allow this. He wanted six men. Eight volunteered, and the party as selected consisted of the original Gardner division of the survey with the substitution of McCreary for a former member of it who broke down in the fight. Such arms and ammunition as the mining camp of Parrott's town could supply were obtained and each man was armed with a breech-loading rifle, except our hunter-cook Charpiot, who despised anything but a double-barreled shotgun. With some difficulty he obtained one and when it was too late discovered that it was no good at all. Necessarily, we had nothing to ride except mules from our already tired-out herd, but the best of them were selected and they carried us through well.

"*The Hayden Survey: A Rescue Expedition*," New York Times, *September 25, 1875.*

## James Gardner ✳

I ordered the four best mules to be chosen and reshod, pack-saddles to be gotten from the miners, and packs of about twenty pounds to be prepared of the provisions most quickly cooked. We were utterly destitute of blankets, cooking utensils, etc., having slept in our saddle blankets since the battle. Messrs. Holmes and Chittenden's party and Mr. Aldrich generously shared with us to fit out our rescue party. We could carry but little and were soon prepared. I estimated the distance to the supply camp at about 280 miles and proposed to march it in seven or eight days. We took one extra mule in case of accident. At noon on the 22nd the party marched to the Mancos.

Leaving the Mancos valley on the morning of August 23rd, we traveled northward, intending to keep this course to the east fork of the Dolores, where I expected to find an Indian trail leading in the direction we wished to go. After crossing several canyons five hundred to six hundred feet deep, we descended into one two thousand feet. A faint trail was found and from here onward we traveled by Indian trails though often very dim.

During the first three days we accomplished but a hundred miles, as our way lay across the great San Juan mountain, through passes nine thousand and ten thousand feet high, and among peaks over fourteen thousand feet. The scenery at the head of the San Miguel is in many respects the finest in Colorado. The mountain crests are apparently vertical walls at whose angles stand needle-like peaks. All around the profound valleys rise pinnacled ridges to the height of thirteen thousand and fourteen thousand feet. At their foot, instead of gray debris, there are slopes of rich green aspen forest mottled with groups of dark spruce while in the valleys are verdant levels or picturesque canyons with sounding waterfalls or shining lakes. The great meadow-like valley at the head of the north fork of the San Miguel is about five miles long by one-half broad. Its elevation is about eight thousand feet while the mountain wall that encircles it on the north, east, and south, is not less than thirteen thousand feet and only distant two to four miles. As we saw these mighty cliffs and peaks, frosted with new snow and wreathed with fleecy clouds contrasted with the brilliant green below, while at the head of the valley a great cascade not less than fifteen hundred feet high came leaping from rock to rock—it seemed as if no mountain view could be more perfect.

We passed the ridge that bounds it on the north, and descended into the waters of Uncompahgre River, as it should be called, the word meaning red spring. The river takes its name from a hot spring above the park. We now traveled forty miles a day down the Uncompahgre and the Gunnison and then across the plateau to the west, till on Sunday afternoon, August 29th, when we were within twenty-one miles of the supply camp.

Suddenly, in turning a point in the canyon down whose grassy bottom we were traveling, I saw a horse feeding in the meadows about a mile ahead. Conjecturing that an Indian camp was hidden by the bushes of a stream near the animal, I ordered the pack train tied up to trees and down we went on the full run with rifles ready, intending, if Indians were there, to surround them in camp, cut them off from their ponies, and kill them among their lodges. Each man strove to be foremost in the charge, but much to our disappointment no camp was there. It is needless for me to say that the peace policy is not now popular with us. Circling around the horse, we found it to be Mr. Holman's, the broken rope showing that he had escaped from his master.

Camp was then made and we retired with the sun, for breakfast was to be at three in the morning. We were twenty miles from the supply camp and my plan was to leave camp in the dark so as to escape the observation of any Indians watching from the cliff, and by rapid riding, prevent any successful ambush being laid. Packs and pack-mules remained at camp. Each man carried one hundred rounds of ammunition and two days' bread and ham. We passed down the dangerous canyon as swiftly as the rocky trail would permit, and at last reached a spur at its mouth, five miles from the Dolores River, no fresh Indian signs being seen. This spur was the key to the whole canyon—two men could hold it against twenty. So I ordered Kelsey, who was mounted on Holman's fresh, swift horse, and Mills, who was on a good mule, to keep a little in our rear in case of a fight, and when the Indians tried to flank us they were to fall back and hold this hill so that our retreat would not be cut off. From here we went on as fast as our mules could go over the smooth valley, hoping to surprise any Indians that might be at the river.

The supply camp was on the western side in a grove. We soon reached the high eastern bank, and as no fresh Indian signs were seen, I gave a loud shout for Holman and Dallas. It was a moment of intense anxiety as we stood listening for the answer, which we knew would come if they were alive. No response came and again I shouted. The echoes came back from the great red cliffs that overlook the river, but no answer. As the third attempt seemed to prove the absence of all life, a deep gloom settled over us. We did not know what dreadful spectacle was awaiting us under the deep shade of those cottonwoods. Doubt was torture; we dashed at a gallop across the ford, on toward the grove, and through it, then catching sight of boot tracks on the sand, we turned abruptly toward the left around some thick-growing trees and bushes. The men we had ridden so hard to save stood before us, alive and well, with all their natural hair.

They had thought us Indians and preferred seclusion. It was a happy moment for all. The Sierra La Sal Indians had not passed that way, but only a week before a band of White River Utes with a certificate of good character, etc., from their agent, had stopped there and threatened to kill them, and at last set fire to the high grass around the tents, hoping to burn them and the supplies. With great difficulty Messrs. Holman and Dallas extinguished the flames. Mr. Holman was stationed at the White River Agency in the summer of 1874 and knew a number of these Indians by name. He insisted that he knew them and called them by name. What they would have done had they not feared he might leave some note or record of their visit by which, if they murdered him, they could be identified, it is impossible to say. Their whole conduct showed that they wanted to hurt them but did not dare. Our whole experience shows that these people have no friendship for the whites; fear of the consequences is the only thing that keeps them from carrying out their savage propensities to rob and murder the Americans. When they are far away from the agencies under circumstances where their evil deeds can be hidden or the responsibilities shifted on to some other tribe, they are not to be trusted.

We had brought down with us two extra mules and they had one at the supply camp. Two of these had to be used for saddle animals for Messrs. Holman and Dallas. On the other we packed such provisions as we could and destroyed the remainder, so that nothing might be left for the Indians. Then bidding adieu to the Rio Dolores, which had nearly proved a river of grief to us, we retraced our steps to camp, reaching it about sunset. This was Monday, August 30. In eight days we had ridden 310 miles over these mountain trails; since the morning of the 15th we had ridden 540 miles. Few can realize the anxieties of this march when each of us felt that our comrades' lives depended upon the judgment with which the trail was chosen and speed in following it. Now they were safe and the great load was lifted. Next day we rested, as only such tired men can rest, in a green meadow by the side of a shaded mountain brook which noble granite cliffs two thousand feet high, ever varying in color and form, rose solemnly around.

"*The Sierra La Sal Utes*," Rocky Mountain News, *September 17, 1875.*

*Cuthbert Mills* ✳

Indians had come in [to Parrott City] at noon and reported "heap white man coming—surveyors—one sick." The Indian indicated a bandage around the head, and pointed to the sun—meaning that the sick one was suffering from sunstroke. They knew the survey outfit as it was the only one in the country mounted on mules; but the fact that they saw one of the party had his head bandaged (it was hurt by a fall from the saddle) showed that they must have been very near us. We did not see them, though it may well be believed the party did not travel without keeping a sharp lookout. They probably saw the train from some distant point and crawled on foot to some ravine near the trail for closer inspection. It seemed from this that our movements were likely to be watched and the more so that a short time after reaching the camp an Indian appeared on the bench above evidently taking notes of the party.

The workmen opened their eyes a little when they heard of our difficulty, but it was deemed advisable not to tell more of the present mission than that the [Holman rescue] party was on the way to Los Pinos, expecting to meet our supply train on the way. This was the truth, but not quite all of it. Next morning (Friday) the same Indian who had been observed on the watch came in at breakfast accompanied by another. As we moved off, he interrupted something McCreary was saying with the abrupt inquiry: "Where you go?" The answer was one not calculated either to mollify or inform and the party was riding down the valley before any other questions could be put. It was a hard forty-five mile ride that day, and the next threatened a harder one, for there was a thirty mile drive to be made up the Gunnison Valley over an absolutely dry alkali plain. By starting at daybreak the worst of this ride was made before the heat grew too much for comfort and Saturday afternoon camp was made on the west side of the Gunnison, where a grove of cottonwoods offered good shade and lodging ground. As the party was now approaching what was regarded as doubtful ground, the guns were carefully cleaned, and some practice made at long ranges, judged to be "good Indian distance."

Almost from the bank of the Gunnison at this point, that great cross canyon in which the Gannett and Gardner parties met on the 5th of August cuts through for forty-five miles to the Dolores. It is simply a deep furrow in the plateau between those rivers, and the most direct route of travel from one to the other. Many trails cross it north and south, particularly toward its western end, and there we looked for trouble if any trouble was to be had. Fifteen miles down the canyon where it widens into a beautiful valley was the little creek on which the two parties had camped together.

To reach this place was an easy Sunday morning's ride, and just as Mr. Gardner was turning the point which gave a view of the spot, he suddenly pulled up his mule, signed to the others to keep back, and looked through his field-glasses. "There is an Indian horse feeding down there," he remarked, handing the glasses to Shep Madera, who inspected the animal also. Someone suggested that it might be Holman's horse, and on re-examination, this was found to be correct. Holman was the quartermaster at the supply camp, twenty miles below. How was it his horse was here? If any Indians were about, they were in camp on the other side of the line of trees along the creek, "and if they are," added the leader of the party, "we may as well go at them at once. Tie the pack mules in this brush—quick, boys, they may see us. Charpiot, you stay here. Now, boys, ready! Come on!" and out of the brush dashed the six, across the open, down to and past the astonished horse, into and through the creek and its fringe of brush and trees, and then pulled up on the other side. There was never an Indian, nor a sign of one! Our brave charge had been made on a solitary horse. Everybody laughed but Charpiot, who was enraged because he had been left out in the cold. To console him, Mr. Gardner consented to his accompanying the rest of the party down to the camp next day, which was a variation from the original program.

At three next morning the party was eating breakfast and as soon as there was light enough to see the trail, the pack mules were made secure; each man put eighty rounds of ammunition in his belt and saddle pockets and away they went on a sharp trot down the valley. It may be said that while all were prepared for one, none really expected a fight, because no fresh Indian sign had been seen anywhere along the trail. As each cross trail was passed it was examined, but none of them showed any but old tracks. The assurance that the boys were safe had become almost complete, when, about two miles this side of their camp, the pony tracks of a numerous Indian party were observable in the sandy soil. They were only a few days' old, came in on a big trail from the north, and went toward the river. Full of anxiety, all pressed on at full speed till the river was reached, where the great canyon ended as it began, in a vast amphitheater, across which the Dolores flows from south to north.

Along so much of it as was visible, there was the usual fringe of cottonwoods, but no tents could be seen under any of them. Our shouts produced no response. The river was crossed and the Indian tracks followed up on the other side toward a small grove. "Oh! Boys, the deed's done!" cried McCreary in a tone of mingled rage and despair. "They've scalped the boys and there's where they burned the stuff they couldn't carry away," pointing to a large patch where the grass had been burned off. "No!" shouted Kelsey. "Here's fresh boot tracks!" In another moment the whole party rushed through the brush into the opening shadowed by the cottonwoods and gave a hearty cheer at the sight of the two tents and Mr. Holman and his young assistant standing in front of them, the latter looking rather scared and the former with a rifle in his hand, a big revolver and bowie-knife buckled on his belt.

When the greetings and explanation of this sudden visit had been briefly made, the quartermaster explained that he had not answered the shouts, having mistaken them for those of Indians. This impression had been confirmed when he saw a party of horsemen come flying along, whooping and yelling, in a cloud of dust, in which nothing was distinguishable but the flashing of their gun-barrels in the sun. Had he seen any Indians? Yes, a party of Utes, twenty or more, had come in a few days before from the White River Agency, they being on their way south to the Navajo country to trade. Mr. Holman, having spent some months at that agency, knew many of his visitors personally and addressed them by name when they came in. He was inclined to think that this fact saved him some unpleasantness for the Indians were extremely angry at finding white men apparently established in this remote section, and exhibited much insolence of demeanor. They threatened that if he did not leave by to-morrow's sun they would "heap kill"; demanded food, which he refused; tobacco, which was also refused; and finally a drink of water, which was given them. They seemed to waver between a desire to do something and fears of its discovery if they did. As a specimen of shallow cunning and what they would do if they dared, I may mention that one of the Indians asked Mr. Holman to write him a note, which ran to this effect: "White man come in here—pretty soon pony get heap hungry—white man get head hungry—pretty soon die. Tell Washington all right. Ute no kill him."

It was not till he had seen the Indian quietly slip this paper under the cover of the camp table that the thought flashed across him what it was intended for, and snatching it out, he ordered the fellow out of the tent and tore the paper to pieces. The whole band went off next morning, after hinting at the probable visit of certain Utes who would "heap scalp," and attempting to burn out the camp by firing the brush and grass about it. As a matter of course, the Indians had passes from their agency, stating that they were peaceable and well-disposed, that they were on their way to the Navajo country to trade, "and though off their reservation," added the agent, "I hope they will not be molested."

No other Indians but these had passed the camp. All things considered, this was fortunate, and also that our visit was not made at the same time as that of the gentlemen from White River. It was certainly not Mr. Gardner's desire to get into trouble with Indians known to be Utes for whose conduct the tribe is responsible to the authorities, but the orders given to his following that day practically amounted to "shoot at anything wearing a red blanket," and they would have been obeyed to the letter.

All harsh feelings, however, were forgotten in the pleasure of finding the boys safe. Everyone fell to work with lighter heart than any had known for many days. One loose mule had been brought down and this was packed with such things as were deemed desirable to preserve. Everything else, except what each man could carry away on his back or in his saddle-pockets, was destroyed so that it should not fall into the hands of the Indians. This task seemed peculiarly congenial to Charley McCreary, who declared it was the best thing he had struck since Sherman's raid. First he carefully "went through" the camp with an eye for what might be personally useful and then raged around with a big axe, smashing and ripping things generally and cursing the Indians with every stroke. In two hours nothing was left of the supply camp but what was blazing on a huge fire built where it had stood.

"Mount, boys," said the leader of the party and every man was in the saddle. "Now give them a salute," and all the echoes slumbering in the canyons for a mile around were roused in sudden thunder with the simultaneous discharge of the rifles. While trotting back to camp someone suggested it, and after a festive dinner, at which four apple-pies figured, some brief resolutions of thanks to our commander were scribbled on a soiled fragment of note paper and presented to him by Adams in a neat little speech. This practically ended the rescue expedition. It had been a rough one but full of excitement. Two nights we had been nearly washed out of our blankets by heavy rains, one night had been almost frozen, two days had been long drives across a dry country under a scorching sun, and every day had been in the saddle almost from sunrise to sunset.

*"The Hayden Survey: A Rescue Expedition,"* New York Times, *September 25, 1875.*

## Jackson's Return

Holman and Dallas were safe, but what of Jackson? Gardner knew well that Jackson and his division had been scheduled to pass through the exact area where the fight had taken place. He had serious concerns for their safety, knowing that one of the Utes was either killed or wounded, the feelings of animosity held toward surveyors in general, the escalating series of events that had led to the fight, and Jackson's ignorance of what had transpired. With no contact from the Photo-graphic Division for weeks, Hayden sent two experienced frontiers-men, working as miners in Parrott City, to find the endangered group. On August 21, the two departed with a note from Gardner warning of problems, only to return on September 5 without having delivered it. They had found Jackson's party's tracks and followed them for nearly two weeks, traveling from the San Juan River past Blue Mountain but lost them, then ran short of supplies.

*James T. Gardner* ✳ *Parrott City, August 21*

My Dear Jackson: The combined parties of Mr. Gannett and myself numbering 13 men with seven rifles were attacked by the Indians in a canyon fifteen miles north east of the Sierra Abajo known here, I believe, as the Blue Mts. We were besieged in a waterless place. We fought two days and a night without water under constant fire and at last escaped by the bluff by cutting off the packs. None of the men were hurt, 4 animals were wounded and two killed. We rode 200 miles in four days to reach this point, where we met Holmes just coming in. His mules were stolen by the Indians two nights after you left him but were retaken a few moments after their capture. In view of this state of things I think it wise for you to return home as soon as practicable and run no more risks. Mr. Holmes has completed his western work and goes north for 20 days. Two of Gannett's party were left by him on the Dolores to watch supplies. I march tomorrow with six fighting men to rescue them if they are yet alive. I have hired Mr. Giles at six dollars per diem and the other man at $5 to find you. Hoping that my fears for your safety are groundless, I am Truly yrs, Jas T. Gardner.

*Gardner to Jackson, August 21, 1875, RG 57, Howell Papers.*

### *William Henry Jackson* ❋ *August 15*

The route we chose lay to the right [east] of Sierra Abajo [Blue Mountain]. We first put in a day of photographic exploring by going up one of the side canyons on the west until it became impassable with walls a thousand feet or more in height.[4] Many interesting ruins were found—small individual tenements in caves built along high cliffs and perched on isolated rocks. The third day out from the river we came on to a small party of Pah Utes. They first made their presence known by calling down to us in their peculiar, far-reaching cry from far up the bluffs above. It was only after some parleying with Harry that they ventured to come down. They were curious as to where we were going.

The Indians had some buckskins they wanted to sell, but we had nothing with which to trade. Following us to the next water, they were rather insistent that we should camp there, but we preferred to go on further. About supper time the same Indians came into camp, and after being well fed, hung around until long after dark.[5] Our animals, which we allowed to run loose, were restless during the night and made several rushes. Once they stampeded right through camp nearly running over us and scattering pots and kettles in every direction and making a great rumpus for a while. It was the result, probably, of the same Indians prowling around the neighborhood.

*Jackson and Driggs*, Pioneer Photographer, *262–64.*

## E. A. Barber ✹ Sierra Abajo, Utah, August 29

Leaving this spot [the junction of Fish Creek and Comb Wash] we travelled up the canyon for about ten miles farther, when following an old trail, we found a pass through the sandstone ridge on our right. Just before reaching this we met a band of Ute Indians on foot, who begged everything we had about us. They informed us that they were camped on the other side of the cliffs and that they would be over to trade with us when we made camp. Scarcely had we unpacked in full view of the mountain and near an alkaline marsh where we found some questionable water, when three of these Indians approached on two horses, and before they could dismount made [obscure text] errand by uttering the word "bish" [obscure text] some of the others in the band whom we had met at noon would steal our horses unless we kept them picketed close to camp. On their departure they stampeded all of our animals, and as it was now dark, it was with much difficulty that they were collected together and brought to camp.

We had scarcely got to sleep before we were all awakened by a terrific noise as of shouting and much trampling of feet. There stood Bill in the tranquil moonlight, close to the cargo, frantically shouting, waving a blanket in each hand and dancing a hornpipe on his blanket in his bare feet while the mules parted into two bands and rushed past him on either side. We all found ourselves more or less on the defensive when we became thoroughly awakened. One discovered himself sitting bolt upright on his saddle and wondering if anything had happened. Another had hold of a sprig of a bush which grew at the head of his bed, ready to climb up on further developments. One of the party found himself standing in a cactus bed in his stocking feet about five feet from his bed, supposing he had been shot through his pedal extremities. The mules had taken fright at some actual or imaginary noise and attempted a second stampede. The whole fourteen were charging at full gallop, seven abreast, toward us as we lay dreaming peacefully of secure retreats. Bill's effectual horn pipe was the only thing which turned the rushing tide into two channels ere it overwhelmed us and ground us into the dust. Then "silence reigned supreme" for a while, only interrupted occasionally by the suppressed thanks of an obstructed windpipe.

*"Hayden Survey: The Caves of the Rio De Chelly,"*
New York Herald, *October 3, 1875.*

### *William Henry Jackson* ✤ *August 25*

Skirting the eastern flanks of the Abajo Peak, we rose out of the region of cliff ruins, but found another region of rich, abundant grass, clear mountain streams, and groves of oak and aspens. Game signs were frequent; three deer crossed the trail ahead of us as we were riding along with the train. We met but one other party of Indians, a Weeminuche family with many horses and goats on their way to the Navajo country. Our last camp on the mountain was in a fine grove of scrub oaks where there was luxuriant feed for our animals and plenty of clear, cool water. This was so grateful [*sic,* gratifying] to both man and beast after the desert experiences of the past month that I decided to leave the larger part of our party there to recuperate while I went on a side trip with Harry and Bill for an investigation of the country lying between the Abajo and La Sal mountains.

With two light packs, we struck out across country to pick up the Old Spanish Trail to an upper crossing of the Colorado which Harry said was in this neighborhood.[6] Dropping into a draw or shallow canyon, we came to a copious and remarkably cold spring. As we followed down the gradually broadening canyon, we came on the old trail near a peculiar rock formation known as La Tinaja. We were now in a broad, valley-like-expansion of the gorges leading into the Colorado Canyon, where there was very little grass and no water. A dry camp was made, but we had a heavy shower during the night.

Until noontime we roamed about looking for ruins, but found no indications whatever. The only object that warranted setting up the photographic outfit was a group of red sandstone bluffs with great dome-shaped caves that would have been a fine place for cliff dwellings. Returning by a different route which bore around to the east, we struck an old trail under white sandstone bluffs. This was followed until we came to a side canyon which took us, after a steep and rough climb, to the level, plateau-like summit. Leaving the trail here, we made a beeline in the direction of our camp, but had to tie up for the night when about halfway there.

During our day's rambling we had puzzled much over numerous tracks of shod horses and mules, plainly not Indian, which we found at various points in the vicinity of our first night's camp. There was also a fresh trail going east through the sagebrush on the plateau over which we had just passed. Gardner was to make a station on the Abajo Mountain, but these tracks, if of his party, would indicate that he had not been there.

Returning to our camp among the oaks and after resting the animals a bit, we packed up for our return to the rendezvous camp on the La Plata. A direct route by the way of Montezuma Canyon was taken. Fortunately, we happened on a practicable way down into it. The bottom of the canyon, usual with those in this region, was flat with a deep wash winding from side to side. It was rather narrow where we first entered it, but gradually widened further down. Near sunset we camped at the junction of another large canyon. The main canyon was now some two hundred to three hundred yards wide with the bottom lands literally covered with old ruins.

As this was a dry camp, in the morning I first sent the men up and down the canyon to locate water, but finding none, we started off down the trail. The ruins were so numerous now that frequently one or more were in view as we rode along. Arrow points were so plentiful that there was an active rivalry as to which one of us found the greatest number. Broken pottery of all kinds and beads and other trinkets also were collected. After passing two rather important ruins, we found running water a short distance below and went into camp while we investigated them.

Next morning our camp was moved down the canyon a little way for better grass, while I went back to complete my photographing. Near the previous night's camp there were Indian cornfields, planted in white sand and not thriving very well. Our stock got into the fields during the night, doing no great damage, but it was just as well that the owners were not around. In the afternoon, with Harry and Bill

Large eight-foot blocks of sandstone raised vertically were part of a wall behind which lies a massive prehistoric pueblo complex. Photographed at the junction of Montezuma and Coalbed Canyons, this is also the place where Jackson encountered sporadic Ute cornfields extending for miles down Montezuma Canyon. *Courtesy William H. Jackson Collection, Scan #10028981, History Colorado Center, Denver, Colorado.*

and the photo-pack mule, I started on a side trip down the canyon to look for more ruins. About five miles from camp we came to a right-angle bend to the eastward; and a few miles further on, to a large Indian camp of brush wikiups. Between these two points we had a lively and exciting experience. Soon after passing the big bend, we noticed up in the rocks to the left the head and shoulders of an Indian boy. He beat a precipitous retreat down the canyon on his pony as soon as he saw he had been discovered. A little later a single horseman met us, and after the usual "How-how!" turned back and rode along with us.

While Harry was trying to get some information from the Indian, we saw a cloud of dust down the trail, and out of it came some fifteen to twenty Indians on ponies, rushing full tilt toward us. Shouting their shrill, "hi, hi" and swinging their guns over their heads, they did not stop until they had run right into us and, turning about, surrounded us completely. We had no idea what all this demonstration meant, but there was nothing to do but sit tight and wait to see what happened.

Crowding around us, all of the Indians joined in a noisy chorus of greetings and shaking of hands. Harry thought he recognized one of the men—he claimed acquaintance anyway—and through him replied to some of their questions as to who we were, where we came from, and where we were going. There was some hesitation in saying we were a part of the government surveys as we knew of their hostility toward surveyors in general. Being none too sure of the temper of these young bucks in these remote canyons, Harry told them that we were prospectors bound for Moss's La Plata camp. They appeared to be friendly, however, and finally insisted upon our going to their camp. In a spirit of pure mischief or deviltry they got behind us and with quirt and lariat lashed our horses and mules into a breakneck race, never letting up until we dashed among their wikiups. It was a regular stampede all the way and it was fortunate that the photographic outfit on Blinkey was securely packed, for if anything had gone wrong, that would have been the last of it.

Old Pogonobogwint, their chief who was present, met us with a friendly greeting and by his invitation we joined them in a lunch of boiled green corn.[7] They were insistent that we stop there overnight as they declared there was no water, other than the spring near their camp, within a day's journey. We were equally insistent upon going on, however, and after supplying ourselves with a dozen ears of green corn, we continued down the canyon. In order to get away from the Indians, we were willing to take our chances for water.

All this time we had not told the Indians of the rest of our party that we had left up the canyon. We had a rather hazy purpose in mind of getting back to it by some roundabout, unobserved way and then leaving the country by another route that would pass around the Indian camp. Soon after leaving, we noticed that we were being followed by two Indians on horseback. Spurring up and watching our opportunity, as the deepening shadows of late evening obscured our movements and tracks somewhat, we lost our pursuers by making a quick turn up a small side canyon filled with brush. Up this we

Jackson's painting of the Photographic Division's "stampede" at "breakneck speed" into the Ute camp of Poco Narraguinip portrays what may have been in sport, but also underscores the vulnerability of this small group of travelers. Later discussions about the difference in outcome between the Jackson and Gardner experiences raised questions about why one group encountered so much resistance. *Courtesy Scotts Bluff National Monument, SCBL 279.*

worked our way to the top of the mesa where we unsaddled for a dry camp just as the stars were beginning to shine brightly in a dark blue sky. We had eaten so much corn that we did not prepare supper, and after securely picketing our four animals, we rolled up in our saddle blankets for a sound sleep.

Until late the next afternoon we wandered around among canyons and over mesas. We found many ruins, but discovered no way to rejoin our party other than by going back over the old trail past the Indian camp. Making a virtue of necessity, for our animals had had no water for twenty-four hours, we rode to the spring where they drank deeply. Nearly all the men of the Indian camp were away, but those who were there gave us another noisy reception and also more boiled corn. I do not know what Harry told them, but they seemed friendly enough. When we finally got back to our camp, the boys said that no Indians had been around there.

There seemed to be no other way of avoiding the Indians than by going up the canyon and finding a trail leading over the mesa to the south. We were so opposed to further contact with them that we took desperate chances to keep out of their way. There was no trail, but we began tracking back and forth up the sides of the canyon. Halfway up the pack mules began to weaken, some of them stumbling and falling over loose rocks. We did not give up, however, until Old Mag, carrying a load of bedding in which was packed some of our pottery collections, fell backwards on a steep incline. The mule rolled heels-over-head, making a clear leap of about forty feet over a perpendicular ledge and landed on her back in the top of a thick scrub cedar. I was below, at the rear of the train, when this happened and thought it was surely the finish of Old Mag as I saw her hurtling through the air followed by a clatter of loose rock; but to my utter amazement, she rolled out of the tree and landed right side up in the trail below, none the worse, apparently for her experience. Our difficulties seemed to be growing greater rather than less in trying to get over the mesa, so I ordered a right about and returned to our former camp.

Next morning we decided to strike out straight for the La Plata rendezvous, Indians or no Indians. Passing their camp, we were held up for the damage done to their cornfield by our mules, which had been discovered in the meantime. We had nothing to give them and when they got ugly about it, I had the packers rush the train ahead while Harry and I remained behind to stand them off until we could make a get-away. It was a long, forced ride to Hovenweep. From there we went directly to the La Plata.

*Jackson and Driggs,* Pioneer Photographer, *264–71.*


### *Charles Aldrich* ❈

It seems very singular that Mr. Jackson should have had no trouble from the Indians, but he had with him as a guide Harry Lee, who has long been upon the frontier. He is a "California Americat" and few of the Indians out this way ever molest one of this class of frontiersmen. The party met many Indians in the section where the fight took place and the redskins always came up with their guns unsheathed and their ponies on a sharp gallop or dead run. But through the judicious action of "Harry" and Mr. Jackson, they escaped any molestation. When the Indians asked where they were from, they invariably said "California." As the party had only two or three guns, they could have made but a feeble defense against the bands of Indians who are continually roaming around in the region where the other parties were attacked. The escape of the party seemed almost providential and the boys were warmly congratulated on their return.

*"Ute Warriors: A Band of Renegade Redskins Attack the Hayden Party,"*
Rocky Mountain News, *September 5, 1875.*[8]

Ouray in Washington, 1880, shortly before his death. Of all of the Ute chiefs, he was one of the most tragic figures. He worked to stem the flow of miners in his mountains but failed; he tried to protect his people from the white invasion, yet many thought he was working for the enemy; he tried to maintain peace but was held accountable for the Meeker Massacre. In the end, the government succeeded in evicting his people from their lands. *Courtesy Denver Public Library, Western History Collection, X-30585.*

# CHAPTER 8

# *Back to the Other Side*

## Los Pinos Agency and Washington, D.C.
### AUGUST 22–OCTOBER 20, 1875

### THE FIGHT'S SEQUEL—
### THOUGHTS AND CORRESPONDENCE

GARDNER NOW HAD TIME TO DETERMINE, MORE PRECISELY, just who and what had caused the confrontation with the Utes. He needed to talk to Agent Bond and Chief Ouray, soon and personally. Then all of what he learned needed to be explained to Hayden, who was likely to read about events as soon as the eastern papers got their reporters' posts. Gardner wanted the director to hear his side of things first. Still, there were questions that needed to be answered, among which were how could Jackson have come through unscathed, while the Gardner-Gannett parties fought their way through the same territory? How did the Utes think about different groups of white men passing over their land? And what type of punishment should the recalcitrant Utes/Paiutes receive? The following ruminations show that he had established at least a partial explanation of what had happened and what should be done in the future.

### *James Gardner* ✳

I authorized Mr. Holmes to finish that part of his district which lay about the head of the Dolores River where the Utes would probably not molest him, and to leave unfinished a small piece in Utah, south

of the Sierra Abajo where the hostile Indians are likely to range. Mr.
Gannett, Dr. Peale, Mr. Atkinson, and Mr. Pearson accompanied
him to complete a small unfinished portion of Mr. Gannett's district
about the head of the San Miguel. The only portion of our sheets left
blank will be a very small and unimportant area in Utah near the
Colorado boundary. . . . Next morning we all started for the Los Pinos
Agency, but not by the direct route of the Gunnison River. I turned
northward and followed the high plateau that divides the waters of
the Uncompahgre from the Dolores, wishing to examine all the trails
which connect the valley in which the new agency is to be placed with
the western waters on which live the hostile bands. Having finished
this examination, we crossed the Uncompahgre Valley into which a
fair road is now built. Over it they are hauling material for the new
agency building. We reached Los Pinos on the 10th and were warmly
welcomed by Mr. Bond and his family. The friendly agent was about
to go in search of us, but fortunately all cause for anxiety on the part
of our friends is now passed.

In an interview with Ouray, chief of the Utes, he informed me that
this Sierra La Sal band is well known to him and that they procure
their ammunition and arms by trading with the Utes. It is therefore
evident that the powder and lead that was so freely used upon us on
the 15th and 16th of August, was indirectly furnished by the government. The recklessness with which they used it at long range showed
clearly that they must have some ample source of supply. How easily
the Utes could control them is evident by the trails that I found in our
homeward journey; the farms of these Sierra La Sal Indians are within
a day's ride of the Uncompahgre Valley. Ouray himself acknowledged
to me that this was the case.

The miners have, within the past few years, been coming through
from Salt Lake to the San Juan district by trails that pass near the
Sierra La Sal, and Ouray tells me that he knows of their having been
killed by this same band. I would respectfully suggest that measures
be taken to bring this gang of outlaws to justice. Severe punishment
summarily meted out to them would have a very salutary effect upon
all of the Indians. If their rascality goes unpunished all the lawless
spirits of the Colorado and Utah tribes will gather about them as a
nucleus and serious trouble will result. We now have the means of

furnishing a careful map of the region they occupy and are acquainted with almost every trail. We had ridden, up to this time of our arrival at Los Pinos, eight hundred miles in the past four weeks on the same mules that had previously carried us seven hundred miles.

"*The Sierra La Sal Utes,*" Rocky Mountain News, *September 17, 1875.*

## *James Gardner to F. V. Hayden* ❋ *September 18*

Having had until now no access to the newspapers for many weeks, I am surprised to learn from the *New York Herald*'s Washington correspondent of September 5th that the acting Secretary of the Interior, in a conversation with the correspondent, seemed to understand me as placing upon the Ute tribe the responsibility of the attack on our party. He very justly says that a powerful people like them, familiar with every foot of the country, could certainly have killed every one of our little band of explorers had they intended to. It was not my intention to make the Utes, as a tribe, responsible for the outrages, nor do I consider them so, except in the same sense that the community of Washington would be responsible for a band of highwaymen infesting the road to Arlington Heights.

For the past thirteen years I have been conducting geological and geographical explorations among the Arapahos, Cheyenne, Sioux, Shoshones, Pah Utes, Apaches, and Utes, often trusting to the rifle alone for security, and often shot at by Indians simply to frighten. The difference between an attack to kill and an attempt to intimidate becomes very obvious after a varied experience with these tribes. During the past few years our work has been among the Utes, requiring us to traverse every part of the reservation. Although the explorations have been objected to by the more ignorant part of the nation, yet we have had the constant support and protection of the most powerful chiefs, Ouray and Douglass, providing good treatment at the hands of their followers. Our intercourse with these chiefs has led me to think highly of their wisdom and to regard them as true friends of the whites and of peace. That it may be clearly understood to whom we are indebted for the warm reception we received at the Sierra La Sal, I will give in a condensed form such information as I have been able to gather about them.

[Gardner recalled Ouray's earlier warning, then proceeded.] From these warnings it is evident the band who attacked us has an established reputation as robbers and murderers, whatever may be the tribe to which they originally belonged. It was this knowledge which caused me to join Mr. Gannett's party with my own. After our fight and the rescue of Messrs. Holman and Dallas from their perilous position at the supply camp, I marched at once to the Los Pinos Agency, reaching there September 10. Agent Miles acting as special commissioner to investigate the Utes was at the agency when I arrived. Agent Bond sent for Ouray, chief of the Utes, and Mr. Harris, the well-known interpreter; I had a long talk with Ouray in the presence of Agent Bond and Commissioner Miles.

I told the chief all that had occurred. He immediately asked if the leader of the band was an old man of unusually dark complexion, and if he had several young men with him of similar appearance. This very dark complexion had been noticed by our party as a characteristic of the old leader and two of the younger men when they came to shake hands with us before the firing commenced. It was this old man and a boy that we had seen at a corn patch on the south end of the Sierra La Sal. There could be no mistake about the identity and Ouray said that the old man and his family had been farming around these mountains for many years; that he was a very bad man who had robbed and murdered for a long time. Three years ago he paid Ouray a visit and the chief advised him to stop raiding and join the reservation Indians. He answered that he was not a dog to eat bread from the hands of the white men, but intended to live at war with them. Since that time Ouray has not seen him, but through his Utes he learned that last year the band killed certainly one and perhaps more miners on their way from Salt Lake to the San Juan mines.

Ouray seemed surprised that the number of the band had increased to fifteen lodges, which he said would represent twenty-five to thirty fighting men. The success of this old desperado and his family has attracted the lawless spirits of the surrounding tribes, probably both Utes and Pah Utes. He has gone so many years unpunished that his evil example is beginning to tell powerfully on his neighbors. Ouray had supposed that there were only seven or eight men when he advised me that seven of us would be safe. He recalled this to me and said though mistaken in the number he had nevertheless stated explicitly that they would either kill or rob if they got an opportunity.

I then told him that it was as much for the interest of the Utes to suppress this band of guerrillas as it would be for that of the whites to capture any band of Americans who should go about shooting and robbing Indians, and that if he would furnish me some Utes to serve as scouts so that I might be able to tell the difference between Ute and renegade camps, I would immediately return with five of my men and undertake to kill the whole of the gang. To this he answered that the old man, their leader, was a Pah Ute, and that the Pah Utes, who had never been his friends, would consider that he was making war upon one of their sub-chiefs. If the government would supply regular troops and make a formal request of him, he would supply Ute guides who knew every trail around the Sierra La Sal. I then asked where these renegades got so much ammunition, and he said, "by trading with the Utes."

Ouray did not express the slightest doubt but that they would have killed us, as they did the others before. It was certainly the best opportunity for plunder that they ever had. To murder a prospector is to secure but poor pay, a few pounds of flour and bacon, a blanket or two, a frying pan and a shovel, with a few burros, comprising his all. But here were eighteen heavily loaded pack mules with provisions, tents, blankets, ammunition, etc., sufficient to last them for an indefinite period; fifteen saddle animals, seven good rifles, and last, but not least, thirteen scalps to capture which would make them noted braves for life. Already reckless from years of unpunished crime, secure in their mountains and canyons which no white men had before entered, [these Indians would receive] certain wealth and reputation if they could only hold us twenty-four hours in that cliff-walled desert valley.

No robber band ever came nearer realizing their fullest ambitions. That they fought so long without killing any of us—for which we seem to owe the public an apology—is due to the fact that they shot at such long range, all but one being armed with muzzle-loading rifles and that they were shooting at objects moving across the line of fire. It is a mistake to suppose that Indians are good shots when under excitement. They are not nearly equal to practiced white men. I have many times been shot at for the purpose of frightening by Indians, and they always shot far overhead or off to one side. But the second shot which I saw these fellows fire, coming obliquely from behind passed between two of the men who were so close that it must have been aimed at the foremost of the two.

We then drove them to such a distance that their muzzle-loaders were of no use except to bombard the camp in a general way, hoping that a stray ball might take effect somewhere in so large a group as was formed by our mules and men. At night all firing at two hundred yards and over is mere chance, for one can neither see the sight of their gun clearly nor can they see where the balls strike so as to get the correct elevation. In the night the bullet which by accident lodged in our bell mare would have hit a man had it gone a foot to the left. Next morning we again kept driving them to a distance by the accurate long range practice of our fine breech-loaders. . . .

The whole history of the frontier proves that where the Indian and white come face to face in equal fight, his nerve fails before that of the Anglo Saxon. In this trying time, when the enemy was within a hundred yards [on the cliffs above], Mr. Mills was so anxious to get a shot at an Indian that the bullets cut the twigs first on one side of his head and then on the other before his comrades could persuade him to seek complete shelter. After we had abandoned the packs, is it probable that the Indians would have ridden twenty-five miles to cut us off from the next water unless they had wanted rifles, mules, or scalps? . . . If this renegade band, after their former record and this attack upon the United States Geological and Geographical Survey, are allowed to escape punishment, their success will embolden every desperate character in the neighboring tribes to join them or imitate their example. No amount of whitewashing can make these fellows pass as injured brethren. The Sierra La Sal lies on the most direct and what would be the best trail—were it not for these robbers—from Salt Lake to the newly discovered mines in the La Plata Mountains and at the head of the San Miguel and Dolores Rivers. The route is practically closed by this handful of renegades who are bringing disgrace on the peaceful tribes about them and who the head chief of the Utes has promised to assist in catching. Their home is within a day's ride of the new Uncompahgre Agency to which a wagon road has been built. Their country being thus accessible, I would respectfully suggest that it be urged upon the government to take immediate steps to punish the renegade band occupying the region around the Sierra La Sal.

"*The Old Man of the Mountains,*" Rocky Mountain News, *September 22, 1875.*

### Charles Aldrich ✸ Parrott City, Colorado, September 8

It seems very singular that Mr. Jackson should have had no trouble from the Indians, but he had with him as a guide Harry Lee who has long been upon the frontier. He is a "California Americat" and few of the Indians out this way ever molest one of this class of frontiersmen. The party met many Indians in the section where the fight took place and the redskins always came up with their guns unsheathed and their ponies on a sharp gallop or dead run. But through the judicious action of "Harry" and Mr. Jackson, they escaped any molestation. When the Indians asked where they were from, they invariably said "California." As the party had only two or three guns, they could have made but a feeble defense against the bands of Indians who are continually roaming around in the region where the other parties were attacked. The escape of the party seemed almost providential and the boys were warmly congratulated on their return.

"*The Hayden Survey: Completion of the Season's Work in the Mountains of Southwestern Colorado,* Chicago Daily Inter-Ocean, *September 25, 1875.*

### E. A. Barber ✸ Camp on the La Plata River, Parrott City, September 6

Much excitement has probably been raised ere this by the recent outrage perpetrated upon the two divisions of the United States Geological Survey by a band of renegade Utes, Pah-Utes, Navajo, and Apache Indians near the Sierra La Sal in Utah. Great indignation has been felt and exhibited at the manner in which these parties were attacked, plundered, and driven out of the country, with only sufficient provisions to last them until they reached a point of safety. But could the whole truth and all its facts be known, it would occasion no surprise that such a thing had occurred.

This state of affairs has been brought about by the dilatory action of the government in regard to fulfillment of its contracts with these

Indians, or its failure, or that of its employees, to meet the requirements of its treaty with them. These Indians claim that they were promised by the treaty annuities amounting to $30,000 per annum, and that out of $60,000 previously owed them, they have received but $25,000. For more than a year they have been trying in a peaceable manner to obtain their rights but not succeeding, and being unable to obtain any satisfaction, they have become dissatisfied and suspicious. It cannot be supposed that an uneducated savage will understand the delay of a prompt fulfillment of promises made them, and when they sell their land to "Washington Americats" and receive nothing for it, the blame is likely to fall upon the heads of innocent parties. Thus, when they meet a party of men on their reservation, and, upon inquiry, are told that they are Washington men, these Indians reason: "You are Washington Americats; therefore you are the men who bought our land; now, pay us what you owe us."

The two divisions of the survey in charge of Mr. Gardner and Mr. Gannett, running across a band of these dissatisfied Indians, were commanded to settle the debt, and because they were unable to do so, fell a prey to the wrath of the band and escaped miraculously with barely their lives. It is not the intention here to uphold the conduct of these Indians or to shield them from the punishment they deserve, but justice, at least, is due them. In not recognizing their rights the government withdraws its protection from all whites, even those whom it sends into the country, and irritates the feeling of animosity which exists between the two races.

To show how peaceful these Indians are disposed to be toward all those who are not concerned in defrauding them, we may take as an illustration the photographic party of the survey, in the charge of Mr. W. H. Jackson, which has just returned to the La Plata. Scarcely a week after the fight we [Jackson] approached the Sierra Abajo, from the ruins in Arizona, and encamped in those mountains for three days. A side trip was made for two days north to the foot of the Sierra La Sal, and the very ground was passed on which the other parties had been attacked. Descending into the Montezuma Canyon we drove unconsciously into the very camp of these identical Indians, number about one hundred men, women, and children. The first sight they obtained of us on our approach brought them armed and mounted toward us.

At first we were startled by the sight of twenty savages galloping toward us, whooping, yelling with drawn guns; but, not suspecting any harm, we rather enjoyed the sight. Being asked from whence we came we replied, "California," and were immediately taken into their camp and to the wickiup of Poco Narraguinip, the captain of the band, where we were treated hospitably and well. Here were three men, hundreds of miles from any settlement, surrounded by a band of renegade Indians in their own wilds, who had only a few days previously raised their hand against the representatives of the United States Government. In the camp at this very time, were secreted all the captured cargo of the other parties, although we suspected nothing for they conveyed us in a circuitous way up to the captain's lodge. Had we told them that we had come from Washington, things most probably would have terminated in a more serious manner.

Upon the arrival of the plundered parties at the La Plata River two men, well-acquainted with the country and known to the Indians, were dispatched in search of us, as it was feared that some danger might have befallen us, especially as we were to pass through the same section in the vicinity of the Sierra Abajo and Sierra La Sal. Trailing us down into Arizona and back as far as the first mentioned of these mountains in Utah, the men fell short of provisions and were compelled to return to the La Plata with no satisfactory news of us. They had been out fifteen days and could have been but a day or two behind us when they gave up the hunt. At the very time when we unconsciously camped within a distance of three or four miles of the Indians, who had preceded us down the canyon of the Montezuma two days at the furthest, as we could see by their trail, on their return from the battle.

This incident will show the peaceful disposition of the Utes generally, taking this most dangerous band as an example. Much surprise was manifested on both sides on our return. All were astonished to see us come in safely, and we were equally surprised to hear of the events of the past two weeks. We arrived just in time to stop another party which was to start out for us the next morning, and as the three parties of the survey sat around the campfires that night, on the banks of the La Plata, the time was passed in recounting the events of the battle with much merriment at the expense of some of the participants.

This is but the prelude to an Indian war, unless things are more satisfactorily arranged. This seems inevitable from the general feeling of the whole tribe, and to fight four thousand Utes in their own country where water only occurs at long intervals, hidden in some unlikely spot only known to them, would cause much suffering and inconvenience. There should be at least an immediate inspection of affairs here, and whatever is wrong should be righted as speedily as possible.

[No title], New York Herald, September 22, 1875.

#        #        #

In offering his opinion about the causes of the fight with the Utes, E. A. Barber hinted at what was to become, in the ensuing months, an unsettling problem for F. V. Hayden. The director had always been intensely concerned with his Survey's public image, which meant that he had to balance cultivating a public fascination for the "wild" West with assurances to funders that science could be conducted safely and efficiently in remote regions. The encounter near the La Sals might be used by Hayden's critics as evidence that civilian scientists shouldn't be the ones doing survey work in hostile areas. News of the attack came at a particularly difficult moment for Hayden. Just as news of these events was hitting the eastern papers, his longtime supporter, Secretary of Interior Columbus Delano, was forced from office after facing charges of corruption.

For the Hayden Survey's sister agency in the Interior Department, the Office of Indian Affairs, the event threatened to antagonize what was already a complex situation. The government had, only the year before, succeeded in reducing the boundaries of the Ute Reservation, and there was little doubt that white settlers would demand further changes. The Commissioner of Indian Affairs was anxious that the incident near the La Sals not be an excuse to further inflame passions, either white or Indian, in the region. The national climate was also problematic for the Indian bureau. President Grant's Indian policy had lost political support, as had the Grant administration as a whole, so the bureau faced constant criticism in the press about corruption among Indian agents. News of "Indian trouble" in Utah and Colorado was likely to only add fuel to a growing fire.

## REPORTS AND REACTIONS

When Gardner arrived at Parrott City on August 21, he wrote to Hayden (who was in Denver), promising a fuller report later, once all members of the Survey were accounted for. Hayden's first response to the news was to downplay its severity. He, and the Indian Bureau, sought to purge the event of any larger political meaning—it was not part of the "Indian problem" but the result of "outlaws" among the Indians behaving badly, out of personal greed, against the wishes of government-friendly tribal leaders. Hayden also implied that Gardner may have panicked during the encounter with the Indians and then exaggerated the story to cover his embarrassment, an interpretation seemingly shared by Jackson and Holmes. The U.S. Army, long Hayden's rival for authority in western surveying, chimed in with a facetious article about the "Great Battle."

Gardner responded to the report of this criticism in the press with a lengthier and more strident defense of his actions. He didn't hesitate to share with reporters his reports and correspondence to Hayden. For the eastern press this was all just too good to be true—"savage Indians," "intrepid explorers" heroically escaping the jaws of death, combined with a whiff of scandal and bureaucratic infighting. We have included here excerpts from the correspondence between Hayden, his superiors, and his men in the field, as well as newspaper reports hinting at disagreements within the Survey. Since both Hayden and Gardner sought to use the press to present their own viewpoints, we have tried, whenever possible, to include the original date and location for reports and correspondence as well as dates when those materials appeared in print.

### F. V. Hayden ✳ Denver, August 24

Sir [Secretary of Interior Delano]: I have the honor to report that recent letters have been received from two of the parties connected with the survey, and that the reports are very favorable indeed. Mr. Gardner has ascended the highest peak of the Sierra La Sal in Utah, thus connecting Major Powell's work with our own. He will undoubtedly complete the primary triangulation of the entire Southwest, which will enable us to finish five out of the six sheets of our atlas next winter. A report from Mr. Gannett's party is also most favorable. He will complete the area west of the junction of the Gunnison and Grand Rivers. He informs me that he has made fifty-four stations, extending his survey over about three thousand square miles. He has discovered some of the most remarkable canyons on the continent, fully equal to those of the Colorado River. I enclose a copy of Mr. Gannett's letter.

In the South and Southwest the parties are discovering an almost unlimited number of the ancient ruins, a glimpse of which we obtained last year. This subject will be thoroughly investigated, and sketches, photographs, and other materials will be secured for a most valuable report. The subject is one which is attracting the attention of the entire intelligent world. The results of the explorations of the survey for the present season will be fully equal to those of any previous year.

*Hayden to Secretary of the Interior, August 24, 1875,*
*appearing in the* New York Times, *August 31, 1875.*

### *F. V. Hayden* ✳ *Denver, September 5*

Sir [Secretary of Interior Delano]

I telegrammed you last evening a brief account of the attack of the Utes on the combined parties of Messrs. Gardner and Gannett, near the boundaries of Utah and Colorado. I was absent on duty more than one hundred miles from this point and did not arrive in Denver until about nine o'clock last evening. In the meantime Mr. Sullivan had sent a number of messages to the friends of the party by special request and the letter of Mr. Gardner was just in type at the news office. I enclose a printed copy which appeared in this morning's "News."

The news passed over the lines from the south yesterday, the same day that Mr. Gardner's communication came to this office. I do not think the results will be very disastrous. We lost four mules, the packs of eighteen animals, and much valuable time. A more extended report is expected. The force of the survey is now directed toward bringing out of the dangerous country the other parties. The ones in the south will go on to completion.

I trust that the Commissioners now on their way to make a treaty with the Sioux will be instructed to require of the Indians full permission for scientific parties under the government to pass over their country without molestation. I hope this arrangement will be made with all other tribes in the West that require any favors of our government.

*Hayden to Secretary of the Interior, August 24, 1875,*
*appearing in the New York Times, August 31, 1875.*

### *"A Scientific Adventure"* ✳ New York Times, *September 9*

Something of the old-time thrilling interest attaches itself to the story of the Indian attack on a detachment of the Hayden survey, told in our columns today. Of late years the risks taken by exploring parties on the frontier have disappeared. The Indians have melted away, or have become subjugated and coerced into peaceable behavior. In the sterile fastness so graphically described by our correspondent, there yet linger some of the remnants of wild tribes. These, for the sake of plunder, have forgotten ancient feuds, and often combine in bands which are the terror of the few white men who have occasion to penetrate that forbidding region. The Utes and Paiutes are known to plainsmen as the meanest and most rascally of all red men. They are only a few removes above the miserable Diggers, found further West. They are thieving, but cowardly; they will steal anything and everything they can carry away, even while professing friendship and honesty. They will fly before any well-organized, well-armed force, however small; and they do not hesitate to shoot a white man from an ambush, provided they can snatch his mule, rifle, or clothing, and be off before overhauled by an avenger. They are the true Arabs of the American desert. They can subsist on roots and insects, hide in the sagebrush, and scale the rocky cliffs of the region with the agility of the tiger-cat. No wonder the frontiersmen call these creatures "vermin."

*Editorial,* New York Times, *September 9, 1875.*

### *Cuthbert Mills* ✳ New York Times, *September 9*

It would have been lamentable if any of this peaceful party, bent only on a peaceful errand, had been killed. And it would have been a great pity if the records of the scientific work already accomplished had been destroyed or lost. Fortunately, the adventurers got away with their lives, working memoranda, and animals enough to bring them back to a place of safety. There was no special reason to anticipate any trouble in that region, except such as might come from brigands and guerillas, of any color. The tribes to which these predatory bands belong are nominally at peace with the United States Government. The acts of the plunderers cannot be charged to the account of any known tribe; and their attack on the Hayden Survey party was just such a one as a pack of wolves might make on a solitary traveler in the snow. But it is one of the perils of the frontier—this possible swooping down of a predatory horde of savages who have no visible connection with any known tribe, no abiding place where they may be followed and punished, and no lair from which they may be driven. It is most likely they thought that this party of daring civilians, wandering so far into the wilderness of rock and sand, would be an easy prey. The red rascals did not want to take the lives of the white men, unless it was necessary to do so in order to get at the booty. They secured a rich prize, after all, but they must have been astonished at the stubbornness with which the white explorers fought. Certainly, considering the odds against them and the great disadvantages of their position, the little band of scientific adventurers showed pluck and courage worthy of the highest praise.

*"A Scientific Adventure,"* New York Times, *September 9, 1875.*

## Army and Navy Journal ✳ *September 18*

The latest and best record of rifle practice at long range comes to us from the borders of Colorado and Utah, as being made by the now renowned Hayden exploring expedition. Professor Hayden most unhappily was not with the party that made it, but he has dispatched full accounts of the practices; and, thanks to the *Inter-Ocean*, all the morning papers last week teemed with accounts of "Hayden's Indian Fight," in which Hayden was not present. . . . It seems that a section of the Hayden party, headed by Professor Gardner, and numbering seven professors, with six rude mountain men to tend mules and baggage, was followed for some days by a party of Utes or Diggers, it is uncertain which. These red sons of the desert followed Professor

Gardner's party for several days in quest of bones and other refuse food, but owing to the appetites of the professors and mountain men, found their chances of starvation excellent. Then it was that, having tried in vain to strike up a trade, the hungry Indians opened fire on the professors at long range, and the fun commenced. . . .

Four long days was the fight kept up, and the Indians were completely defeated, while the professors did not lose a man in all the fighting. At last, after threading a canyon 1,000 feet deep, with ruthless Digger Indians firing at them from the summit of every precipice, the bullets dropping around them in showers, but nobody hurt, the great Hayden survey party emerging from the jaws of death and out of the mouth of hell, so to speak, leaving behind them only the baggage on three mules, with the mules themselves.

It is reported that Professor Hayden intends to apply for a scalp contract to the U.S. Government on the ground that with his small party of professors he can dispose of the whole body of Western Indians in a better and cheaper manner than the effete and worn out regular army.

[*No byline, no title*], Army and Navy Journal,
*September 18, 1875, Box 9, Howell Papers.*

### John D. Miles [*U.S. Indian agent and special commissioner*] ✢ Denver, September 20

Sir [Commissioner of Indian Affairs]: I met the Utes in council at the Los Pinos Agency on the 10th inst. They refuse to accept the southern boundary of the San Juan cession as located. The north line is not yet surveyed. They positively affirm that they will not accept any portion of the compensation guaranteed by the Treaty of 1873 until the lines are established as agreed upon with Messrs. Brunot and Cree, in which they claim that no agricultural lands were to be ceded. I am unable to find that they have ever-yet had an opportunity to receive any portion of the pay guaranteed by the government for the San Juan cession. There are causes for pretty general dissatisfaction at present.

Ouray, the chief, designates the band who attacked the Gardner and Hayden surveying party as a band of outlaw Paiutes whom he knows to have committed frequent murders and thefts during the past few years. He says he has no doubt they meant it for an attack and that he will furnish guides for troops which may be sent to punish them.

Miles to Commissioner of Indian Affairs, September 20, 1875,<br>photocopy in RG 57, Howell Papers.

## *Editorial* ✳ Rocky Mountain News, *September 21*

Elsewhere the *News* publishes today an official letter from Prof. J. T. Gardner to Dr. Hayden respecting the Sierra La Sal Utes and their recent attempt to destroy his party, of which full accounts have been published. Some of the wise men of Washington who know so much about Indian affairs, made haste to publish the opinion that the attack was intended only for a "scare." We should like to see such very knowing gentlemen under Indian fire once and then hear their opinion. It is true that Indians very frequently fire over the heads, or in the neighborhood, of white men for the purpose of scaring them, but it is very easy to tell the difference. Old plainsmen and mountaineers cannot be fooled in that way. Besides they never follow up a party simply for the purpose of scaring them. There is not a shadow of a doubt that the intention of the Sierra La Sal robber band was to kill all the white men and capture their valuable outfit as booty. It is the duty of the government to root out at once the nest of freebooters and murderers. If the Indian department sees fit to question the veracity of Professor Gardner or his men, let it do so. The people of Colorado believe them, and many know from other sources the character of the red devils who infest that country. The agency band of Utes, under Ouray, Piah, and their sub-chiefs, should not, however, be held in the slightest degree responsible for this outrage.

Editorial, Rocky Mountain News, September 21, 1875.

## *Robert Adams* ✳ Philadelphia Inquirer, *September 28*

A letter from Indian Agent Thompson, Denver, Colorado, says that the reports of the attack upon Gardner's division of Hayden's surveying party has created an intense feeling of animosity toward the Utes for which those Indians should not be held responsible. "Big Head," the leader of the attacking party, is a half-breed of Weeminuche and

Navajo, and has been for a long time regarded as an outlaw by the agency Utes and has not been allowed to come among them. His followers, about twenty in number, are renegade Paiutes, Jicarilla Apaches, and Navajos, there being no Utes among them.

The agent asks that these renegades be punished and that the rather bombastic account of the fight be discounted at its proper value. Professor Hayden states in relation to the account in the papers of the fight alluded to above, that it hardly seemed probable that such a fight could have been continued so many hours, so fiercely as reported, and nobody getting hurt. He thinks his party, being terribly frightened, ran away, left their instruments, and told the big story to justify their conduct.

*"The Hayden Expedition: The Indian Attack—How the Utes Have Been Wronged,"*
Philadelphia Inquirer, *September 28, 1875.*

### John D. Miles ✳ Washington, D.C., September 28, special dispatch to New York Times

Prof. Hayden denies the statement printed in the general press dispatches yesterday from Washington in relation to the attack made on a section of his expedition by Ute Indians, and which quotes him as saying that the party being badly frightened ran away, left their instruments, and told the big story to justify their conduct. Prof. Hayden says he has not even intimated that there was any lack of courage in his party or that they told the story of their battle to justify the loss of the instruments. He speaks in the highest terms of the endurance and bravery of the entire party in their conflict with the Indians, and regards it as quite remarkable that so much of the property was saved upon the occasion.

*"The Hayden Survey Battle," reprinted in* New York Times, *September 29, 1875.*

### Commissioner of Indian Affairs to John D. Miles ✳ October 2

Tell Ouray the Brunot Treaty very carefully defines the boundary of the cession, and the surveyors are following the line exactly and must not be disturbed. Also, that the President regards the attack upon Hayden's party by the Utes as a bad violation of treaty, expects Ouray to secure the capture and punishment of the bad Indians, and recover the valuable surveying instruments which Hayden lost.

*Commissioner to Miles, October 2, 1875, photocopy in RG 57, Howell Papers.*

## *James B. Thompson [Bureau of Indian Affairs]*
## *to F. V. Hayden* ❋ *October 9*

My Dear Sir: Your letter of 27th inst. satisfies me that you do not altogether endorse the statements made by members of your survey engaged in that desperate conflict with Indians in the Sierra La Sal country. I greatly regret the occurrence, and the feelings that have grown out of it toward our Ute Indians. I hope thus in the future prosecution of your surveys you may be personally spared any annoyance of a similar nature, and that such steps may be taken by the Department as will lead to the speedy punishment of the outlaws who attacked the party under Mr. Gardner.

As to the past, I have taken in this matter. I have nothing to retract.

*Thompson to Hayden, October 9, 1875, photocopy in RG 57, Howell Papers.*

## *Henry Gannett* ❋ *Bath, Maine, October 15*

Dear Dr. Hayden: I received your letter of Oct. 9, two or three days ago. As I understand, the Department is trying hard to persuade themselves that those Indians simply played a game of bluff on us; that they, while they wanted our property, wouldn't have harmed a hair of our heads on any account. This is all very reasonable and agrees perfectly with the facts, doesn't it? It was simply and solely pure luck that no one was hit. But enough of this subject. Gardner has made himself, and all of us, ridiculous enough, while Adams and Mills have added their quotes. The only hold that the Engineers [U.S. Army Corps of Engineers] can gain by this is that an escort is necessary; yet they, themselves, have worked without an escort the last two years, '74 and '75. This is a small affair and if Gardner hadn't made such a fuss about it, it could have been easily slurred over so that it would have excited little comment.

*Gannett to Hayden, October 15, 1875, photocopy in RG 57, Howell Papers.*

Henry Gannett (1846–1914) did not suffer from the notoriety connected with the Ute fight as did Hayden and Gardner. Gannett went on to become a charter member of the U.S. Geological Survey Department and one of the founders of *National Geographic*. He is viewed by many as the "father" of topographical maps. *Courtesy Henry Gannett Photofile, American Heritage Center, University of Wyoming.*

*William H. Jackson* ❖ *Philadelphia, October 19*

My Dear Dr. [Hayden]: I arrived here this A.M. My arrival in Denver, departure from there, and progress east have followed so closely upon each other that I could not get you in a letter ahead of myself. From here I go down to my father's one day to settle some private matters and then on the Baltimore to meet Mrs. J. & then to Wash'n. I rec'd your letter of the 26th last in D. on my way in.

I have been entirely successful upon my whole trip. Succeeded fully in all my undertakings. I brought everything back in good shape. I will prepare a full statement at first leisure moment. In regard to the "fight" I entertain only the prevalent opinion that it has been made a complete farce and is a subject no one upon the Survey who has any self-respect likes to say much about to any outside the pale. But I shall be in W. [Washington, D.C.] so soon that it is not necessary to go into any details here.

*Jackson to Hayden, October 19, 1875, typescript copy in RG 57, Howell Papers.*

## Completing the Survey

As Hayden worked to calm the eastern press and mitigate the implications of the incident in the La Sals for the Survey and the Department of the Interior, the divisions in the field continued their business, finishing remaining tasks. Holmes, Gannett, Chittenden, Pearson, and Peale completed surveying around Lone Cone.[1] With this work done, Holmes spent time investigating the La Plata mining district, while the others prepared to return east. Jackson made several short photographic expeditions and then headed home. The ever-curious Charles Aldrich, accompanied by T. S. Brandegee, took a quick trip to the ruins at Mesa Verde, unwittingly putting the lie to his own conclusion that southwestern Colorado "has few attractions for the tourist." As diary entries, field notes, and newspaper articles from this period indicate, the crews had no difficulty resuming the routines of work and proceeding without concern for difficulties with the Utes.

### William H. Holmes ✳ August 21

Busy all day getting ready for the next trip. Mr. Gardner is making up a party of seven to rescue the boys at the supply camp. He took only part of his provisions; we take the remainder. It is arranged (at my suggestion) that Gannett goes with us on our trip to Lone Cone, also that Mr. Atkinson assist him and that Mr. Pearson takes the place of Brandegee, who is to remain with Mr. Aldrich, to accompany him on a trip to Mancos Canyon and do some topography in the LaPlata Mountains.

It is thought best that the survey of the dangerous area west of the Dolores be given up for the present, as the risk seems too great. It is calculated that fifteen days will be sufficient to finish our work in Southwest Colorado.

August 22nd—Saw the outfit off to Mancos Camp and then began my writing: First, my report to Dr. H. Second, my newspaper correspondence then my miscellaneous letters. At sundown I was not done, but it was high time to be off in company with Gardner, Adams and Mills. I set out. Reached Mancos at about 10 o'clock.

August 23rd—Said good-bye to Gardner's party and lit out for the Dolores. Reached it early, and marched five miles up. Camped in the large park at the point where we left the valley on our first mountain trip. . . . A family of Utes were camped by the river at the crossing, but they kept out of sight. They have come over to hunt and fish and gather berries. They must be short of food . . . as they have a number of [lengths of] pine tree bark, the inner pulpy part of which is used for food. Berries are very scarce.

*Holmes, Field Notes, Howell Papers.*

### *A. C. Peale ✳ Dolores River, August 24*

We came up the Dolores today through thick brush and without a trail most of the way. I travelled with the train, as did Holmes. The topographers were all away making stations. Holmes led the train.

*Peale Diary, August 24, 1875, Howell Papers.*

### *William H. Holmes ✳ Lone Cone, August 26*

Saddled early and rode out with Gannett, Peale, and Chit. toward Lone Cone. The mountain is very fine. The bare summit rises abruptly from the timbered slopes and is unusually symmetrical—a triangular pyramid rather than a cone. The upper part, some 500 feet of the summit, is of solid-rock crossed by almost vertical crevices and gulches (after the manner of trachyte) from which long slides of debris sweep down to the timber. In rising from the meadows the first slopes are grassy and parked, the groves of aspens giving the most charming variety to the scenery. Higher up are the parked pine forests and about the summits of the ridge, dense timber. Small streams of icy water run down the slope on all sides. Ten acres of this parked upland transplanted into some Eastern estate would rival the finest product of the horticulturalist's hand. A well beaten Indian trail crosses the divide just east of the peak. . . . The Sierra Abajo and La Sal Mountains are in view.

*Holmes, Field Notes, Howell Papers.*

*A. C. Peale* ✳ *Head of Dolores River, August 26*

Early this morning we were up and Gannett, Chittenden, Holmes and I started for Lone Cone. Holmes and I climbed from the east, the other two boys going up on the west slope. The climb was comparatively easy. We had to ride four or five miles from camp to the base of the mountain. We were on top at 11 o'clock and left about half past three. The mountain is an isolated cone of trachyte seeming in places to rest on Cretaceous shales.

*Peale Diary, August 26, 1875, Howell Papers.*

*William H. Holmes* ✳ *August 28*

September 1st.—Reached Mancos Camp in good time. Peale and Gannett went ahead to catch the out-going mail.

September 2nd.—Found affairs at the LaPlata Camp about as usual, but no word from Jackson. Brandegee and Aldrich have returned from their Mancos trip. Mr. A. declares himself much pleased.

September 5th.—Sunday. Made a section from camp down a mile. (On the Rio) Made some photo views also. Moss and a couple of Mining Engineers from San Francisco came in yesterday evening. Jackson came in all right today. Camped two or three days, almost in sight of Gardner's battle field and among the same rascals that did the mischief. Heard nothing of the trouble until reaching Mancos Camp. His collection of pottery is good. His views he reports fair. Harry Lee gave me a bowl and spoon of Moqui manufacture. I am to send him a copy of Powell's Report. Mr. Barber and Bill Whan have very nice collections of arrowheads, etc.

*Holmes, Field Notes, Howell Papers.*

*Charles Aldrich* ✳ *August 25–September 5*

After the departure . . . of Messrs. Holmes and Gannett to finish up their work, an interval of two weeks was to elapse before the return of the last-named gentlemen, when it is expected that we will all start for the other side of the mountains, and then for our several homes. I have long desired to see the ruins in the valley of the Mancos, a few of which were last year photographed by Mr. Jackson . . . and by him first brought to the notice of the outside world.

[Accompanied by T. S. Brandegee and Charles Bennett, assayer for the La Plata Mining District,] I left this "city" on the evening of the 25th. . . . Our outfit was not very pretentious. We were each mounted on a mule, carrying our blankets and our arms. Of the latter had only a shotgun with a few buckshot cartridges, and a small revolver. A pick, shovel, and hatchet completed the equipment. Each of us also carried a common grain bag, in which was stowed away some bacon and boiled mutton, sundry loaves of camp-made bread, a little tea, coffee, and sugar, three tin cups, and a coffee pot, rations for three to five days, depending upon our appetites.

The ride to the Rio Mancos was a pleasant one. The air was cool and balmy, after a heavy storm the day before. Wagons have occasionally gone through, but the road is simply an Indian trail, a very old one, for in some places it is worn to the depth of a foot or more. Sometimes one is passing through little savannahs, where the grass is rank and green, and the flowers gay and beautiful; again, through magnificent openings or parks, where the lordly pines rise on every hand as from a luxuriant meadow; and yet again through a tangle of oak brush, high as your head, which seems to aspire to pull you off your mule, and which would be well-nigh impervious but for the trail. So you go on, uphill and down dale, at a swinging trot through the level reaches, letting your careful animal pick his own way in the rough, stony places. . . .

On the south side of the ravine two great semi-circular alcoves have been worn into the white sandstone. The highest of these was about 100 feet below the top of the mesa, and about 100 feet long from north to south. In its widest part its depth back was some ten feet, though in front of this flat portion, the harder red rock sloped down at an angle of sixty to seventy degrees. In this hard, steep rock, steps had been cut, or rather shallow depressions for the toes. Just on the edge of the flat portion a wall one foot in thickness had been carried up some ten feet high, forming the front of the dwelling. As the alcove narrowed toward either end, of course, this wall decreased in height. On the north side it finally ran out, when a low wall was laid along the edge for thirty or forty feet to where it again deepened,

Two Story House, as it appeared in 1874, located on Soda Point at the southern edge of Mesa Verde. It was undoubtedly visited the next year by Aldridge and his companions. This Pueblo III (1150–1300 A.D.) ruin is characteristic of the period—carefully faced walls, protected access, and defensible posture. *W. H. Jackson, Courtesy Palace of the Governors Photo Archives* [NMHM/DCA], *#49787.*

and there was perched another little house six feet long and three feet wide. From the front wall partitions were built to the solid rock in the rear, and thus the space was divided into rooms, of which there were four, though that at the south end was more properly a sort of entrance, the wall fronting which was quite low and loosely laid up. Of the three rooms proper, the first was 8 × 11 feet, and the other two 8 × 8 approximately. In the large room there were evidences that fire had been used, for it was blackened overhead as if by smoke. In the next beams and beam posts were found in the dirt, and dirt at the bottom, so Brandegee named it the "Beam Room." In the next corn and cobs and husks were found in excellent preservation, and that was christened the "Corn Room." In excavating here a stone hammer, squash seeds, a quantity of very small rope, of some fiber unknown to us; the remains of a calabash, a bodkin made of bone, some pointed sticks, evidently used in knitting or weaving, and small fragments of very coarse matting, were also found.

The next house examined was in an alcove or grotto, directly under this first one. The alcove was higher and three or four feet deeper. The house contained five or six rooms; it was two stories in height, and more complicated and finished in its general design and make-up. One of the rooms was circular in form, plastered inside, and we thought at first it was used as a cistern [actually, a kiva], but this could not have been the case, for the "outside door" opened into it. This circular room, the doorway, and fireplace had been vandalized by time or some previous visitor so that we could not form absolutely correct opinions in regard to it. But it seemed quite evident that the doorway was through a small passage fifteen inches wide by two feet high. This passageway was five or six feet long, roofed overhead with little bows of cedar imbedded in the clay. These pieces of cedar had been chopped off with stone axes, and, despite their great age, are yet red inside and as odoriferous as ever. The rock at the bottom was not level, nor was the front wall straight. It bent inwardly at one point, evidently to secure greater strength, and at another there was a square angle, made for the purpose of extending the house out on a jutting piece of rock to gain more room. We found some remains of broken pottery about this house and strewn among the rocks below, one or two very rude stone hammers, a fresh kernel of corn, a lot of cobs, and a quantity of cedar bark which may have been used for roofing or bedding.

These two houses were by far the largest in these cliffs. The others were very much smaller, and wholly inaccessible. One was perched near the top of cliffs, 200 feet above us, and looked not larger than a bushel basket. It had a small door half way up the side, like the entrance to a swallow's nest. Small as it looked it was probably five feet high and six or seven feet wide. How the cliff dweller who occupied this perch ever got to it is difficult now to determine. He may have used ropes, or have had steps cut in the rocks which the winds have worn away. But once up there he was safe from any disturbance from the elements or from savage beasts, or still more savage enemies of his own race. In a cleft of the rocks directly under this house, I found a stone which had evidently been used as a scraper or cutting tool, and some curious pieces of pottery, one of the last of which was more elaborately painted than any I had yet seen.

The other houses, of which there were four in this locality, were from twenty-five to fifty feet above us, and we could devise no means of reaching them. A piece of the wall of one of them had fallen out, but the others were in an excellent state of preservation. On the north side of the ravine, beneath a widely projecting shelf of the rocks, we discovered a small spring, the water from which disappeared entirely some thirty or forty feet below. It was evident that, carefully saved, it afforded water enough for a limited supply for a community like these cliff men, who probably did not carry cleanliness to the extent of modern civilized communities. These houses were no doubt located just here on account of this hidden spring.

While we were searching among these rocks, we found upon some of their smooth faces many rude attempts at drawing or picture-making. Among these were very uncouth images of men, the outline of a dog, and some other drawings which it would be hard to define or describe. Some were cut into the rocks and others painted with colored clays. The latter were on the hard, red sandstone rocks, which formed the roofs of some of the houses. These specimens did not give us a very high opinion of the artistic talent of the cliff men, but it was suggestive of dawning intelligence, considering that they lived in the Stone Age. There was one feature of these pictures which we did not overlook: all the men were painted or engraved with tails, and one of our party felt quite confident that they must have formed that missing link in the Darwinian theory of the development of the human race, and that possibly they wore their tails off in climbing about among the rocks!

When we finally descended to our camp it was quite late in the afternoon, and we were all too tired to do more that night than to prepare our supper and go to bed on the ground. [After two days exploring the cliff houses, Aldrich and the others headed back toward the La Plata mining district. On their last night, the group] camped for the night in the mouth of a small side canyon, where the grass was plenty and very excellent. From the abundance of "wicky" poles and deer bones strewn about, it is no doubt a favorite camping place for the Utes. About fifty feet from where we slept was an old ruin, but the ghosts of its former proprietors did not disturb the sound sleep which blessed us after the labors of the day. Our breakfast the next morning used up all our provisions except a little can of salt, and we therefore left early, and traveled rapidly until we reached Parrott City.

*"The Hayden Survey: The Cliff Dwellings in Southwestern Colorado,"*
Chicago Daily Inter-Ocean, *September 24, 1875.*

## Reflections and Heading Home

As the 1875 field season of the Hayden Survey drew to a close and members left the "wilderness" for homes and families in an America poised for the Gilded Age explosion of industrialization and urbanization, they reflected on the accomplishments of the season. Charles Aldrich summarized the important aspects of the season's work.

### *Charles Aldrich ✻ September 25, 1875*

Yesterday a party started for the other side, comprising the topographers of the two parties, viz.: Messrs. Gannett, Chittenden, Brandegee, Atkinson, and Pearson. They go out via Silverton and Del Norte. Tomorrow morning Mr. Jackson starts out on the same route. He goes as far as Silverton, but will stop and do some work on the way. Tomorrow morning the geologists, Messrs. Holmes and Peale, will take up their line of march via Tierra Amarilla, Abiquiu, and Correjos [New Mexico]. It is with this latter party that I expect to travel, at least as far as Del Norte. . . .

These scientific gentlemen go through on this route for the purpose of completing the section of the rocks from the upper cretaceous through the bone beds of tertiary origin. When this is done data for a complete section of the rocks of Colorado from the oldest to the most modern will have been secured. They hope also to obtain some evidence in relation to the age of the lignitic beds. This has long been a disputed question. Dr. Hayden has described them as lower tertiary, and Professor Lesquereux, from the investigation of the collections of fossil flora, coincides with him in this opinion. Professor Cope, however, basing his opinion on the vertebrate remains found in the beds, considers them as upper cretaceous. In this opinion he is not alone, several geologists, Professor Stevenson among them, holding the same views. It is in these strata that the immense coal beds of the Rocky Mountains are found, and the question of their proper location geologically, as I have stated, has been for some time unsettled and in dispute. Messrs. Peale and Holmes hope to secure further data upon the subject—possibly to solve the knotty problem. Their conclusions will be looked for with much interest by a large number of scientific people.

Messrs. Holmes and Chittenden have been fortunate in completing the survey of the district assigned to them. Mr. Brandegee, who has filled the positions of assistant topographer and botanist, will be able to report fully upon the flora of this section of Colorado. He has found several entirely new species, among which is a large and very beautiful Datura. This district comprised about 5,000 square miles in southwestern Colorado, with about 1,500 in the adjoining corners of New Mexico, Utah, and Arizona.

Mr. Holmes has not only looked up the geology of the district very thoroughly, sketching the important features of the whole region, but has investigated its mineral resources as far as practicable, making sections of all the coal expanses, gathering specimens of its fossils, minerals, and rocks, but has given particular attention to the old ruins, a few of which I have sent the readers of the *Inter Ocean* brief descriptions. He has drawn ground plans of all that present special features of interest, aside from making sketches and watercolor drawings of a great many of the cliff houses. Some of the latter he has drawn from the valleys below, showing how they are perched on the high ledges, and others from closer points of observation. He has also copied hundreds of the quaint picture-writings with which the old cliff dwellers ornamented the rocks in the neighborhood of their houses. In short, he goes home with his sketchbook filled with rare, curious, and valuable materials for the next annual report of the Hayden Survey, as well as for articles for some of the illustrated magazines or papers when he has time to work them up. In addition to his position as working geologist on the survey, he is fortunate in being an artist of very excellent talent, and is equally at home whether sketching from a mountaintop a territory with a radius of a hundred miles, or making a watercolor painting of an object near at hand. In the last edition of Dana's work on geology—probably the best work of the kind the world has yet seen—that great author copies several of Holmes' drawings, aside from mentioning him in terms of high compliment. This is a distinction of which any man might well be proud; but as Mr. Holmes is still a young man, higher and brighter honors in the world of science will yet reward his decided talents and most persevering and untiring industry.

In the line of topographical work Mr. Chittenden has been quite as fortunate, though his work is not of a character to attract as immediate notice as that of his associate in this district. But upon his observations during the past summer will be based the representative map of Southwestern Colorado, which will take the place of all others at once upon its publication. Few men upon our public surveys have brought to their work more decided taste and talent in the direction of their profession, and no one has worked with more unflagging industry. He has climbed the high and steep mountains, threaded and meandered the streams and canyons not traceable from these elevations, and made sketches of the physical features of the country which in point of truth to nature and accuracy and minuteness of detail will place him on one of the "front seats" as a topographer. He is one of the few who have really "done the state some service," and they will know it one of these days. With all his merit as a scientist, he is one of the most genial and merry-hearted fellows in the wide world—the light of whose countenances never fails to make him a chief favorite, whether he is in the rough camp on the frontier, or in the cultured society of Washington, or his New England home. The best wishes of his associates in the South will follow "Chitty" wherever duty or fortune may lead him. . . .

Our train is packed and in a few minutes is to move forward on the journey to the other side of the mountains. We go down the Rio La Plata some distance, striking across to the Hermosa and then to the San Juan, expecting to pass through Tierra Amarilla, Abiquiu, and Correjos. The various parties employed in the survey will reach Denver from the 1st to the 20th of October. Aside from the interruption caused by the Indians, the work has been done in the most thorough and efficient manner in southwestern Colorado.

*"The Hayden Survey: Completion of the Season's Work in the Mountains of Southwestern Colorado,"* Chicago Daily Inter-Ocean, *September 25, 1875.*

# Conclusion

A S DUST SETTLED IN THE TRACKS OF THE 1875 HAYDEN Survey in the West, it was time to finalize reports in the East. Each specialist now had the responsibility of submitting detailed accounts on the geology, botany, and archaeology of the region they had passed through, while the topographers drafted maps of heretofore slightly known areas. Newspapers abandoned the controversy surrounding Hayden, Gardner, and the fight for newer, more interesting topics. Alexander Graham Bell patented the first telephone, the National Baseball League played its first game, and Colorado received statehood, all occurring in 1876. These and other events signaled change, the repercussions from which could only be guessed. The end of the Hayden field season, while appearing to bring closure to events in the Four Corners region, also set in motion uncalculated change.

The change of greatest and most immediate consequence fell upon the Utes, much as they had feared and predicted. Under the terms of the Brunot Agreement, the government was to pay the Utes a $25,000 annuity to be used to purchase horses, sheep, and guns, but the commissioner of Indian Affairs would not grant permission for the purchases until the attack on the Hayden Survey party had been explained. The formal Ute response was to pin the blame on "a little patriarchal band of outlaws, called by the head chief Ouray, Pi-Utes, but admitted by many others to be Weeminuche Utes. Up to within a few months, they acknowledged allegiance to no one. . . . According to their story, which can hardly be credited, all the shooting was done by one man, and he a Pi-Ute from Nevada."[1] This group visited the agency in 1876, received some goods, and promised that there would

be no more trouble. Of far greater import than the tiff over the annu-
ity payment, however, was the fact that the Survey's activities greatly
facilitated and expedited the whole land-loss process. No wonder the
Utes were suspicious of tripod legs sticking out from under a canvas
tarp on the back of a mule.

The five years following the Hayden Survey's work in southwestern
Colorado saw rapid expansion onto Capote and Weeminuche lands.
The San Juan mining area was "filling up with surprising rapidity; the
roads are filled with trains of emigrants, and that whole region bids
fair to be soon well-peopled."[2] By 1879, the entire San Juan region was
filled with prospectors working claims.[3] As new mines were opened
and towns were constructed, the Denver & Rio Grande Railroad
pushed farther west. Settlers gobbled up agricultural land and pastur-
age, creating an expanding network of unauthorized roads into Ute
territory. The area of Farmington, New Mexico, on the San Juan River
saw rapid settlement, once it was officially opened to homesteading
in 1875. In 1874, the Mancos Valley sported a small ranch and farm,
but by 1876–77, large numbers of settlers had claimed property that
removed the land from Ute use. Ranches established at this same
time on the Dolores River took advantage of a huge open range that
spread cattle across southwestern Colorado and into southeastern
Utah. These ranches also served as a springboard for settlements along
the Utah portion of the San Juan River; by 1879 there were eighteen
families living in the vicinity of McElmo Creek and Riverview, today
the community of Aneth. A year later, a Mormon contingent of settlers arrived to establish Bluff. Two years earlier, a small handful of
people had begun building in the Moab region at the base of the La
Sals. Paradox Valley at the southeastern end of the La Sals welcomed
its first settlers in 1877.

The Utes were angry as they watched their treasured lands disappear.
When Ouray had "given away" much of the Utes' farming land, many
Indians did not understand or agree to it. But what the treaty accords
were affecting on the recently surveyed lands was abundantly clear.
Ossipawiz, a medicine man in Ignacio's Weeminuche band, was tired
of the immigrant flow. He was ready to enlist all of the young warriors
to push the whites out of the "lower country," but wanted either Ouray's
help or at least his young chiefs to assist. His visit to the Tabeguache

In 1875, Jackson took the earliest photograph of "Punch and Judy," known today as the "Navajo Twins." Five years later, approximately 250 Mormon settlers established the town of Bluff nearby, beginning the rapid transition of southeastern Utah from being known as a blank spot on a map inhabited only by American Indians to a land of spectacular scenery and potential resources. *Courtesy U.S. Geological Survey, W. H. Jackson Photo 00536.*

camp was not only unsuccessful in enlisting aid, but Ouray killed him for attempting it. There were other problems. The three southern bands reiterated that they had not been consulted about losing the San Juan country, which they viewed as having prime hunting grounds and campsites. Nor had their expected payments yet arrived. "The Great Father talks to Ouray only [who] discards their rights and they all say that he has a giant pocket in which everything goes."[4] Ouray was seen as the great friend of the white man, who valued his services in restraining the young warriors. And from the white man Ouray received an annual salary of $1,000. Still, the Utes had no interest in assuming the trappings of civilization—speaking English, going to school, farming land, or accepting Christianity. The old ways were tried and proven and intertwined in the fabric of their culture.[5]

Settlers and miners demanded protection from the Utes. The citizens of Parrott City sent a petition to Gen. William Tecumseh Sherman, commander-in-chief of the army, asking for a military post in their proximity. After stating that the undersigned had settled the valleys of the Pinos, Florida, Animas, La Plata, and Mancos Rivers as well as their tributaries in Ute country, the petitioners went on to say that it was time for the military to defend their lives and interests. They were all about progress—agriculture, mining, and livestock—but now the Indians were taking their possessions, killing their cattle, and threatening their families. They had "so far patiently borne their insults and divided with them our last mouthful of flour, when we did not know where the next was to come from nor how soon our children would be crying for bread."[6] They believed that the Indians had become bolder because they had met little resistance. In an attempt to keep Ute activities under control, the government maintained the new agency on the Los Pinos, and, two years later, the U.S. Army established a cantonment at Pagosa Springs, fifty-two miles from the agency. The structure soon received the name of Fort Lewis, the first of two establishments to have this title.[7]

Yet other storms brewed. Some of the smaller agencies that had been serving the Jicarilla Apache and some Southern Ute bands were closed, forcing the Indians to move onto other Utes' territory. Lack of knowledge of intratribal politics, and the Ute situation in general, led government officials to toy with the idea of consolidating all of the agencies into one at White River. The Indians would forfeit the southern part of Ute lands totally. Some whites cried foul and offered the possibility of at least allowing the Southern Utes to move to the headwaters of the Navajo, Chama, Piedra, and San Juan Rivers. On May 3, 1878, Congress empowered a commission to hold talks with all of the bands at Los Pinos; Agent Francis Weaver received instructions to have all three Southern Ute groups present. On November 9, the Indians reached an agreement. No doubt the $2,000 worth of gifts helped, although the signers feared deceit and would not at first accept them. Eventually, all consented to giving up their holdings on the Consolidated Ute

Reservation in southwestern Colorado and moving by the summer of 1879 to the headwaters mentioned. They also accepted that traffic on either already existing or newly constructed roads across their land would not be molested. One hundred Muaches, eighty-seven Capotes, and thirty-seven Weeminuches signed the agreement. By doing so, they gave up a reservation of 1.1 million acres for one of 700,000 acres.[8]

But these problems were dwarfed by comparison with those played out with the White River Utes and their agent, Nathan C. Meeker, in what is known as the "Meeker Massacre." Events leading up to and involving a number of bloody incidents have been aptly described elsewhere.[9] Briefly, a new zealous, reform-minded agent, Nathan Meeker, insensitive to Indian wishes and cultural protocol, alienated many of the White River Utes. Events escalated both on and off the reservation to the point that, when Maj. Thomas T. Thornburgh crossed the reservation boundaries, he was summarily attacked. On September 29, Thornburgh and ten of his men died; his four troops of the Fourth Cavalry remained pinned down for six days. Other units joined the fray, but were unable to initially break through to the agency. On the same day, the Utes killed Meeker and ten civilians.

Soldiers poured in from Texas, Oklahoma, and New Mexico, as well as Colorado, all deployed to Ute country. Ouray ordered the Southern Utes to remain on their reservation and not to participate in any of the war talk. Still, six White River Utes rode 250 miles, appearing at the agency to hold a victory dance over Thornburgh's losses and to attract more men for the fight. The temptation proved too great and "many young warriors left with them."[10] Chiefs Savan (Capote) and Aguila (Muache) arrived at the agency the next day to say that they were doing all they could to control their young men, but it was proving to be impossible. Ute leaders and warriors attended a second meeting on October 13, again promising to be quiet.[11] The Indians reported that "Ignacio's band is, with few exceptions, on the reservation near the agency; Pi-Utes on the Mancos and Dolores."[12] These same leaders went with Agent Page to visit General Hatch to ensure that their peaceful motives were understood. It is important to recognize that Poco Narraguinip was among them and was considered influential enough to represent the "renegade Utes" (not Pi-Utes) at this time.[13]

Military forces traveled quickly and could be massed at any sign of insurrection.[14] A year-end report to General Sherman outlined the troop disposition: on the Animas River, three companies of the 15th Infantry, one mounted company of the 19th Infantry, and two troops of 9th Cavalry—a total of 234 men; at Fort Garland, five troops of 4th Cavalry, five companies of 19th Infantry, and two companies of 16th Infantry—in all 542 men; expected shortly were five infantry companies from the Department of the Platte and five more from the 23rd Infantry from Oklahoma, with a grand total of 942 men.[15] The Indians soon realized the futility of resisting the mounting odds and surrendered. With the return of some hostages taken by the Utes and a meeting with Indian commission representatives and the military, the two groups signed an agreement on November 10, 1879, ending the Meeker affair to the satisfaction of the government. It served only as a prologue to even more disturbing events for the Utes.

Movement to displace the Indians came at dizzying speed. In January of 1880, Ouray, his wife Chipeta, and eight other Utes traveled to Washington with their agent, W. H. Berry. There they met with federal officials as well as Colorado governor Frederick W. Pitkin and Otto Mears, two men "on the make." After grilling the Utes about events surrounding the Meeker Massacre, the topic of land exchange arose. On March 6, the nine Ute men signed an agreement that eventually resulted in removing all of the Northern Utes from the state of Colorado into Utah. Congress ratified the agreement on June 15, 1880, setting in motion the wheels of a process that was not completed until 1882. The Southern Utes at the same time received a reservation in the corner of southwestern Colorado along the Los Pinos, Animas, La Plata, and Mancos Rivers. This land was eventually divided into the Southern Ute and Ute Mountain Ute Reservations of today.[16] As for Ouray, on August 24, 1880, he died of natural causes at the age of forty-seven, never to see the effect of the agreement.

Thus ended a half decade during which the Utes saw sweeping changes. By 1882, their lands had shrunk from roughly the western third of the state of Colorado to the total expulsion of the northern bands to Utah, with the Southern Utes tucked into a corner of southwestern Colorado. Hunting and gathering for most became impossible following these land losses. The government gained stewardship and general control over most of the Indians, while towns, railroads, and road networks sliced through their territory. Miners and ranchers rejoiced at the vast potential of the lands now opening to expansion. With bewildering speed following the eventful 1875 field season, the white entrepreneurs and settlers who were the intended beneficiaries of the Hayden Survey's scientific endeavors had succeeded in driving the Utes from their traditional homelands.

This same field season marked a turning point for F. V. Hayden's fortunes as well. In some ways, 1875 was a high point in his survey work, the Colorado effort garnering for Hayden and his scientists widespread attention and public acclaim. But the events in Colorado exacerbated some existing problems, including internal differences among employees and the ever-simmering competition with the other federal surveys. Thus, while Hayden could point to that year's work as a prominent example in his long record of working in the West, it also marked the beginning of the end for the Survey. When the 1875 fieldwork concluded, his scientists returned to their offices in Washington and began processing the data they had gathered in Colorado, preparing maps, and drafting official reports. Quick publication of each season's work had been a hallmark of the Hayden Survey, in part because the director understood how persuasive printed maps, reports, and photographs were in convincing congressional supporters that the Survey was a professional, efficient, and productive part of the federal bureaucracy. As always, Hayden had to balance the appeal of exoticism and adventure that the Survey's work represented with the reassurance of consistent professionalism that stable funding required.

For the Hayden scientists, transitioning from the rigors of fieldwork and settling into the routines of office employment was especially important in the winter of 1875–76. The men who labored for Hayden were dedicated scientists, loyal to the director and mostly admiring of him, but they were also young and ambitious, ready, anxious even, to make their personal marks in the professional world of science. Hayden, a man of considerable self-assurance and ambition, often struggled to manage conflicting temperaments and desires within his team; the events of the 1875 field season had strained some of the bonds of camaraderie.

This was especially true for James Gardner. He resented criticisms about his conduct in the La Sals, while Hayden was angered by

Gardner's defense of his actions. Their relationship further soured when Hayden, ever sensitive to his own reputation, had begun to believe that Gardner was too ambitious and was inappropriately claiming more credit for the Survey's work than he deserved. He made his concerns known to Gardner and, more frequently, to others.

In October, as the field scientists gathered for the winter's work in Washington, Hayden openly criticized Gardner's report on the Colorado coalfield study, suggesting that he had "sold the Survey out to a private corporation." Given Hayden's own friendship with William Palmer and William Blakemore, this seems an odd accusation. Although historians disagree about Hayden's role in arranging for the study, Gardner's publication of the *Report upon the Southern Coal and Iron Field of Colorado Territory* infuriated Hayden. It is unclear whether Hayden truly believed that the coal survey crossed the line between scientific study for benefit of the general public and promoting the interests of a single company or whether he was merely deflecting that very charge from himself onto a subordinate. Perhaps it was simple jealousy over any acclaim that publication of the work might bring.[17]

Gardner bristled at Hayden's criticism, although there is no doubt that he had his own professional, as well as business, ambitions. And it was clear to many of the scientists working for the Hayden Survey and their colleagues in the increasingly professionalized scientific communities of geology, geography, cartography, and anthropology that the Survey's work had improved under Gardner's oversight. The growing suspicions and resentments between two ambitious men were exacerbated by the lingering consequences of the encounter with the Utes near the La Sals. Usually pleased with publicity about the Survey's activities, in this instance, Hayden found the dramatic retellings of the "Indian fight" in the eastern press counterproductive. From his perspective, all these newspaper stories did was antagonize the Bureau of Indian Affairs, one of the Geological and Geographical Survey's sister agencies in the Department of Interior, and fuel the Army Corps of Engineers' ambitions to assume responsibility for surveying the West. Hayden sought to quiet excitement over the fight, but Gardner's strident defense of his actions the previous August threatened these efforts. Gardner's willingness to give interviews and provide copies of his correspondence with Hayden about the matter to reporters, which made it difficult for the director to control the message, seemed a final proof of insubordination.

By mid-October, Hayden determined that Gardner had to go. In his biography of Hayden, James Cassidy suggests that the Survey director allowed Gardner to resign, rather than fire him. Whatever the case, Gardner left the Hayden Survey in November to take up a post directing the state land survey of New York, a job that presumably would not involve confronting hostile Indians, parched deserts, or the vicissitudes of bureaucratic politics. In his later life, Gardner went on to be a successful businessman in the mining industry, with particular interests in development of coal resources. Although he offered to complete the report on his division's 1875 fieldwork despite his separation from the Survey, Hayden turned the task over to A. C. Peale, while leaders of the other divisions worked on the reports for their respective regions of work.

Preparation of the official reports on the 1875 fieldwork was slowed by two special projects. Of most immediate concern was the upcoming International Exhibition of Arts, Manufactures, and Products of the Soil and Mine—most often referred to as the Centennial Exposition—which was scheduled to open in Philadelphia in May 1876. With the likelihood that millions of people, including the important national politicians who held the Survey's purse strings, would visit the six-month-long fair, Hayden saw the Exhibition as an opportunity to publicize the Survey's work. Nations from around the world had been invited to prepare exhibition halls representing their culture, arts, and industries, but the United States was to be the star, with separate halls for each of the states and a massive building devoted to modern technology taking up most of the 285-acre site. It was, after all, the nation's centennial and the fair's organizers sought to distract attention from the still-painful memories of the Civil War with dazzling displays of American accomplishments and progress. Congress appropriated a modest sum for building an exhibition hall dedicated to the activities of the federal government, with about $1,500 going to the Hayden Survey. Hayden supplemented that with an additional special appropriation and private donations. He wanted something spectacular to show off the Survey's more than twenty years of work. Hayden assigned the job of preparing the exhibit to Jackson.

With the help of Holmes and a bevy of craftsmen, Jackson came up with what proved to be one of the most popular exhibits at the gathering. The Survey was assigned space at the western end of the Government Building. Jackson took advantage of the light in that location and erected a wall display of glass transparencies. Visitors to the building were immediately attracted to the luminous display of his photographs. On the side walls, Jackson mounted large-format prints, some of Yellowstone but most of his work in Colorado. In the center of the room were displayed six large plaster and papier-mâché relief maps and models. One was a contour map of Yellowstone and another of Colorado Territory.

What most impressed visitors, however, were models of Mesa Verde cliff houses and several of the Canyon de Chelly ruins. One of these showed the ruins in their present condition, while another was an imagined re-creation of its ancient glory. As one guidebook described the display, the "second cast was the same as the first, restored to its probably original state, and tiny men and women were to be seen at their daily work, grinding corn, carrying water, etc. This has been reconstructed after the manner of the houses now occupied in Arizona and New Mexico by the Moqui and Pueblo tribes."[18] Situated below the models were display cases filled with pottery and implements collected in the field.

The Survey's Centennial exhibit not only delighted fairgoers, but impressed the renowned international scientists who visited as well. Hayden capitalized on their interest by trading copies of the models for specimens and publications from museums in Europe and across America. According to Cassidy, the Centennial Exhibition greatly assisted Hayden in "translating the disparate items he and his men collected in the West into the political influence necessary to gain the appropriations for continuing his work."[19]

Equally important in bringing the Survey's information to the public was the second project that took Hayden and his staff's attention away from completing reports on the 1875 fieldwork. This was Hayden's long-planned Atlas of Colorado. He intended the atlas as not only the culmination of the Survey's work in Colorado but also as an exemplar of his entire approach to science: data made useful for practical purposes through mutually informing science and art.

William Henry Holmes oversaw the preparation of the *Atlas*, leaving Washington only for an abbreviated field season back in Colorado in the summer of 1876; he remained in Washington throughout the summer of 1877 to prepare the final pages for publication that fall. The *Atlas* consisted of a series of colored maps, half of which portrayed land use and the others geological features. The pages with the geological maps also included sections. Holmes drew the colored maps, choosing a chromatic schema suggested by the natural features represented—green for forests, yellow for mineral deposits, reds for eruptive formations. These color choices, artistically pleasing but also, in Holmes' view, true to the landscape being represented, were soon adopted as standard in cartography. The *Atlas* also included seven black-and-white maps and seven panoramic views of the Colorado Rockies. Holmes prepared these from sketches in his field notebooks, adding a more readily accessible sense of three-dimensionality to the graceful, but less visually sensible, contours of the maps. According to Kevin J. Fernlund, Holmes's biographer, his "fidelity to nature and his ability to present an enormous quantity of information with economy, taste, and elegance help account for why the Atlas has long been regarded as a masterpiece of cartographic art."[20]

Hayden's determination to complete the *Atlas of Colorado*, even to the extent of delaying publication of the official reports on the 1875 fieldwork, was due in part to growing conflict with the other western surveys. The long-standing competition among Hayden, Powell, Wheeler, and King was coming to a head, reaching by 1876 a particularly fevered pitch of personal antagonisms as the different surveys sought congressional appropriations. King's survey of the Sierras had been completed, but he remained a respected and outspoken figure in the field of western surveying. The Army Corps of Engineers, with King's backing, continued to press its case that all surveying in the West should be the military's responsibility. Powell, whose work in the Colorado River basin was coming to a close, made a bid to have his assignment expanded to all of the Rocky Mountains. Congress rejected Powell's request, noting that the Rockies were Hayden's domain. King had never been reluctant to express his dislike of Hayden to fellow scientists and political backers, but Powell, though no fan of Hayden's, had always been reticent to openly criticize

Holmes sketching under a piñon pine, 1874. His "fidelity to nature," understanding of geologic principles, and painstaking effort made him an invaluable asset, not only in the field but also as a cartographer. *Courtesy F. M. Fryxell Collection, Fryxell Oversize Box F-20, Neg. #10164, American Heritage Center, University of Wyoming.*

his rival. Even so, in 1876 Powell became more vocal and more vicious, particularly with accusations about Hayden's failings as a scientist. Hayden, in turn, pressured the secretary of the Interior to hand Powell's Colorado work over to him.

Bickering among the leaders of the western surveys was particularly troublesome for the Department of the Interior. Hayden's long-standing supporter, Columbus Delano, who had served as secretary of the Interior since 1870, had been forced to resign in September of 1875, partly the result of charges that he had accepted bribes from Colorado mining interests. Following the presidential election of 1876, which was largely a reaction to corruption scandals, including those in the Interior Department during the presidency of U. S. Grant, the new administration appointed Carl Schurz as secretary of the Interior. Schurz instituted civil service reform in the department and sought to rationalize and professionalize its work.

For several years, Schurz tried to manage internal rivalries over western surveying by negotiating agreements between Powell and Hayden, but by 1879 he had grown weary of the infighting. Schurz backed a proposal, which had been considered before, to combine all the western surveys under a single department. That year Congress voted to create a new agency within the Department of the Interior devoted to all surveying tasks. Hayden and his supporters hoped that he might be appointed to head the U.S. Geological Survey, but the job went to Clarence King. When King resigned after only two years, Powell replaced him. Hayden received a position as a geologist in the new agency, but his assignment was only to finish up work previously conducted. Accompanied by A. C. Peale, Hayden returned to the Yellowstone area several times in the early 1880s, but by that time his health had deteriorated. He resigned from the U.S. Geological Survey in December 1886 and passed away a year later.

By the time of his death, Hayden's reputation had waned. His work has been eclipsed by that of his rivals, especially Powell, so that today the Hayden Survey is most remembered for the Yellowstone expeditions. Although some members of the 1875 Survey went on to notable scientific careers, only the photographer, William Henry Jackson, achieved lasting stature. Jackson's imagery, some created as part of the Hayden Survey and some through his private photographic studio, helped integrate the far West into a nineteenth-century Euro-American culture of meaning, representing, as Peter Hales has suggested, one of the "core myths of American civilization: the fabled ground upon which could be enacted American destiny."[21]

In recent years, scholars of the American West and of the history of science have re-examined Hayden's career and the contributions of his work. These scholars have highlighted his role in the professionalization of scientific endeavor and the concept that within a democratic nation, science is properly the pursuit of the civilian government. Hayden successfully institutionalized this concept by making his Survey part of the federal bureaucracy and forging a link between science conducted in service of the public to the use of public revenues.

The Hayden Survey's role in the bureaucratization of civilian science is certainly of historical significance. But we should not overlook the fact that Hayden's work had much more immediate and profound consequences for the people of the Four Corners region. The Survey's work in Colorado was to incorporate an indigenous space into an Anglo-American system of thought and utility. Doing so required reimagining the geography of the Four Corners in terms of Western scientific understandings of nature, space, and time. Translating the region into maps—with the land's vast and strange topography tamed by measured lines and colorful contours—made the area knowable in a larger ideological and historical context. The Survey's work portrayed the Four Corners as just one more neat chunk in an orderly, predictable progression of meridians that constituted the space, the idea, and the way of being that was America.

Much of what Hayden envisioned has, in fact, taken place. Yet it is worth noting that the Four Corners region is today a unique place—a physical and cultural landscape forged jointly, if not always cooperatively or fairly, by diverse peoples. The participants in the events of 1875, Native and white, would probably recognize this place. Stand at the juncture of the four states, just as William H. Holmes did in 1875, and one is struck by the paved road, busy parking lot, and jangle of tourists. But lift your eyes and look out across the distance, as Holmes did, into an enduring vastness whose timelessness humbles most notions of human consequence.

# *Postscript*

FOUR HUNDRED FEET ABOVE THE ROLLING SAGEBRUSH PLAIN of Dry Valley sits the terminus of a deer trail that winds through the sandstone cap of a series of sheer cliffs. Today, only the deer use it as they move from the wide, vegetated rock shelf to the piñon, juniper, and grass plain above. Not so in mid-August 1875, when thirteen men believed themselves snared and at the mercy of the Utes above and below. This trail became their literal lifeline out of the trap and back to their friends and associates in Parrott City. Before grasping that lifeline, they left behind unnecessary baggage rendered useless so that the enemy could gain no benefit. There, in scattered heaps along the rock shelf lay the battered equipment—everything from cooking gear to survey instruments, cans to panniers, and mess kits to horseshoes. For close to ninety years, the elements had their way, weathering this refuse through sun, rain, and snow. Nothing, including the deer, gave much notice.

Then, during the uranium boom of the 1950s, a prospector named Reef Eggers stumbled across an old transit (theodolite) abandoned about twenty miles north of the town of Monticello, Utah.[1] This find piqued the interest of a uranium geologist who had spent a great deal of time in the same area. Perry Hurlbut, a resident of Roswell, New Mexico, who worked for Cities Service Oil Company (CITGO), was also a history buff; in the early 1960s he became interested in trying to identify the precise location of the encounter between the Utes and the Hayden crew. Hurlbut spoke with Eggers and contacted two scholars who were in the process of writing a comprehensive history of the Hayden Survey, J. V. Howell (a geologist in Tulsa, Oklahoma) and Fritiof M. Fryxell (professor of geology at Augustana College,

Rock Island, Illinois). With Eggers's recollections and copies of some of the documents that are now included in this book, Hurlbut set out in August 1964, with his three teenage sons, to find the site.[2]

Hurlbut's intimate knowledge of the area helped him to identify on the ground the descriptions in the old documents. As dramatic as the original descriptions of the fight were, they were not, understandably, precise in giving the geographic location of the events. Eggers's recollections were also problematic. As those familiar with the region know, pinpointing a specific draw, rock formation, or deer trail without the modern convenience of a global positioning system (GPS) can be difficult. But Hurlbut was convinced that his own experience in the area made locating the site possible, at least sufficiently so that it was worth devoting a portion of his family vacation to the task.

The Hurlbut family camped on the mesa above the valley described in the documents and began searching for a cut in the plateau that might have been the route used by the Hayden men. Armed with some of Gardner's men's accounts, the family was hopeful. On their first day of searching, Hurlbut's sixteen-year-old son spotted a well-used deer trail descending the cliff. The boys, with father following, dashed down the trail and soon stumbled across the scattered remains of the Hayden crew's equipment.

> Doug suddenly yelled—"Dad, there's the boxes!" We were at the site. Lying before us was a rotted box, old square nails visible. . . . All around were items: rusted cans, more boxes, broken glass, much of it turned deep purple by the sun and time. I found zinc plates approx. 3 1/2" × 6", presumably from the "dry plates." We found cartridge cases, mess gear such as metal plates, lids, and the large iron lid for a Dutch oven. . . . One large mason jar was dated 1858, and several smaller jars were recovered. We found glass tubes, from the "cistern barometer," plus many steel points.[3]

Ironically, this was on August 17, 1964, eighty-nine years to the day after the equipment's abandonment.

Hurlbut immediately recognized the artifacts as those listed as being lost during the fight with the Utes. "All types of material were scattered about the site, which we hastily examined. . . . In the ensuing thirty minutes we accounted for many of the items presented in the official list of abandoned equipment."[4] The family packed up as many of the artifacts as they could and the next day continued their vacation

Remnants of the nonessential gear Gardner had his men jettison before ascending the slope and leaving his Ute antagonists behind. Eighty-nine years later, P. K. Hurlbut visited the spot, eventually collected much of the material, and sent it to the University of Wyoming, where it resides today. *Courtesy J. V. Howell Collection, Hayden Party Photo File 3, American Heritage Center, University of Wyoming.*

with a trip to Mesa Verde. From there, Hurlbut telegrammed Howell about the find. Howell confirmed that most of the items mentioned appeared on the official list of abandoned equipment filed by Hayden in 1875.

The following spring, Hurlbut, this time accompanied by Fryxell, returned to the site to look for more artifacts. The 1875 fight had been spread over miles so it was possible that the Hayden men dropped equipment along the escape route. Also, it was possible that the Utes had gathered the abandoned equipment and moved it elsewhere to examine and assess its value. On this trip, Hurlbut and Fryxell made additional finds. Fryxell made a subsequent trip to the area in 1966 to trace other campsites and found some objects he believed to have been from the Hayden crew.[5]

Bates Wilson, the legendary first superintendent of Canyonlands National Park (established in 1964), also took an interest in locating the route of the Hayden "Indian fight." He took Boy Scout groups into the area on artifact hunts, but found nothing. For a time in the mid-1960s, Wilson, Hurlbut, and Howell fielded numerous reports from local history buffs about supposed relics from the Hayden Survey, but no additional objects surfaced. Eventually, the American Heritage Center at the University of Wyoming received the vast majority of the artifacts along with copies of most of the written materials from and about the 1875 Survey. Today, a much smaller collection of artifacts also resides at the Monticello (Utah) Visitor's Center. As for the trail, the deer still have right-of-way.

Little else of the 1875 Hayden Survey likely remains in the Four Corners.

# Notes

### PREFACE

1.  "A Scientific Adventure," *New York Times*, September 9, 1875.
2.  Conversation with Cleal Bradford, executive director of the Four Corners Heritage Council, May 11, 2015; statistics from Karen Yazzie, Four Corners Monument Tribal Park manager, May 11, 2015.
3.  Sprague, *Great Gates*, 215–16.

### INTRODUCTION

1.  For a discussion of the finances of the Hayden Survey, see Foster, *Strange Genius*, 284, 310–12. The Survey received annual appropriations from Congress, but Hayden often sought supplemental funds from federal and private sources.
2.  On Hayden's decision to refocus the survey on Colorado, see Cassidy, *Ferdinand V. Hayden*, 122–23.
3.  Ibid., 126.
4.  On Hayden's association with Blackmore and Palmer, see Cassidy, *Ferdinand V. Hayden*, 126, 148–49, and Foster, *Strange Genius*, 158–60. The coal survey is discussed by Cassidy, 191–93.
5.  Gardner's family name was spelled "Gardiner" until his father dropped the "i." In documents relating to his work with the Hayden Survey, the name is sometimes spelled with the "i" and sometimes without. Later in his life, Gardner resumed the older spelling. Throughout this book, we have used "Gardner."
6.  These are 1878 figures gathered by Jesse V. Howell as part of his study of the Hayden Survey. "Members of Hayden Survey Parties," Box 25, Papers of Jesse V. Howell, American Heritage Center, University of Wyoming, Laramie (hereafter Howell Papers). Generally, the Hayden crews worked well together and with admirable efficiency. There were occasional disputes, with some packers unable to work together, for example, and some contention among the scientists for credit. Peale expressed concern in 1875 that he wasn't being given sufficient credit or independence. See Holmes to Hayden, June 13, 1875, Records of U.S. Geological Survey, Record Group 57, Howell Papers (hereafter RG 57, Howell Papers).

7. On the importance of nonscientific members of the Survey, see Cassidy, *Ferdinand V. Hayden*, 143–50.
8. Hayden, *Ninth Annual Report*, 21.
9. Stubbs, *Uto-Aztecan*, 3–4.
10. Goss, "Traditional Cosmology, Ecology, and Language of the Ute Indians," 36.
11. Conetah, *History of the Northern Ute People*, 19.
12. "Abiquiu Agency Report," Arny to Norton, June 24, 1867, 206.
13. Thompson, *Southern Ute Lands*, 5.
14. Kappler, "Treaty with the Ute, 1868," 990–96.
15. Hafen, "Historical Summary," 21–22.
16. "Negotiations with Ute Indians," January 6, 1873, 2.
17. Ibid., 5–6.
18. Ibid., 7–8.
19. Ibid., 2.
20. *Report of the Commission*, October 15, 1873, 6.
21. Ibid., 19.
22. Ibid., 22.
23. Ibid., 31.
24. By 1875, Hayden was spending less time in the field, his energies taken up with the executive duties of the Survey, overseeing publications, and lobbying. Also, it was around this time that Hayden contracted syphilis, and his health began to decline.
25. Since this volume concerns the work of the Hayden Survey in the Four Corners region, no excerpts from the work of the Bechler and Wilson divisions are included here.
26. Robert Adams, Jr., was a graduate of the University of Pennsylvania, although his field of study was law, not geology. He was admitted to the Pennsylvania bar in 1872 but spent summers working with the Hayden field crews in Yellowstone and later in Colorado. After the 1875 field season, Adams returned to Philadelphia, earned a degree from the Wharton School of Economics and Finance, and went on to a career in business and politics. He served as U.S. minister to Brazil, 1889–90, and was elected to the U.S. House of Representatives in 1893. He served in the House until 1906, when he committed suicide over a failed business venture.
27. Gannett became an important figure in the U.S. Geological Survey, which replaced the Hayden Survey in 1879. He was the geographer for the 1880 U.S. Census, helping to modernize the process with the use of precisely enumerated districts. He served as chief geographer of the U.S. Geological Survey from 1882 to 1896. Gannett was one of the founding members of the National Geographic Society, the American Association of Geographers, and the American Statistical Association.
28. Peale was the great grandson of the renowned Revolutionary era painter, Charles Wilson Peale. His great-uncle, Titian R. Peale, was with the 1819–20 expedition of Stephen Long to the Rocky Mountains, and in 1841 he served as naturalist on the Wilkes expedition in the South Pacific.
29. Jackson and Driggs, *Pioneer Photographer*, 217.

30. Hough, "Edwin Atlee Barber," 588. Barber served as curator of ceramics at the Pennsylvania Museum and School of Industrial Art and published numerous works on Native cultures in the Southwest.

31. Hayden, *Ninth Annual Report*, 1.

32. Ibid., 5.

33. "A Scientific Adventure," *New York Times*, September 9, 1875.

34. Jackson, quoted in "Peaks and Canons: Work of the Hayden Survey in Southwestern Colorado," *Chicago Daily Inter-Ocean*, August 19, 1875.

35. On changing ideas about the canyon country's aesthetics, see Nelson, *Wrecks of Human Ambition*.

### 1. An "Outfit of Special Character"

1. The byline for Mills's articles read, "From our own correspondent." Hereafter, unless otherwise noted, all *New York Times* articles carried this byline.

2. Manitou Springs, founded in 1872, is still a major tourist and rest area, famous for its mineral springs.

3. The byline for Adams's articles read, "Special Correspondent of the *Philadelphia Inquirer*," but were signed, "Botanicus."

4. No byline accompanies this article, but in past years Robert Adams had submitted articles to the *Rocky Mountain News* as well as to the *Philadelphia Inquirer*.

5. Located at the northern end of the San Luis Valley, Colorado, Saguache is a town filled with western history. The name derives from the Ute language and is variously interpreted as "Blue Earth" or "Green Place." The town, located in the proximity of a stopping place on the Old Spanish Trail, was the scene of intense mining and ranching activities during the last half of the nineteenth century, and today is noted for its beautiful scenery and outdoor recreation.

6. Otto Mears (1840–1931) is a well-known entrepreneur of southwestern Colorado. Among other ventures, he is famous for creating a series of toll roads in the San Juan Mountains that promoted agricultural interests and mining industry through a network of supply roads. One of the first such roads was the one over Poncha Pass, where elements of the Hayden Survey traveled. Eventually, the Denver & Rio Grande Railroad expanded its line into the southwestern corner of Colorado; part of this rail line followed roads pioneered by Mears. For an account of this activity based on interviews with Mears, see Jocknick, *Early Days*.

7. Rev. Henry F. Bond of the Unitarian faith assumed responsibility for the Los Pinos Agency on July 3, 1874. He had his work cut out for him. Coming at a time when the Utes were feeling the full impact of the Brunot Agreement, were living at an agency where the government's program of agriculture was an impossibility because of the cold temperatures at that high altitude, and were promised annuities that had not appeared, the new agent faced less-than-ideal conditions. When the Hayden Survey parties arrived, the reverend was in the process of selecting a new site for the agency in the Uncompahgre Valley, a much warmer and practical climate. By

November of 1875, the Utes had completed their move to the new site, but in the fall of the next year, Bond resigned under charges of graft. See Houston, *Two Colorado Odysseys*, 43–54.

8. This article reprinted a letter from J. T. Gardner to F. V. Hayden, dated September 18.

9. Adams is somewhat off in his chronology, but is referring to an attack on El Pueblo, where seventeen Mexican men, women, and children, who had allowed a group of Muache Utes and Jicarilla Apaches into their community, were massacred. Only two young boys and a woman survived, and later, the woman was also killed. This was in December of 1854. Other conflicts followed to the point that Col. Thomas T. Fauntleroy pursued the Utes and Apaches and, in a series of engagements, killed a sufficient number to bring the fighting to a halt by July 1855. See Simmons, *Ute Indians*, 101–102.

10. Ouray (1833–80) was born to a Jicarilla Apache (not Navajo) father and a Tabeguache (band) mother. He spoke Ute, Spanish, and English fluently and eventually ascended to positions of leadership that were recognized by the U.S. government for treaty negotiation purposes. Although he resisted the sale of land during the discussions that resulted in what is called the Brunot Agreement (1873), he is viewed by many Utes as having given away a large piece of territory promised in earlier treaties. Though not all of the various bands of Utes accepted him as their spokesman, there is no doubt that he was influential among them, in part because of his connection with the powers of the federal government. See Smith, *Ouray*.

11. The term "Snake" Indians refers to the Shoshonean people, including the Shoshone, Bannock, and Northern Paiute.

## 2. "Grand and Beautiful Scenery"

1. Canon City received its name from the Mexican word of "cañon" (canyon) in 1860, when miners and settlers founded the town. Many people who wrote about the community dropped the Spanish accent mark without bothering to add a "y," and so the spelling has remained unchanged.

2. Lt. William L. Marshall was part of a military survey team under the direction of Capt. George M. Wheeler. From 1872 to 1879, Wheeler directed the mapping of a huge geographical area west of the 100th meridian and was in direct competition with the assignment of the Hayden Survey, which was operating during the same time frame and in the same region. The duplication became most obvious during the 1873 season, but government intervention was not enough to calm the rivalry between the two groups of military and civilian scientists/topographers.

3. William Jackson Palmer (1836–1909) was founder of Colorado Springs (1871) and co-founder, with William Bell, of the Denver & Rio Grande Railroad. By 1883, this railroad had joined the Rio Grande Western line, becoming Colorado's only railroad across the mountains. During the Civil War, Palmer received brevet rank of general, as well as a Medal of Honor, allowing him to use the honorific title of "general." After the war, Palmer became a chief promoter not only of the railroads

but also of coal and steel production, among other businesses in Colorado. After amassing a great deal of wealth, he became very involved in numerous philanthropic enterprises. For an excellent study of his role in railroad development, see Athearn, *Denver and Rio Grande Western Railroad*.

4. For a history of early Hispanic settlement in southern Colorado, see Lecompte, *Pueblo, Hardscrabble, Greenhorn*; as a companion piece that examines Hispanic settlement in northern New Mexico and southern Colorado, see Swadesh, *Los Primeros Pobladores*.

5. Aldrich is referring to the Panic of 1873 that led to a depressed economy from 1873 to 1879. Among the reasons for this condition were post–Civil War inflation, economic stagnation, trade deficits, and overspeculation, but one of the most important reasons was the government's having moved from a bimetallic (gold and silver) standard to one based solely on gold. The West played a part in this with all of the silver mining in Nevada and Colorado that dumped large amounts of the metal on the market, causing it to be devalued.

6. Lafayette Head (1825–97) fought in the Mexican War, earning the rank of major. In 1854 he settled in the San Luis Valley of Colorado, and by 1859 he was an agent for the Capote Utes and Jicarilla Apaches in that area. Head served in that position until 1868, at which time the Utes signed a treaty in Washington, D.C., that promised them approximately the western third of the territory of Colorado. It did not take long before much of this land was lost through subsequent treaties. In 1876, the same year that Colorado became a state, Head became the first elected lieutenant governor.

7. There is no byline on this, the first article on the Hayden Survey to be published in the *Daily Inter-Ocean*. Most subsequent articles carried the byline, "David Grey."

8. This technique, called "rough-locking," was used to limit the speed and maximize control for wagons descending steep slopes. Chains were placed on the back wheels, often with a log tied to them, so that they did not move, while the front wheels and wagon tongue were left free to steer the vehicle. On extremely steep inclines, the animals could be used in the rear of the wagon to provide more braking power.

9. This Latin phrase is translated as "the descent to Avernus is easy," meaning "the road to evil is easy."

10. The brothers of the Pious Fraternity of Our Father Jesus the Nazarene (Los Hermanos de la Fraternidad Piadosa de Nuestro Padre Jesus Nazareno), also known as "The Brotherhood" or "the Penitents," is an offshoot of traditional Roman Catholic beliefs practiced in the small mountain villages of northern New Mexico and southern Colorado. The roots of this belief extend back to as early as the thirteenth century in Europe, but the practice first started in New Mexico during the eighteenth century, most likely because of the scarcity of ordained clergy in the small villages scattered throughout rural frontier communities. Initially committed to assisting people in need as well as to continuing worship services, the dedicated practitioners became involved in flagellation, re-enacting parts of Christ's mortification, and bearing a cross in remembrance of the events leading to the crucifixion. The Catholic Church attempted first to control and then to stop the practice. In 1851, the Church began

excommunicating members of the Penitentes. Times softened the reproach, and in 1946, the brotherhood was recognized as an order and received official status within the Church. See Swadesh, *Los Primeros Pobladores*, 72–80.

11. Soap-weed, or narrow-leaf yucca (*Yucca glauca*), is used to create an effective shampoo by digging up its roots, smashing them, and then swishing the pulp in water, which is poured over the hair and then rinsed. The plant's narrow spines, when softened, can be woven into cordage and mats.

12. This reference to "Carter" is unclear.

13. This is a reference to syphilis, known historically as the "French disease" because it was spread in Europe by French soldiers returning from a campaign in Naples, Italy (1494–95). The sexually transmitted disease may have come from America as part of the Columbian exchange.

14. "Hounds" are two pieces of wood that extend in a triangular form on the bottom of the wagon to hold the tongue stationary between the two end points.

### 3. "The View from the Top"

1. The Ute people believe that Sleeping Ute Mountain, near Cortez, Colorado, is formed by one of seven giants who fought against other tribes' gods during the time of creation. As these forces struggled, their feet and bodies pushed against the land, forming mountains and valleys. The Great Warrior grew tired from the battle and fell into a deep sleep on the spot. Blood poured from his wounds, creating streams of water. Sticks and leaves covered his body as he slept, with his head to the north, face toward the sky, arms across his chest, and legs to the south. During the four seasons, he changes his blankets—light green in the spring, dark green in the summer, yellow and red in the fall, and white in the winter. Some people say that the Sleeping Ute will one day awake to fight his people's enemies.

2. Narraguinip was a local Ute leader who could command between fifty to one hundred warriors during times of trouble. Generally peaceful, this man, whose name translates as "Storyteller," played a friendly role during the settlement of southeastern Utah and southwestern Colorado.

3. McElmo Canyon took its name from an old miner who died and was buried there. The canyon is wide and winding, serving as a major thoroughfare between southeastern Utah and southwestern Colorado. An intermittent stream flows through the canyon and is paralleled by a road that has been both a shipping route and a connecting link for farms and ranches spread throughout the canyon since the late 1870s and early 1880s. Between its head near the foot of Sleeping Ute Mountain and its mouth on the San Juan River, there were also a number of springs, many of which gave rise to earlier Ancestral Puebloan communities.

4. Hovenweep is a Ute word meaning "Deserted Valley," most likely in reference to the Ancestral Puebloan dwellings abandoned by 1300 A.D. In 1923, this collection of homes, towers, and kivas was so impressive that they became part of the national park system. Jackson was among the first to record information and then popularize the existence of this archaeological treasure.

5. A bell horse (or mule), usually referred to as a bell mare, had a bell placed around its neck, helping the owner to know the speed and direction of the herd. Calm in nature and often white for visibility, the bell mare kept the animals together.

6. Holmes is correct in that Capt. John N. Macomb, during his 1859 mapping expedition ordered by the U.S. War Department, traveled from Abajo (Blue) Mountain down Recapture Canyon to the San Juan River. He called it "Ritito de Sierra Abajo" (Small River of the Abajo Mountain). He complained about the water at his campsite, but enjoyed a good night's sleep, noting that the coolness of fall was "bracing" on that September 2 morning. See Madsen, *Exploring Desert Stone*, 163.

## 4. "Making Stations"

1. Peale Diary, July 25, 1875, Howell Papers.
2. This rugged mountain range is located in west-central Colorado and now comprises much of the White River National Forest and Gunnison National Forest.
3. A letter from Gardner to Hayden, reporting on the conflict with the Utes in the La Sal Mountains in mid-August, appeared in this article in the *Rocky Mountain News*.

## 5. Vestiges of Bygone Ages

1. George Chittenden gave a lengthy report on the ruins encountered by the Holmes Division to Charles Aldrich after the group returned to Parrott City. Aldrich quoted Chittenden verbatim in an article for the Chicago *Daily Inter-Ocean* entitled, "Peaks and Canons: Work of the Hayden Survey in Southwestern Colorado," which appeared on September 26, 1875.
2. The Moqui, Ancestral Puebloans or Anasazi, evolved from the Archaic Indian culture, developing through a growing technological sophistication, cultural change, and societal transformation. Beginning around 1000 B.C., these people moved from a strictly hunting and gathering experience to an increasing dependence on agriculture—primarily corn, beans, and squash—that fostered different types of sedentary dwellings and lifestyle patterns. Archaeologists classify the different stages as Basketmaker II and III (BM I is the hypothetical transition stage from Archaic), then Pueblo I, II, and III. By this time—1300 A.D.—these people living in the Four Corners had abandoned the area. After a series of migrations, they settled where they are found today in New Mexico and Arizona. The Hopi, Zuni, and people of Acoma are classified as the Western Pueblos, while those groups living along the Rio Grande are the Eastern Pueblos, but all of them composed the ancient people now called the Anasazi.
3. Anasazi sites often have elements left over from various phases, so that there may be remnants of Basketmaker ruins mixed (below) with Pueblo phases. Many of the most dramatic and highly defensible communities belong to the last phase (Pueblo III) before the general abandonment. Many archaeologists today agree that a great deal of conflict and turmoil seems to have accompanied this last period, although there is no real indication that the warfare was conducted by outsiders.

4.  The name Moqui (spelled various ways—Moki, Moquis, Moquitch, etc.) is correctly spelled "Mokwič" or "Muukwitsi." It is a Ute/Paiute term, and means "the dead." Ute and Paiute oral tradition varies as to the relation these people had with the Anasazi, some indicating that they were enslaved by them, others viewing them more as relatives, while others considered them powerful and warlike. Some say that they were driven out of the area by "tribes from the north," others suggest their removal was self-imposed, but few disagree that the puebloan peoples of today are their descendants. The Hopi refer to themselves by that name or *Hopiit*, meaning "The Peaceful Ones." This, and the two preceding endnotes, raises substantial questions not easily handled by short answers. For further information, see McPherson, *Viewing the Ancestors*.

5.  Because Canyon de Chelly connects with the southern part of Chinle Wash, Barber, as with other nineteenth-century explorers, lumps the two under the title of Rio de Chelly.

6.  Barber raises two points of importance. The first concerns Navajo (Diné) history and that era known as "The Long Walk." Starting in the mid-1850s and lasting for ten years, these people faced increasing pressure from the U.S. government and its allies, the New Mexican volunteers, Utes, Hopis, and other tribes that joined as auxiliaries against their enemies. The Navajos call this the "fearing time"; it culminated for many, but not all, in a four-year incarceration (1864-68) at Fort Sumner on the Pecos River in east-central New Mexico. An estimated third of the tribe fled to peripheral areas to avoid detection and wait for the return of the others in 1868. Barber refers to this evacuation of previously occupied Navajo territory—in this case, because of pressure by the Utes.

    The second issue is the relationship of the Navajo to the Anasazi, a Navajo word glossed as "ancestral aliens or enemies," but also "those who live beside us but not among us." The Navajos have an extensive oral tradition about who these people were, what happened to them, and how their objects and sites should generally be avoided by the uninitiated who do not understand how to control spiritual power. For a detailed discussion of Navajo, Ute, and Hopi beliefs concerning these prehistoric peoples, see McPherson, *Viewing the Ancestors*.

7.  The diamond fields is a reference to a hoax perpetrated in the early 1870s by hucksters wishing to lure unsuspecting entrepreneurs to a site where diamonds had been "salted." Eventually, it became apparent that the whole scheme, much of which was centered in Wyoming, was a fraud. A site on Chinle Wash was a part of this elaborate falsehood.

8.  Today, this area is still called the community of Many Farms.

9.  The Hopis live atop three mesas in Arizona, fittingly named First, Second, and Third. Jackson's party encountered the easternmost First Mesa, which has the three villages of Walpi (founded around 900 B.C. and one of the oldest continuously inhabited cities in the United States), Hano or Tewa (inhabited by a group of Tewa-speaking people from the Rio Grande who came to help defend the Hopis during prehistoric times), and Sichomovi. On Second Mesa the villages are Shongopavi, Mishongnovi, and Shipaulovi, while on Third Mesa sit Hotevilla, Bacavi, Moencopi, and Oraibi.

This latter village split in 1906 because of rivalry between traditionalists and those embracing elements of the white society, leading to an Old and New Oraibi.

10. Barber, obviously smitten with the "princess," provides an interesting contrast to the party's comments about the Utes. The dichotomy between civilization and barbarism, a contemporary anthropological notion of the time, is evident.

11. Barber is describing what is called a "butterfly" hairdo (*poli'ini*) worn by a young, single Hopi woman of marriageable age. A wooden hoop provides support for the whorls on each side of the head. Not only does this hairdo announce her availability for marriage, it is also viewed as highly attractive, as Barber attests.

12. Barber is describing the ceremonial chamber called a kiva, found in both prehistoric and contemporary puebloan villages. Hopi kivas may differ in construction from those of other pueblo groups, but all of them serve as the place where primarily men perform sacred ceremonies and rituals important in the annual cycle of religious beliefs that have been passed down through the various Hopi clans.

13. The "boomerang" here is a throwing stick used while pursuing small game and has no aerodynamic features that would make it return like a boomerang of an Australian Aborigine.

14. The Hopis used arrowheads for both hunting and warfare in prehistoric and historic times. Because Barber is looking at arrows used for hunting rabbits, which do not necessarily require stone or metal points, he jumps to an inaccurate conclusion.

15. Most likely, Barber and Jackson were seeing either turkey pens or jacal structures, without the mud attached.

16. These kachina dolls, carved out of cottonwood root, are not worshipped but are used to teach children about the appearance of some of the many Hopi gods. When the kachina spirits visit the Hopi mesas during certain times of year related to agricultural ceremonials and rain, men dressed as these gods perform traditional dances and songs (prayers) in the plaza. Because of their familiarity with the kachina dolls, the people recognize the various gods.

17. Truax was actually the agency doctor, and Keam was the younger brother of Thomas V. Keam, the trader.

18. Barber is referring to pahos, or prayer sticks, that are placed about at springs, shrines, and other special locations as a prayer and invitation for the kachinas and other spirits to come and bless the Hopis with rain and other things that they stand in need of. The pahos are an invitation to participation. As Barber notes, feathers and paint applied in a particular way are all part of the pahos "message" or summons.

19. This reference to cranial size reflects a popular belief in the nineteenth and early twentieth centuries of a pseudoscience called phrenology. One of its basic concepts is that the more advanced a people or an individual is in intellectual capacity, the greater the size of the skull. By measuring cranial capacity, one could tell how far a people has progressed in becoming "civilized" on an evolutionary scale.

20. Either Jackson is mistaken or the names of the two mountain ranges had been combined in the past. There is a distance of approximately fifty to sixty miles between the two. Today Blue Mountain (singular) is the range farther south; one of its peaks is named Abajo but in the past, the entire range was also called by that name.

## 6. "Something Serious Had Occurred"

1. The Macomb map, recorded in 1859, played an important part in what was about to happen. As Gardner noted, this was the only specified source of water—Cold Spring (today, Peters Hill Spring)—in the area, and it lay at the end of an increasingly steep hill with an exit at the top that was significantly narrowed by two rock walls.

2. Mills filed a short dispatch to the *New York Times* on August 23 (posted from Pueblo, Colorado, on September 4) that appeared in the paper under the headline, "A Battle with Indians," on September 5. Mills's much more detailed description of the fight with the Utes was published on September 9, 1875.

3. Peale's diary includes daily entries until August 14. There are no entries for the dates August 14 to 19.

4. "The Hayden Survey: What the Sierra La Sal Indians Did for It," *New York Times*, September 9, 1875.

## 7. Getting Everyone In

1. After posting this article from Parrott City on August 21, Peale notes in his diary that he had prepared a story for the *Philadelphia Press*, though the article appeared under the byline, "From a Regular Correspondent of the *Press*."

2. The Dreyse Needle Gun received its name from its long firing pin, which struck a percussion cap that ignited the black powder charge, sending a .61 acorn-shaped round at a muzzle velocity of 1,000 feet per second. This breech-loading, bolt-action rifle increased the rate of fire over muzzle-loading weapons with a five-to-one superiority, leading eventually to a standardized cartridge. This rifle was used in both the Austro-Prussian and Franco-Prussian wars. By 1871 the Prussian military had replaced it with improved weaponry, but surplus needle guns made their way to the United States. From "Franco-Prussian War: Dreyse Needle Gun," http://militaryhistory.about.com/od/smallarms/p/needlegun.htm?p=1.

3. This article carried no byline, stating instead that "A *News* reporter called upon Mr. Gardner at Charpiot's Hotel [in Denver] and interviewed him in reference to the recent attack upon his men by the Sierra La Sal Utes." Following this brief introduction by the unnamed reporter, the article printed a first-person account by Gardner under the subheading, "An Interesting Narrative." This account provided yet another version of the initial attack and described in detail the subsequent effort to find the men left behind and Gardner's visit to the Los Pinos Agency.

4. Jackson's camp at this point had moved approximately fifteen miles above the San Juan River going north. He was traveling up what in those days was called Epsom Creek because of the poor-tasting water, but is known today as Comb Wash. This prominent feature has an intermittent stream that parallels Comb Ridge. There are also a number of side canyons that feed into the wash from the west. The one on which Jackson took a "side trip" of eight to ten miles is known today as Fish Creek. The date was August 22.

5. At this point, the party had passed out of Comb Wash and was camped at a spring in the Cottonwood Creek drainage, most likely Whiskers Spring at Whiskers Draw. The date was August 23.

6. This approximately 1,200-mile trail linked Santa Fe, New Mexico, to Los Angeles and southern California by passing through parts of New Mexico, Colorado, Utah, Nevada, and California. It is actually a combination of a number of different trails, most of which could only be traveled by pack train and not by wheeled vehicles. The Old Spanish Trail, as a singular unit, was traveled primarily from 1830 to 1848. The end of the Mexican War decreased the necessity for using such a difficult trail— although, for years to come, many explorers and mapmakers would use sections of it and note its existence on their maps.

7. Pogonobogwint is most likely a mistranslation of Poco Narraguinip, or Slow Story-teller. Each band of Utes had a man, usually an elder, who kept the group's history, mythology, and teachings, to pass on during winter nights. This was a position of honor and leadership.

8. This article printed, in full, a letter signed by James T. Gardner and dated August 22, 1875, La Plata River Mining Camp.

## 8. Back to the Other Side

1. Lone Cone is a 12,618-foot peak at the western end of the San Miguel Mountains in southwestern Colorado. As its name suggests, it stands alone, visible from great distances as a prominent landmark.

## Conclusion

1. Bond, "Los Pinos Agency," September 30, 1876.

2. Pope, "Indian Affairs—Utes in Colorado," September 26, 1876.

3. See Biggs Family, "Our Valley"; Rickner, *History of the Pioneers*; Palmer, "Mormon Settlements"; Silvey, "History and Settlement of Northern San Juan County"; Deets, "Paradox Valley," 186–98; O'Rourke, *Frontier in Transition*.

4. Unnamed 2nd lieutenant, 3rd Artillery, "Relations between the Utes and Settlers," November 13, 1877, in Record Group 98, Letters Received—Adj. Gen. Office, 1871–80 (hereafter Letters Rec'd—AGO), Washington, D.C.

5. Page, "Annual Report," August 28, 1879, 16–17.

6. Petition to William T. Sherman, February 14, 1877, Letters Rec'd—AGO.

7. Smith, *A Time for Peace*, 7–10.

8. Pope, "Report of General John Pope," 41; Acting Commissioner of Indian Affairs to Francis Weaver, June 26, 1878; "Articles of Convention and Agreement," November 9, 1878; Edward Hatch to Assistant Adjutant General, November 25, 1878, and Ute Commissioner to Assistant Adjutant General, December 4, 1878. All found in Letters Rec'd—AGO.

9. The best detailed account is by Sprague, *Massacre*. Also see Emmitt, *Last War Trail*; Marsh, *Utes of Colorado*; Smith, *Ouray*; and Simmons, *Ute Indians*.

10. Philip H. Sheridan to H. McCrary, October 3, 1879, and Hatch to Adjutant General, October 16, 1879, Letters Rec'd—AGO.
11. Page to E. A. Hayt, October 13, 1879, Letters Rec'd—AGO.
12. Valois to Assistant Adjutant General, October 15, 1879, Letters Rec'd—AGO; "Ute Indians in Colorado," 87.
13. Ibid.; Page to Hayt, October 21, 1879, 163, Letters Rec'd—AGO.
14. For both the personal experience of a man stationed at Pagosa Springs during the conflict and an example of the rapidity with which he and his unit were deployed, see Athearn, ed., "Major Hough's March," 97–109.
15. Pope to Sherman, December 31, 1879, Letters Rec'd—AGO.
16. See Simmons, *Ute Indians*, 190–97.
17. James G. Cassidy argues that Gardner undertook the coalfield survey on his own initiative, "without consulting Hayden" or informing Charles Endlich, the geologist in charge of the 1875 field division assigned to the region in which the coal and iron deposits Gardner studied were located. It was this act of insubordination that angered Hayden. Cassidy, *Ferdinand V. Hayden*, 191. In his biography of Hayden, Mike Foster says that the coal survey threatened to expose Hayden's link to Palmer and Blakemore and that the director's criticism of Gardner was an effort "to avoid embarrassing questions by shifting the focus" onto his subordinate. Foster, *Strange Genius*, 262.
18. Ingram, *Centennial Exposition*, 148.
19. Cassidy, *Ferdinand V. Hayden*, 237.
20. Fernlund, *William Henry Holmes*, 80.
21. Hales, *William Henry Jackson*, 4.

POSTSCRIPT

1. Eggers also found some steel tape, glass jars, and cartridge cases. The transit bore the marking, "U.S.C.S 103"; this was mistyped in some of the correspondence about Eggers's find as "USGS," instead of the abbreviation for United States Coastal Survey. See Hurlbut to Howell, August 13, 1964, and Howell to Hurlbut, August 17, 1964, Howell Papers.
2. "Story of Hayden Survey Is Told to Geologists," *Durango-Cortez Herald*, February 19, 1967; Hurlbut to Howell, August 13, 1964, Howell Papers.
3. Hurlbut to Howell, August 19, 1964, Howell Papers.
4. Hurlbut, "Where the Canon Narrowed," 56–57.
5. Hurlbut to Fryxell and Howell, April 8, 1965; Hurlbut to Howell, March 6, 1965; Howell to Hurlbut, March 9, 1965, Howell Papers.

# Bibliography

A LL PRIMARY SOURCE MATERIALS CITED IN THIS TEXT ARE located in the Papers of Jesse V. Howell, American Heritage Center, University of Wyoming, Laramie, as typescripts or photocopies of the originals. This includes all correspondence related to the Hayden survey, the field notes, the diary of A. C. Peale, and the vintage newspaper articles. Where any of these materials appear in the extract notes and endnotes, they are cited as "Howell Papers."

⁂      ⁂      ⁂

Abbott, Carl. *Colorado: A History of the Centennial State*, 5th ed. Boulder: University Press of Colorado, 2013.

"Abiquiu Agency Report," June 24, 1867. *Report of the Commissioner of Indian Affairs—New Mexico*. Washington, D.C.: Government Printing Office, 1868.

Athearn, Robert. *The Denver and Rio Grande Western Railroad*. Lincoln: University of Nebraska Press, 1977.

———, ed., "Major Hough's March into Southern Ute Country, 1879," *Colorado Magazine* 25, no. 3 (May 1948): 97–109.

Bartlett, Richard A. *Great Surveys of the American West*. Norman: University of Oklahoma Press, 1962.

Biggs, J. T., Family. *Our Valley*. Mesa, Ariz.: Self-published, 1977.

Blair, Bob, ed. *William Henry Jackson's "The Pioneer Photographer."* Santa Fe: Museum of New Mexico Press, 2005.

Bond, H. F. "Los Pinos Agency," September 30, 1876. *Report of the Commissioner of Indian Affairs*. Washington, D.C.: Government Printing Office, 1877.

Cassidy, James G. *Ferdinand V. Hayden: Entrepreneur of Science*. Lincoln: University of Nebraska Press, 2000.

Chambers, Frank. *Hayden and His Men: Being a Selection of 108 Photographs by William Henry Jackson of the United States Geological and Geographical Survey of the Territories for the Years 1870–1878*. N.J.: Francis Paul Geoscience, 1988.

Conetah, Fred A. *A History of the Northern Ute People*. Fort Duschesne, Utah: Uintah-Ouray Ute Tribe, 1982.

Decker, Peter R. *"The Utes Must Go!": American Expansion and the Removal of a People*. Golden, Colo.: Fulcrum Publishing, 2004.

Deets, Lee Emerson. "Paradox Valley—An Historical Interpretation of Its Structure and Changes." *Colorado Magazine* 11, no. 5 (September 1934): 186–98.

Emmitt, Robert. *The Last War Trail: The Utes and the Settlement of Colorado*. Norman: University of Oklahoma Press, 1954.

Fernlund, Kevin J. *William Henry Holmes and the Rediscovery of the American West*. Albuquerque: University of New Mexico Press, 2000.

Foster, Mike. *Strange Genius: The Life of Ferdinand Vandeveer Hayden*. Niwot, Colo.: Roberts Rhinehart, 1994.

Goetzmann, H. William. *Exploration and Empire: The Explorer and the Scientist in the Winning of the American West*. New York: Alfred A. Knopf, 1966, 2006.

Goss, James A. "Traditional Cosmology, Ecology, and Language of the Ute Indians." In William Wroth, ed., *Ute Indian Arts and Culture, from Prehistory to the New Millennium*. Colorado Springs, Colo.: Colorado Springs Fine Art Center, 2000.

Hafen, Leroy R. "Historical Summary of the Ute Indians and the San Juan Mining Region." Unpublished manuscript, Utah State Historical Society, Salt Lake City, n.d.

Hales, Peter B. *William Henry Jackson and the Transformation of the American Landscape*. Philadelphia: Temple University Press, 1988.

Harrell, Thomas H. *William Henry Jackson: An Annotated Bibliography, 1862–1995*. Nevada City, Calif.: Carl Mautz Publishing, 1995.

Hayden, F. V. *Ninth Annual Report of the United States Geological and Geographical Survey of the Territories: Embracing Colorado and Parts of Adjacent Territories; Being a Report of Progress of the Exploration for the Year 1875*. Washington, D.C.: Government Printing Office, 1877.

Hough, Walter. "Edwin Atlee Barber." *Dictionary of American Biography*, vol. 1. New York: Charles Scribner's Sons, 1928,

Houston, Robert B. *Two Colorado Odysseys, Chief Ouray and Porter Nelson*. Lincoln: University of Nebraska, 2005.

Hurlbut, Perry. "Where the Canon Narrowed." Four Corners Geological Society, *Guidebook*, Eighth Field Conference, 1975.

Ingram, J. S. *The Centennial Exposition, Described and Illustrated: Being a Concise and Graphic Description of This Grand Enterprise, Commemorative of the First Centenary of American Independence*. Philadelphia: Hubbard Bros., 1876.

Jackson, William Henry, and Howard R. Driggs. *The Pioneer Photographer: Rocky Mountain Adventures with a Camera*. New York: World Book Company, 1929.

Jocknick, Sidney. *Early Days on the Western Slope of Colorado and Campfire Chats with Otto Mears the Pathfinder from 1870 to 1883, Inclusive.* Glorieta, N.M.: Rio Grande Press, 1913, 1968.

Kappler, Charles. "Treaty with the Ute, 1868." In *Indian Affairs—Laws and Treaties.* Washington, D.C.: Government Printing Office, 1913, 990–96.

Lecompte, Janet. *Pueblo, Hardscrabble, Greenhorn, the Upper Arkansas, 1832–1856.* Norman: University of Oklahoma Press, 1978.

Madsen, Steven K. *Exploring Desert Stone: John N. Macomb's 1859 Expedition to the Canyonlands of the Colorado.* Logan: Utah State University Press, 2010.

Marsh, Charles S. *The Utes of Colorado: People of the Shining Mountains.* Boulder, Colo.: Pruett Publishing Company, 1982.

McPherson, Robert S. *As If the Land Owned Us: An Ethnohistory of the White Mesa Utes.* Salt Lake City: University of Utah Press, 2010.

———. *Viewing the Ancestors, Perceptions of the Anaasází, Mokwič, and Hisatsinom.* Norman: University of Oklahoma Press, 2014.

"Negotiations with Ute Indians," January 6, 1873. *Report of the Secretary of the Interior,* H. Ex. Doc. 90, 42d Cong., 3d Sess.

Nelson, Paul T. *Wrecks of Human Ambition: A History of Utah's Canyon Country.* Salt Lake City: University of Utah, 2014.

Noel, Thomas J., and John Fielder. *Colorado, 1870–2000, Revisited: The History behind the Images.* Englewood, Colo.: Westcliffe, 2001.

O'Rourke, Paul M. *Frontier in Transition: A History of Southwestern Colorado.* Bureau of Land Management Cultural Resource Series 10. Denver: Bureau of Land Management, 1980.

Page, Henry. Annual Report, August 28, 1879. *Report of the Commissioner of Indian Affairs.* Washington, D.C.: Government Printing Office, 1880.

Palmer, John Franklin. "Mormon Settlements in the San Juan Basin of Colorado and New Mexico." Unpublished master's thesis, 1967, history department, Brigham Young University, Provo, Utah.

Pope, John. "Indian Affairs—Utes in Colorado," September 26, 1876. *Report of the Secretary of War,* H. Ex. Doc. 1, part 2, 44th Cong., 2d Sess., 449.

———. "Report of General John Pope," October 4, 1878. *Report of the Secretary of War,* 45th Cong., 3d Sess., 1878.

"Relations between the Utes and Settlers in the San Juan Region," November 13, 1877. Record Group 98, Letters Received—Adjutant Generals Office, 1871–80, National Archives, Washington, D.C.

*Report of the Commission to Negotiate with the Ute Tribe of Indians,* October 15, 1873. Washington, D.C.: Government Printing Office, 1873.

Rickner, Mrs. Thomas. *The History of the Pioneers of the Mancos Valley.* Mancos, Colo.: Self-published, 1910.

Sandweiss, Martha A. *Print the Legend: Photography and the American West.* New Haven, Conn.: Yale University Press, 2002.

Silvey, Frank. "History and Settlement of Northern San Juan County." Self-published: n.d.

Simmons, Virginia McConnell. *The Ute Indians of Utah, Colorado, and New Mexico.* Boulder: University Press of Colorado, 2000.

Smith, Duane A. *A Time for Peace: Fort Lewis, Colorado, 1878–1891.* Boulder: University Press of Colorado, 2006.

Smith, P. David. *Ouray, Chief of the Utes.* Ouray, Colo.: Wayfinder Press, 1986.

Sprague, Marshall. *The Great Gates: The Story of the Rocky Mountain Passes.* Lincoln: University of Nebraska Press, 1964.

———. *Massacre: The Tragedy at White River.* Lincoln: University of Nebraska Press, 1957.

Stubbs, Brian D. *Uto-Aztecan: A Comparative Vocabulary.* Blanding, Utah: Self-published, 2008.

Swadesh, Frances Leon. *Los Primeros Pobladores, Hispanic Americans of the Ute Frontier.* London: University of Notre Dame Press, 1974.

Thompson, Gregory Coyne. *Southern Ute Lands, 1848–1899: The Creation of a Reservation.* Occasional Papers of the Center of Southwest Studies, No. 1. Durango, Colo.: Fort Lewis College, 1972.

"Ute Indians in Colorado." Letter from the Secretary of the Interior, S. Ex. Doc. 31, 46th Cong., 2d Sess., 87.

West, Elliott. *The Contested Plains: Indians, Goldseekers, and the Rush to Colorado.* Lawrence: University of Kansas Press, 1998.

# Index

Page references in *italic type* indicate images.

Adams, Charles, *26*
Adams, Robert, Jr., 28, 39, 43, 52–54,
 109, 117–19, 123, 156, 158, 160, 162–65,
 168–70, 172, 174, 176, 193, 202, 230,
 232, 262n26, 263n4; writings of,
 44–45, 55–60, 169–70, 175–77, 179–80,
 184, 189, 228–29
adobe construction, 48, 71, 72, 74–78
adobe ovens, 75
Aguila (Muache chief), 247
Aldrich, Charles, 34, 38, 49, 50, 61–62,
 69, 89, 91, 95, 185–87, *191*, 193–94, 232,
 234, 238–39; writings of, 69–87, 90,
 92–99, 188–92, 210–11, 219, 234–42
American culture, shifts in, 7
Anasazi, 21, 267nn2–3 (chap. 5); culture
 of, archaeological study of, 133; ruins
 of, 17
Ancestral Puebloans, 21, 89, 128, 267n2
 (chap. 5)
Aneth (Utah), 244
Animas River (Colo.), 68, 248
Animas Valley (Colo.), 69, 108
anthropological theory, 128
Apaches, 215
aparejo, 41, *47*
Arapahos, 215

archaeological theory, 128
Arkansas Valley (Colo.), 112
*Army and Navy Journal*, 226–27
Arny, W. F. M., 22
art, science and, 62
Atkinson, W. R., 30–31, 39, 49, 50, 123,
 162, 168, 169, 179, *191*, 193, 214, 232, 239
*Atlas of Colorado*, 252–53
Aztecs, 89, 128

Baird, Spencer Fullerton, 29
Baker's Park (Colo.), *19*
Bar, the, 86–87
Barber, Edwin Atlee, 32, 91, 99, 128,
 130, *131*, 137, 152–53, *191*, 234; writings
 of, 128–52, 204–5, 219–22
bears, 112–13, 117–19
Bechler, Gustavus R., 27, 38, 39
Bell, William Abraham, 15, 264n3
bell horse, 100, 101, 267n5
Bennett, Charles, 235
Berry, W. H., 248
Big Head, 228–29
Big Hill, 75
Blackmore, Blanche, 15
Blackmore, William Henry, 13–14, 28,
 250

King, Clarence, 8, 9, 15, 16, 189, 255
kiva, 269n12

Lake San Cristobal (Colo.), 63
La Plata Camp, 234
La Plata Mountains (Colo.), 34, 84, 92
La Sal Mountains (Colo./Utah), 54, 104
Las Animas Mining District, 23
La Tinaja, 205
leather, Indians' interest in, 135, 136, 137
Lee, Harry, 32, 89, 99, *131*, 137, 142, *191*,
 203, 205, 206–8, 210–11, 219, 234
Lesquereux, Leo, 240
lignitic beds, age of, 240
Lone Cone (Colo.), 232–34, 271n1 (chap.
 8)
Long, Stephen, 262n28
Long Walk, 268n6
Los Pinos Indian Agency, 28, 38, 43, 49,
 51–60, 104, 106, 109–10, 246, 263n7
Los Pinos Valley (Colo.), 23, 105

Mack, Dr., 50, 51, 57, 107
Macomb, John N., 8, 102, 267n6
Madera, Shepard (Shep), 28, 45–46,
 *47*, 109, 111, 117–21, 158–62, 164–66,
 168–69, 171, 174, 176–77, 190, 193, 199
Mancos Camp. See Parrott City (Colo.)
Mancos River (Colo.), 30, 93, 184
Mancos Valley (Colo.), 89, 92, 93, 244
Manitou Springs (Colo.), 15, 45
mapmakers, 26
mapping, process of, 95–96
Marshall, William L., 67, 264n2
Mason, Charles, 17
McCook, Edward M., 23
McCreary, Charles, 31, 123, 159–64, 168,
 193, 194, 198, 200, 201
McElmo Canyon (Utah/Colo.), 97,
 266n3
Mears, Otto, *26*, 48, 106, 248, 263n6
medicine men, 57
Meek, Fielding Bradford, 8, 29
Meeker, Nathan C., 247
Meeker Massacre, 212, 247, 248
Merritt Ranch, 185

Mesa Verde (Colo.), 94–96, 130, 232, 252
Mexico (mule), 139
Miles, John D., 216, 227–30
Mills, Cuthbert, 28, 37, 38, 43, 54, 123,
 156, 165, 166, 179, 180, 190, 193, 218,
 230, 232; writings of, 39–43, 46–48,
 104–12, 113–19, 120–26, 156–68,
 170–78, 186, 193–94, 198–202, 225–26
mining, *7*, 244; laws about, 85–86; on
 Ute land, 23–26. See also gold; silver
mirages, 72, 120
Mishongnovi, 147, 149
Mitchell, Bob, *131*
Moab (Utah), 244
Montezuma Canyon (Utah), 206, *207*
*Moonstone* (Collins), 38
Moquis (Moquitch), 127–29, 132,
 141–46, 151–52, 267n2 (chap. 5), 268n4
Moran, Thomas, 11
Mormons, 12
Moss, John, 34–35, 61, 68–69, 64, 86, 89,
 186, 234
"Mountain of the Holy Cross"
 (Jackson), 17, 32
mountain spruce forests, navigating
 through, 114–17
Mount Peale, 155
Mount Tukuhnikivatz, 155
Muache Utes, 247, 264n9
mules, 111–12, 190; admiration for,
 67; behavior of, 40, 41; importance
 of, 18; riding of, 41; selection of,
 41; stampeding of, 204–5; work of,
 63–64, 65

Na-kwap-she-o-ma, 149
Narraguinip. See Poco Narraguinip
narrow-gauge railway, 14, 70
nature, Western concepts of, 7
Navajos, 6, 54, 100, 104, 125, 133–37,
 268n6
"Navajo Twins," *245*
Nebraska, survey of, 9
Newberry, John S., 7–8
newspapers, reporting on survey
 attacks, 187